To the Instructor

Thank you for your interest in the Townsend Press vocabulary series—so successful that it now appears in a Fourth Edition. Our goal in this series has been to produce nothing less than excellent books at nothing more than reasonable prices.

About the Book

Notice that the introduction to students (page 1) immediately makes clear to them just why vocabulary study is important. Students are motivated to learn by the four compelling kinds of evidence for word study. The back cover as well convinces students that "a solid vocabulary is a source of power."

You may want to look then at the preface, starting on page vii, which describes in detail the nine distinctive features of the book.

There are thirty chapters in the book, divided into five units. You'll note that while each chapter takes up only four pages, those pages contain a great deal of hands-on practice to help ensure that students master each word. And you'll find that the practice materials themselves are far more carefully done, and more appealing, than the run-of-the-mill items you typically find in a skills text. The quality and interest level of the content will help students truly learn the words, without either boring them or insulting their intelligence.

Supplements to the Book

Adding to the value of *Advancing Vocabulary Skills* is the quality of the supplements:

- An **Instructor's Edition**, which you hold in your hand. The *Instructor's Edition* is identical to the student text except that it includes the answers to all of the practices and tests.

- A combined **Instructor's Manual and Test Bank**, free with adoptions of 20 or more copies. This supplement contains a general vocabulary placement test as well as a pretest and a posttest for the book and for each of the five units in the text. It also includes teaching guidelines, suggested syllabi, an answer key, and an additional mastery test for each chapter as well as an additional mastery test for each unit.

- **PowerPoint presentations and Blackboard cartridges** are available for the book and may be downloaded from the "Supplements" area for instructors at **www.townsendpress.com**.

- **Online exercises**, available at **www.townsendpress.com**, which provide a general placement test and two additional tests for each vocabulary chapter in the book. These exercises contain a number of user- and instructor-friendly features, including actual, audible pronunciations of the words; brief explanations of answers; a sound option; frequent mention of the user's first name; a running score at the bottom of the screen; and a record-keeping file.

Adopters of *Advancing Vocabulary Skills* can obtain the print supplements by calling our toll-free number, 1-800-772-6410, or by e-mailing Customer Service at **cs@townsendpress.com**.

D1385314

(Continues on next page)

New Features of the Book

Among the changes in this Fourth Edition of *Advancing Vocabulary Skills* are the following:

- **A full-color design.** Color has been carefully used throughout, not as window dressing but to add clarity and readability to the different parts of each chapter and the different sections of the book.

- **Thirty new graphics.** To engage today's visual learners, a full-color illustration has been added to the Final Check story in each chapter.

- **Additional multicultural names and repeated words.** To broaden both the appeal and the effectiveness of the practice materials, ethnic names have been used more frequently, and even more vocabulary words have been repeated in the Final Checks.

- **Revised and updated practice items.** As always, a number of practice items throughout the book have been revised or updated to ensure that each item works as clearly and effectively with students as possible.

A Comprehensive Vocabulary Program

There are nine books in the Townsend Press vocabulary series:

- *Vocabulary Basics* (reading level 4–6)
- *Groundwork for a Better Vocabulary* (reading level 5–8)
- *Building Vocabulary Skills* (reading level 7–9)
- *Building Vocabulary Skills, Short Version* (reading level 7–9)
- *Improving Vocabulary Skills* (reading level 9–11)
- *Improving Vocabulary Skills, Short Version* (reading level 9–11)
- *Advancing Vocabulary Skills* (reading level 11–13)
- *Advancing Vocabulary Skills, Short Version* (reading level 11–13)
- *Advanced Word Power* (reading level 12–14)

Note that the short versions of the three books are limited to 200 words, as opposed to the 260 words and 40 word parts in each of the long versions. For some students and classes, the short versions of the book will provide an easier, more manageable approach to vocabulary development.

Instructor's Edition

Advancing Vocabulary Skills

Fourth Edition

Sherrie L. Nist
Professor Emerita, University of Georgia

Townsend Press Reading Series
Groundwork for College Reading with Phonics
Groundwork for College Reading
Ten Steps to Building College Reading Skills
Ten Steps to Improving College Reading Skills
Ten Steps to Advancing College Reading Skills
Ten Steps to Advanced Reading

Townsend Press Vocabulary Series
Vocabulary Basics
Groundwork for a Better Vocabulary
Building Vocabulary Skills
Building Vocabulary Skills, Short Version
Improving Vocabulary Skills
Improving Vocabulary Skills, Short Version
Advancing Vocabulary Skills
Advancing Vocabulary Skills, Short Version
Advanced Word Power

Supplements Available for Most Books
Instructor's Edition
Instructor's Manual and Test Bank
Online Exercises
PowerPoint Presentations
Blackboard Cartridges

Copyright © 2010 by Townsend Press, Inc.
Printed in the United States of America
9 8 7 6 5 4 3 2 1

ISBN-13 (Student Edition): 978-1-59194-193-4
ISBN-10 (Student Edition): 1-59194-193-8
ISBN-13 (Instructor's Edition): 978-1-59194-196-5
ISBN-10 (Instructor's Edition): 1-59194-196-2

Send book orders and requests for desk copies or supplements to:
Townsend Press Book Center
439 Kelley Drive
West Berlin, New Jersey 08091

For even faster service, contact us in any of the following ways:
By telephone: 1-800-772-6410
By fax: 1-800-225-8894
By e-mail: cs@townsendpress.com
Through our website: www.townsendpress.com

Contents

NOTE: Twenty-six of the chapters present ten words apiece. The other four chapters each cover ten word parts and are so marked. For ease of reference, the title of the selection that closes each chapter is included.

Unit Four

Unit Five

Appendixes

Preface: To the Instructor

The problem is all too familiar: *students just don't know enough words.* Reading, writing, and content teachers agree that many students' vocabularies are inadequate for course demands. Weak vocabularies limit students' understanding of what they read and the clarity and depth of what they write.

The purpose of *Advancing Vocabulary Skills* and the other books in the Townsend Press vocabulary series is to provide a solid, workable answer to the vocabulary problem. In the course of 30 chapters, *Advancing Vocabulary Skills* teaches 260 important words and 40 common word parts. Here are the book's distinctive features:

1 An intensive words-in-context approach. Studies show that students learn words best by reading them repeatedly in different contexts, not through rote memorization. The book gives students an intensive in-context experience by presenting each word in **six** different contexts. Each chapter takes students through a productive sequence of steps:

● Students infer the meaning of each word by considering two sentences in which it appears and then choosing from multiple-choice options.
● On the basis of their inferences, students identify each word's meaning in a matching test. They are then in a solid position to deepen their knowledge of a word.
● Finally, they strengthen their understanding of a word by using it three times: in two sentence-length practices and in a passage practice.

Each encounter with a word brings it closer to becoming part of the student's permanent word bank.

2 Abundant practice. Along with extensive practice in each chapter, there are a crossword puzzle and a set of unit tests at the end of every six-chapter unit. The puzzle and tests reinforce students' knowledge of the words in each chapter. In addition, most chapters reuse several words from earlier chapters (such repeated words are marked with small circles), allowing for more reinforcement. Last, there are supplementary tests in the *Instructor's Manual and Test Bank* and the online exercises that accompany the book. All this practice means that students learn in the surest possible way: by working closely and repeatedly with each word.

3 Controlled feedback. The opening activity in each chapter gives students three multiple-choice options to help them decide on the meaning of a given word. The multiple-choice options also help students complete the matching test that is the second activity of each chapter. A limited answer key at the back of the book then provides answers for the third activity in the chapter. All these features enable students to take an active role in their own learning.

4 Focus on essential words. A good deal of time and research went into selecting the words and word parts in each book in the TP vocabulary series. Word frequency lists were consulted, along with lists in a wide range of vocabulary books. In addition, the authors and editors each prepared their own lists. A computer was used to help in the consolidation of the many word lists. A long process of group discussion then led to final decisions about the words and word parts that would be most helpful for students on each reading level.

5 Appealing content. Dull practice materials work against learning. On the other hand, meaningful, lively, and at times even funny sentences and passages can spark students' attention and thus enhance their grasp of the material. For this reason, a great deal of effort was put into creating sentences and passages with both widespread appeal and solid context support. We have tried throughout to make the practice materials truly enjoyable for teachers and students alike. Look, for example, at the selection on page 11 that closes the first chapter of this book.

6 Clear format. The book has been designed so that its very format contributes to the learning process. Each chapter consists of two two-page spreads. In the first two-page spread (the first such spread is on pages 8–9), students can easily refer to all ten words in context while working on the matching test, which provides a clear meaning for each word. In the second two-page spread, students can refer to a box that shows all ten words while they work through the fill-in activities on these pages.

7 Supplementary materials.

   a A convenient *Instructor's Edition* is available at no charge to instructors using the book. It is identical to the student book except that it contains answers to all of the activities and tests.

   b A combined *Instructor's Manual and Test Bank* is also offered at no charge to instructors who have adopted the book. This supplement contains a general vocabulary placement test as well as a pretest and a posttest for the book and for each of the five units in the text. It also includes teaching guidelines, suggested syllabi, an answer key, and an additional mastery test for each chapter as well as an additional mastery test for each unit.

   c *PowerPoint presentations and Blackboard cartridges* are available for the book and may be downloaded from the "Supplements" area for instructors at www.townsendpress.com.

   d *Online exercises,* available at the Online Learning Center area of www.townsendpress.com, also accompany the book. These exercises consist of two additional tests for each vocabulary chapter in the book. In addition, they include—at the instructor's option—some of the practice material in the book itself. The program includes a number of user- and instructor-friendly features: brief explanations of answers, a sound option, frequent mention of the user's first name, a running score at the bottom of the screen, a record-keeping file, and actual pronunciation of each word.

      Probably in no other area of reading instruction is the computer more useful than in reinforcing vocabulary. These online exercises take full advantage of the computer's unique capabilities and motivational appeal. Here's how the program works:

   ● Students are tested on the ten words in a chapter, with each word in a sentence context different from any in the book itself.

   ● After students answer each question, they receive immediate feedback: The program states that the answer is right or wrong and why, frequently using the student's first name and providing a running score.

   ● When they complete each test, students receive their scores. If they repeat the test, they then receive a new score, labeled "R" on the scores report, with a number following the "R" indicating how many times they have taken the same test. What is so valuable about this, of course, is that the program gives students immediate additional practice with the words they need to review.

   ● In addition, the online exercise program offers a second, more challenging "Word Definitions" test in which students must identify the meanings of the chapter words without the benefit of context. This test is a final check that students have really learned the words. And, again, there is the option of a retest, with its own score.

   ● Finally, if the instructor so chooses, the online program will provide the student with two of the exercises in the book—Sentence Check 2 and the Final Check. Students can take these exercises online and receive immediate feedback and the option of a retest.

      Once students complete these exercises, their knowledge of each word in the chapter will have been carefully reinforced. And this reinforcement will be the more effective for having occurred in an electronic medium that especially engages today's students.

To obtain a copy of either the *Instructor's Edition* or the *Instructor's Manual and Test Bank*, instructors may contact Customer Service at 1-800-772-6420 or at cs@townsendpress.com.

8 **Realistic pricing.** As with the previous editions, the goal has been to offer the highest possible quality at the lowest possible price. While *Advancing Vocabulary Skills* is comprehensive enough to serve as a primary text, its modest price also makes it an inexpensive supplement.

9 **One in a sequence of books.** The most fundamental book in the Townsend Press vocabulary series is *Vocabulary Basics.* It is followed by *Groundwork for a Better Vocabulary* (a slightly more advanced basic text) and then by the three main books in the series: *Building Vocabulary Skills* (also a basic text), *Improving Vocabulary Skills* (an intermediate text), and *Advancing Vocabulary Skills* (a more advanced text). The most advanced book in the Townsend Press vocabulary series is *Advanced Word Power.* There are also short versions of the *Building, Improving,* and *Advancing* books. Suggested grade levels for the books are included in the *Instructor's Manual.* Together, the books can help create a vocabulary foundation that will make any student a better reader, writer, and thinker.

Notes on the Fourth Edition

A number of changes have been made in the fourth edition of *Advancing Vocabulary Skills:*

- **A full-color design.** Color has been carefully used throughout, not as window dressing but to add clarity and readability to the different parts of each chapter and the different sections of the book.

- **Thirty new graphics.** To engage today's visual learners, a full-color illustration has been added to the Final Check passage in each chapter.

- **Additional multicultural names and repeated words.** To broaden both the appeal and the effectiveness of the practice materials, ethnic names have been used more frequently, and even more vocabulary words have been repeated in the Final Checks.

- **Revised and updated practice items.** As always, a number of practice items throughout the book have been revised or updated to ensure that each item works as clearly and effectively with students as possible.

Acknowledgments

I am grateful for the enthusiastic comments provided by users of the Townsend Press vocabulary books over the life of the first three editions. I appreciate as well the work done on earlier editions by Eliza Comodromos, Beth Johnson, John Langan, and, in particular, Carole Mohr. I would also like to thank Kathryn Bernstein, Denton Cairnes, and Rick Moore for design, editing, and proofreading assistance with the fourth edition. And I owe special thanks to two TP editors who brought their exceptional talents to this revision. Barbara Solot is responsible for a four-color text design that is as clear as it is inviting. The result of her artistry is a strikingly attractive book that both students and teachers will enjoy. Janet Goldstein, in addition to providing significant design and content input, has lent her extraordinary editing and proofreading skills to this project. Under her guidance, the vocabulary series has been in the best possible hands.

Sherrie L. Nist

Introduction

Why Vocabulary Development Counts

You have probably often heard it said, "Building vocabulary is important." Maybe you've politely nodded in agreement and then forgotten the matter. But it would be fair for you to ask, "*Why* is vocabulary development important? Provide some evidence." Here are four compelling kinds of evidence.

1 Common sense tells you what many research studies have shown as well: **vocabulary is a basic part of reading comprehension**. Simply put, if you don't know enough words, you are going to have trouble understanding what you read. An occasional word may not stop you, but if there are too many words you don't know, comprehension will suffer. The content of textbooks is often challenge enough; you don't want to work as well on understanding the words that express that content.

2 **Vocabulary is a major part of almost every standardized test**, including reading achievement tests, college entrance exams, and armed forces and vocational placement tests. Test developers know that vocabulary is a key measure of both one's learning and one's ability to learn. It is for this reason that they include a separate vocabulary section as well as a reading comprehension section. The more words you know, then, the better you are likely to do on such important tests.

3 Studies have indicated that **students with strong vocabularies are more successful in school**. And one widely known study found that **a good vocabulary, more than any other factor, was common to people enjoying successful careers in life**. Words are in fact the tools not just of better reading, but of better writing, speaking, listening, and thinking as well. The more words you have at your command, the more effective your communication can be, and the more influence you can have on the people around you.

4 **In today's world, a good vocabulary counts more than ever**. Far fewer people work on farms or in factories. Far more are in jobs that provide services or process information. More than ever, words are the tools of our trade: words we use in reading, writing, listening, and speaking. Furthermore, experts say that workers of tomorrow will be called on to change jobs and learn new skills at an ever-increasing pace. The keys to survival and success will be the abilities to communicate skillfully and learn quickly. A solid vocabulary is essential for both of these skills.

Clearly, the evidence is overwhelming that building vocabulary is crucial. The question then becomes, "What is the best way of going about it?"

Words in Context: The Key to Vocabulary Development

Memorizing lists of words is a traditional method of vocabulary development. However, you are likely to forget such memorized lists quickly. Studies show that to master a word (or a word part), you must see and use it in various contexts. By working actively and repeatedly with a word, you greatly increase the chance of really learning it.

The following activity will make clear how this book is organized and how it uses a words-in-context approach. Answer the questions or fill in the missing words in the spaces provided.

Inside Front Cover and Contents

Turn to the inside front cover.

- The inside front cover provides a _____pronunciation guide_____ that will help you pronounce all the vocabulary words in the book.

Now turn to the table of contents on pages v–vi.

- How many chapters are in the book? ___30___

- Most chapters present vocabulary words. How many chapters present word parts? ___4___

- Four sections follow the last chapter. The first of these sections provides a limited answer key, the second gives helpful information on using _____the dictionary_____, the third contains _____topics for discussion and writing_____, and the fourth is an index of the 260 words and 40 word parts in the book.

Vocabulary Chapters

Turn to Chapter 1 on pages 8–11. This chapter, like all the others, consists of five parts:

- The *first part* of the chapter, on pages 8–9, is titled _____Ten Words in Context_____.

The left-hand column lists the ten words. Under each **boldfaced** word is its _____pronunciation_____ (in parentheses). For example, the pronunciation of *detriment* is _____dĕ′trə-mənt_____. For a guide to pronunciation, see the inside front cover as well as "Dictionary Use" on page 181.

Below the pronunciation guide for each word is its part of speech. The part of speech shown for *detriment* is _____noun_____. The vocabulary words in this book are mostly nouns, adjectives, and verbs. **Nouns** are words used to name something—a person, place, thing, or idea. Familiar nouns include *boyfriend, city, hat,* and *truth.* **Adjectives** are words that describe nouns, as in the following word pairs: *former* boyfriend, *large* city, *red* hat, *whole* truth. All of the **verbs** in this book express an action of some sort. They tell what someone or something is doing. Common verbs include *sing, separate, support,* and *imagine.*

To the right of each word are two sentences that will help you understand its meaning. In each sentence, the **context**—the words surrounding the boldfaced word—provides clues you can use to figure out the definition. There are four common types of context clues: examples, synonyms, antonyms, and the general sense of the sentence. Each is briefly described below.

1 Examples

A sentence may include examples that reveal what an unfamiliar word means. For instance, take a look at the following sentence from Chapter 1 for the word *scrupulous*:

> The judge was **scrupulous** about never accepting a bribe or allowing a personal threat to influence his decisions.

The sentence provides two examples of what makes the judge scrupulous. The first is that he never accepted a bribe. The second is that the judge did not allow personal threats to influence his decisions. What do these two examples have in common? The answer to that question will tell you what *scrupulous* means. Look at the answer choices below, and in the answer space provided, write the letter of the one you think is correct.

    _A_ *Scrupulous* means   A. ethical.   B. economical.   C. unjust.

Both of the examples given in the sentences about the judge tell us that he is honest, or ethical. So if you wrote *A*, you chose the correct answer.

2 Synonyms

Synonyms are words that mean the same or almost the same as another word. For example, the words *joyful, happy*, and *delighted* are synonyms—they all mean about the same thing. Synonyms serve as context clues by providing the meaning of an unknown word that is nearby. The sentence below from Chapter 2 provides a synonym clue for *collaborate*.

> When Sarah and I were asked to **collaborate** on an article for the school newspaper, we found it difficult to work together.

Instead of using *collaborate* twice, the author used a synonym in the second part of the sentence. Find that synonym, and then choose the letter of the correct answer from the choices below.

    _C_ *Collaborate* means   A. to compete.   B. to stop work.   C. to act as a team.

The author uses two terms to express what Sarah and the speaker had to do: *collaborate* and *work together*. Therefore, *collaborate* must be another way of saying "work together." (The author could have written, "Sarah and I were asked to work together.") Since *work together* can also mean "act as a team," the correct answer is *C*.

3 Antonyms

Antonyms are words with opposite meanings. For example, *help* and *harm* are antonyms, as are *work* and *rest*. Antonyms serve as context clues by providing the opposite meaning of an unknown word. For instance, the sentence below from Chapter 1 provides an antonym clue for the word *gregarious*.

> My **gregarious** brother loves parties, but my shy sister prefers to be alone.

The author is contrasting the brother's and sister's different personalities, so we can assume that *gregarious* and *shy* have opposite, or contrasting, meanings. Using that contrast as a clue, write the letter of the answer that you think best defines *gregarious*.

    _B_ *Gregarious* means   A. attractive.   B. outgoing.   C. humorous.

The correct answer is *B*. Because *gregarious* is the opposite of *shy*, it must mean "outgoing."

4 General Sense of the Sentence

Even when there is no example, synonym, or antonym clue in a sentence, most of the time you can still figure out the meaning of an unfamiliar word. For example, look at the sentence from Chapter 1 for the word *detriment*.

> Smoking is a **detriment** to your health. It's estimated that each cigarette you smoke will shorten your life by one and a half minutes.

After studying the context carefully, you should be able to figure out the connection between smoking and health. That will be the meaning of *detriment*. Write the letter of your choice.

    _C_ *Detriment* means   A. an aid.   B. a discovery.   C. a disadvantage.

Since the sentence says that each cigarette will shorten the smoker's life by one and a half minutes, it is logical to conclude that smoking has a bad effect on health. Thus answer *C* is correct.

By looking closely at the pair of sentences provided for each word, as well as the answer choices, you should be able to decide on the meaning of a word. As you figure out each meaning, you are working actively with the word. You are creating the groundwork you need to understand and to remember the word. *Getting involved with the word and developing a feel for it, based upon its use in context, is the key to word mastery.*

It is with good reason, then, that the directions at the top of page 8 tell you to use the context to figure out each word's _____ meaning _____. Doing so deepens your sense of the word and prepares you for the next activity.

- The *second part* of the chapter, on page 9, is titled _____ Matching Words with Definitions _____.

According to research, it is not enough to see a word in context. At a certain point, it is helpful as well to see the meaning of a word. The matching test provides that meaning, but it also makes you look for and think about that meaning. In other words, it continues the active learning that is your surest route to learning and remembering a word.

Note the caution that follows the test. Do not proceed any further until you are sure that you know the correct meaning of each word as used in context.

Keep in mind that a word may have more than one meaning. In fact, some words have quite a few meanings. (If you doubt it, try looking up in a dictionary, for example, the word *make* or *draw*.) In this book, you will focus on one common meaning for each vocabulary word. However, many of the words have additional meanings. For example, in Chapter 13, you will learn that *inclusive* means "including much or everything," as in the sentence "The newspaper's coverage of the trial was inclusive." If you then look up *inclusive* in the dictionary, you will discover that it has another meaning—"including the stated limits," as in "The weekend auto show takes place from Friday through Monday inclusive." After you learn one common meaning of a word, you will find yourself gradually learning its other meanings in the course of your school and personal reading.

- The *third part* of the chapter, on page 10, is titled _____ Sentence Check 1 _____.

Here are ten sentences that give you an opportunity to apply your understanding of the ten words. After inserting the words, check your answers in the limited answer key at the back of the book. Be sure to use the answer key as a learning tool only. Doing so will help you to master the words and to prepare for the last two activities and the unit tests, for which answers are not provided.

- The *fourth and fifth parts* of the chapter, on pages 10–11, are titled _____ Sentence Check 2 _____ and _____ Final Check _____.

Each practice tests you on all ten words, giving you two more chances to deepen your mastery. In the fifth part, you have the context of an entire passage in which you can practice applying the words.

At the bottom of the last page of this chapter is a box where you can enter your score for the final two checks. These scores should also be entered into the vocabulary performance chart located on the inside back cover of the book. To get your score, count the number of items that you answered correctly in each section. Then add a zero. For example, if you got seven answers right in Sentence Check 2, you would write "70" on the first line in the score box.

Word Parts Chapters

Word parts are the building blocks of many English words. Learning word parts can help you spell and pronounce words, unlock the meanings of unfamiliar words, and remember new words.

This book covers forty word parts—prefixes, suffixes, and roots. **Prefixes** are word parts that are put at the beginning of words. When written separately, a prefix is followed by a hyphen to show that something follows it. For example, the prefix *extra* is written like this: *extra-*. One common meaning of *extra-* is "beyond," as in the words *extracurricular* and *extrasensory*.

Suffixes are word parts that are added to the end of words. To show that something always comes before a suffix, a hyphen is placed at the beginning. For instance, the suffix *cide* is written like this: *-cide*. A common meaning of *-cide* is "killing," as in the words *homicide* and *genocide*.

Finally, **roots** are word parts that carry the basic meaning of a word. Roots cannot be used alone. To make a complete word, a root must be combined with at least one other word part. Roots are written without hyphens. One common root is *dorm*, which means "sleep," as in the words *dormant* and *dormitory*.

Each of the four chapters on word parts follows the same sequence as the chapters on vocabulary. Keep the following guidelines in mind as well. To find the meaning of a word part, you should do two things.

1 First decide on the meaning of each **boldfaced** word in "Ten Word Parts in Context." If you don't know a meaning, use context clues to find it. For example, consider the two sentences and the answer options for the word part *ante-* or *anti-* in Chapter 6. Write the letter of your choice.

> Before you enter Tyrone's living room, you pass through a small **anteroom**, where guests can leave their coats.

> A clever saying warns us not to **anticipate** trouble before it happens: "Worrying casts tomorrow's clouds over today's sunshine."

   C The word part *ante* or *anti-* means   A. after.   B. free.   C. before.

You can conclude that if the anteroom is before the living room, *anteroom* means "room before." You can also determine that *anticipate* means "to think about beforehand."

2 Then decide on the meaning each pair of boldfaced words has in common. This will also be the meaning of the word part they share. In the case of the two sentences above, both words include the idea of something coming before something else. Thus *ante-* or *anti-* must mean ___*before*___.

You now know, in a nutshell, how to proceed with the words in each chapter. Make sure that you do each page very carefully. *Remember that as you work through the activities, you are learning the words.*

How many times in all will you use each word? If you look, you'll see that each chapter gives you the opportunity to work with each word six times. Each "impression" adds to the likelihood that the word will become part of your active vocabulary. You will have further opportunities to use the word in the crossword puzzle and tests that end each unit and in the online exercises available at **www.townsendpress.com**.

In addition, many of the words are repeated in context in later chapters of the book. Such repeated words are marked with a small circle (°). For example, which words from Chapter 1 are repeated in the Final Check on page 15 of Chapter 2?

_____*optimum*_____   _____*detriment*_____

Analogies

This book also offers practice in word analogies, yet another way to deepen your understanding of words. An **analogy** is a similarity between two things that are otherwise different. Doing an analogy question is a two-step process. First you have to figure out the relationship in a pair of words. Those words are written like this:

LEAF : TREE

What is the relationship between the two words above? The answer can be stated like this: A leaf is a part of a tree.

Next, you must look for a similar relationship in a second pair of words. Here is how a complete analogy question looks:

LEAF : TREE ::

A. pond : river   C. page : book
B. foot : shoe   D. beach : sky

And here is how the question can be read:

_C_   LEAF is to TREE as

A. *pond* is to *river*.   C. *page* is to *book.*
B. *foot* is to *shoe.*   D. *beach* is to *sky.*

To answer the question, you have to decide which of the four choices has a relationship similar to the first one. Check your answer by seeing if it fits in the same wording as you used to show the relationship between *leaf* and *tree:* A ___ is part of a ___. Which answer do you choose?

The correct answer is *C.* Just as a leaf is part of a tree, a page is part of a book. On the other hand, a pond is not part of a river, nor is a foot part of a shoe, nor is a beach part of the sky.

We can state the complete analogy this way: *Leaf* is to *tree* as *page* is to *book.*

Here's another analogy question to try. Begin by figuring out the relationship between the first two words.

_D_   COWARD : HERO ::

A. soldier : military   C. actor : famous
B. infant : baby   D. boss : worker

Coward and *hero* are opposite types of people. So you need to look at the other four pairs to see which has a similar relationship. When you think you have found the answer, check to see that the two words you chose can be compared in the same way as *coward* and *hero:* ___ and ___ are opposite types of people.

In this case, the correct answer is *D; boss* and *worker* are opposite kinds of people. (In other words, *coward* is to *hero* as *boss* is to *worker.*)

By now you can see that there are basically two steps to doing analogy items:

1   Find out the relationship of the first two words.
2   Find the answer that expresses the same type of relationship as the first two words have.

Now try one more analogy question on your own. Write the letter of the answer you choose in the space provided.

_A_   SWING : BAT ::

A. drive : car   C. catch : bat
B. run : broom   D. fly : butterfly

If you chose answer *A,* you were right. *Swing* is what we do with a *bat,* and *drive* is what we do with a *car.*

Here are some other relationships often found in analogies:

●   **Synonyms:** freedom : liberty (*freedom* and *liberty* mean the same thing)

●   **Item to category:** baseball : sport (baseball is one kind of sport)

●   **Item to description:** school bus : yellow (*yellow* is a word that describes a school bus)

●   **Producer to product:** singer: song (a singer is the person who produces a song)

●   **Time sequence:** January : March (January occurs two months before March)

A Final Thought

The facts are in. A strong vocabulary is a source of power. Words can make you a better reader, writer, speaker, thinker, and learner. They can dramatically increase your chances of success in school and in your job.

But words will not come automatically. They must be learned in a program of regular study. If you commit yourself to learning words, and you work actively and honestly with the chapters in this book, you will not only enrich your vocabulary—you will enrich your life as well.

Unit One

detriment	optimum
dexterous	ostentatious
discretion	scrupulous
facetious	sensory
gregarious	vicarious

Ten Words in Context

In the space provided, write the letter of the meaning closest to that of each **boldfaced** word. Use the context of the sentences to help you figure out each word's meaning.

1 detriment
(dĕ′trə-mənt)
-*noun*

● Loni's purple hair may be a **detriment** when she goes for a job interview.

● Smoking is a **detriment** to your health. It's estimated that each cigarette you smoke will shorten your life by one and a half minutes.

_C_ *Detriment* means   A. an aid.   B. a discovery.   C. a disadvantage.

2 dexterous
(dĕks′tər-əs)
-*adjective*

● The juggler was so **dexterous** that he managed to keep five balls in motion at once.

● Although he has arthritis in his hands, Phil is very **dexterous**. For example, he builds detailed model airplanes.

_A_ *Dexterous* means   A. skilled.   B. educated.   C. awkward.

3 discretion
(dĭ-skrĕsh′ən)
-*noun*

● Ali wasn't using much **discretion** when he passed a police car at eighty miles an hour.

● Small children haven't yet developed **discretion**. They ask embarrassing questions like "When will you be dead, Grandpa?"

_B_ *Discretion* means   A. skill.   B. good sense.   C. courage.

4 facetious
(fə-sē′shəs)
-*adjective*

● Dr. Segura has a **facetious** sign on his office door: "I'd like to help you out. Which way did you come in?"

● My boss always says, "You don't have to be crazy to work here, but it helps." I hope she's just being **facetious**.

_C_ *Facetious* means   A. serious.   B. dishonest.   C. funny.

5 gregarious
(grĭ-gâr′ē-əs)
-*adjective*

● Melissa is so **gregarious** that she wants to be with other people even when she's studying.

● My **gregarious** brother loves parties, but my shy sister prefers to be alone.

_B_ *Gregarious* means   A. attractive.   B. outgoing.   C. humorous.

6 optimum
(ŏp′tə-məm)
-*adjective*

● The road was so icy that the **optimum** driving speed was only about ten miles an hour.

● For the weary traveler, **optimum** hotel accommodations include a quiet room, a comfortable bed, and efficient room service.

_A_ *Optimum* means   A. ideal.   B. hopeful.   C. questionable.

7 ostentatious
(ŏs′tən-tā′shəs)
-adjective

● My show-off aunt has some **ostentatious** jewelry, such as a gold bracelet that's so heavy she can hardly lift her arm.

● The lobby of that hotel is **ostentatious**, with fancy furniture, thick rugs, and tall flower arrangements. The guest rooms upstairs, however, are extremely plain.

__B__ *Ostentatious* means   A. humble.   B. showy.   C. clean.

8 scrupulous
(skrōō′pyə-ləs)
-adjective

● The judge was **scrupulous** about never accepting a bribe or allowing a personal threat to influence his decisions.

● The senator promised to run a **scrupulous** campaign, but her ads were filled with lies about her opponent's personal life.

__A__ *Scrupulous* means   A. ethical.   B. economical.   C. unjust.

9 sensory
(sĕn′sə-rē)
-adjective

● Because our **sensory** experiences are interrelated, what we taste is greatly influenced by what we smell.

● A person in a flotation tank has almost no **sensory** stimulation. The tank is dark and soundproof, and the person floats in water at body temperature, unable to see or hear and scarcely able to feel anything.

__A__ *Sensory* means   A. of the senses.   B. social.   C. intellectual.

10 vicarious
(vī-kâr′ē-əs)
-adjective

● I don't like to take risks myself, but I love the **vicarious** thrill of watching death-defying adventures in a movie.

● If you can't afford to travel, watching videos and visiting tourist websites can give you the **vicarious** experience of traveling in foreign countries.

__B__ *Vicarious* means   A. thorough.   B. indirect.   C. skillful.

Matching Words with Definitions

Following are definitions of the ten words. Clearly write or print each word next to its definition. The sentences above and on the previous page will help you decide on the meaning of each word.

1. _____facetious_____   Humorous; playfully joking

2. _____ostentatious_____   Meant to impress others; flashy

3. _____optimum_____   Best possible; most favorable; most desirable

4. _____detriment_____   Something that causes damage, harm, or loss

5. _____vicarious_____   Experienced through the imagination; not experienced directly

6. _____dexterous_____   Skillful in using the hands or body

7. _____scrupulous_____   Careful about moral standards; conscientious

8. _____gregarious_____   Sociable; enjoying and seeking the company of others

9. _____discretion_____   Good judgment or tact in actions or speaking

10. _____sensory_____   Having to do with seeing, hearing, feeling, tasting, or smelling

CAUTION: Do not go any further until you are sure the above answers are correct. Then you can use the definitions to help you in the following practices. Your goal is eventually to know the words well enough so that you don't need to check the definitions at all.

Sentence Check 1

Using the answer line provided, complete each item below with the correct word from the box. Use each word once.

A. detriment	B. dexterous	C. discretion	D. facetious	E. gregarious
F. optimum	G. ostentatious	H. scrupulous	I. sensory	J. vicarious

_____discretion_____ 1. Any employee who wants to use ___ would simply ignore a piece of spinach on the boss's front tooth.

_____detriment_____ 2. A weak voice is a serious ___ to a stage actor's or actress's career.

_____dexterous_____ 3. Playing with blocks and puzzles makes children more ___ with their hands.

_____gregarious_____ 4. My roommate used to be ___, but since he was mugged, he's begun to avoid people.

_____scrupulous_____ 5. Lonnie is so ___ about filling out his tax return that he even reported the $12.50 he was paid for jury duty.

_____ostentatious_____ 6. Jasmine wants to practice her vocabulary skills, so she's not just being ___ when she uses long words.

_____vicarious_____ 7. Do you think a spectator sport gives the fans ___ triumphs and defeats, or real ones?

_____optimum_____ 8. The ___ order in which to answer test questions is from easiest to most difficult, so that you can write the answers you know before time runs out.

_____sensory_____ 9. Wandering through the bee-filled fields of red and yellow flowers was an amazing ___ experience, one that appealed to the eyes, ears, and nose.

_____facetious_____ 10. The performer Oscar Levant had a tendency to cause disasters. He once made the ___ comment, "In my hands, Jell-O is a deadly weapon."

NOTE: Now check your answers to these items by turning to page 177. Going over the answers carefully will help you prepare for the next two practices, for which answers are not given.

Sentence Check 2

Using the answer lines provided, complete each item below with **two** words from the box. Use each word once.

_____discretion_____
_____scrupulous_____

1–2. "You have to use ___ in choosing your friends," my father said. "If your associates are dishonest, people will think that you also may not be ___."

_____facetious_____
_____dexterous_____

3–4. Tyra is being ___ when she says she's as ___ a dancer as a ballerina. That's her way of making fun of her own clumsiness.

_____optimum_____
_____detriment_____

5–6. When you take vitamins, be sure to take only the recommended dose. Anything more than this ___ amount can be a dangerous ___ to your health.

__gregarious__   7–8. My neighbors give a lot of parties, but not because they're ___. They just
__ostentatious__   want to impress the guests with their ___ home and furnishings.

__sensory__   9–10. Our cousin in Nigeria writes great letters, filled with ___ details that give us
__vicarious__   a(n) ___ acquaintance with the sights and sounds of an African village.

Final Check: Apartment Problems

Here is a final opportunity for you to strengthen your knowledge of the ten words. First read the following selection carefully. Then fill in each blank with a word from the box at the top of the previous page. (Context clues will help you figure out which word goes in which blank.) Use each word once.

Although I'm ordinarily a(n) (1)__gregarious__ person, I'm tempted to move into a cave, far from other people—and landlords. Okay, I admit that I didn't use enough (2)__discretion__ in choosing apartments to rent. But does every one of them have to be a (3)__detriment__ to my health, mental stability, and checkbook?

When I moved into my first apartment, I discovered that the previous tenant had already subleased the place to a very large family—of cockroaches. Although I kept trying, I was never (4)__dexterous__ enough to swat any of them; they were able to dodge all my blows. In time, they became so bold that they paraded across the kitchen floor in the daytime in a(n) (5)__ostentatious__ manner meant to impress upon me how useless it was to try to stop them. As soon as I could, I moved out.

My second apartment was a(n) (6)__sensory__ nightmare—the filth was hard on the eyes and the nose. The place even assaulted the ears, as the walls were as thin as cardboard. My neighbors played music until all hours. Since I was too poor to buy a stereo, I became a dedicated listener. I even attended some of the neighbors' parties, in a(n) (7)__vicarious__ way—with my ear to the wall. When my landlord found out, he tried to charge me seven dollars a day for entertainment, and he wasn't being (8)__facetious__—he meant it. I moved again, hoping to find a decent, (9)__scrupulous__ landlord.

I rented my last apartment because it was supposedly located in an area of (10)__optimum__ safety, considering the rent I can afford. A week after I moved in, I came home to find the locks broken and my belongings all over the floor. On the dresser was an angry note: "What gives you the right to live in such a nice neighborhood and not have anything worth stealing?"

Maybe I should have stayed with the cockroaches. At least they were honest.

Scores   Sentence Check 2 _____%   Final Check _____%

Enter your scores above and in the **Vocabulary Performance Chart** on the inside back cover of the book.

collaborate	rudimentary
despondent	scoff
instigate	squelch
resilient	venerate
retrospect	zealot

Ten Words in Context

In the space provided, write the letter of the meaning closest to that of each **boldfaced** word. Use the context of the sentences to help you figure out each word's meaning.

1 collaborate
(kə-lăb′ə-rāt′)
-verb

- When Sarah and I were asked to **collaborate** on an article for the school newspaper, we found it difficult to work together.
- Several writers and editors have **collaborated** in preparing this vocabulary text, sharing their knowledge and skills.

_C_ *Collaborate* means   A. to compete.   B. to stop work.   C. to act as a team.

2 despondent
(dĭ-spŏn′dənt)
-adjective

- Devon becomes **despondent** too easily. If he gets even one bad grade, he loses all hope of succeeding in school.
- For months after his wife died, Mr. Craig was **despondent**. No matter how hard they tried, his family and friends could not cheer him up.

_B_ *Despondent* means   A. ill.   B. depressed.   C. angry.

3 instigate
(ĭn′stə-gāt′)
-verb

- The rock group's violent performance **instigated** a riot in the audience.
- An English captain named Robert Jenkins **instigated** a war in 1738 by displaying his pickled ear, which he said had been cut off by a Spanish patrol. The horrified British declared war on Spain—the "War of Jenkins' Ear."

_C_ *Instigate* means   A. to prevent.   B. to predict.   C. to cause.

4 resilient
(rĭ-zĭl′yənt)
-adjective

- Children can be amazingly **resilient**. Even after a sad or frightening experience, they often bounce back to their normal cheerful selves.
- Plant life is **resilient**. For example, a few weeks after the Mount St. Helens volcano erupted in Washington in 1980, flowers were growing in the ashes.

_C_ *Resilient* means   A. widespread.   B. slow to recover.   C. quick to recover.

5 retrospect
(rĕt′rə-spĕkt′)
-noun

- After hobbling around on her broken foot for a week before seeing a doctor, Mae then needed surgery. In **retrospect**, it's clear she should have gotten help sooner.
- When I took Ms. Klein's writing course, I thought she was too demanding. In **retrospect**, though, I realize that she taught me more than anyone else.

_A_ *In retrospect* means   A. looking back.   B. looking for excuses.   C. looking ahead.

6 rudimentary
(roō′də-mĕn′tər-ē)
-adjective

- A grammar book usually starts with **rudimentary** skills, such as identifying nouns and verbs.
- I'm so used to adding and subtracting on a calculator that I've probably forgotten how to do those **rudimentary** mathematical calculations on my own.

_A_ *Rudimentary* means   A. basic.   B. intermediate.   C. advanced.

7 scoff
(skŏf)
-verb

- Bystanders **scoffed** at the street musician playing a tune on a row of tin cans, but he seemed unaware that people were making fun of him.
- Tony **scoffed** at reports that a hurricane was coming until he saw the winds knocking down trees and overturning cars.

<u>A</u> *Scoff at* means   A. to laugh at.   B. to watch.   C. to take seriously.

8 squelch
(skwĕlch)
-verb

- My history teacher shot me a dirty look during class when I couldn't quite manage to **squelch** a burp.
- Decades of communism in Eastern Europe didn't **squelch** the desire for freedom. As soon as they could, the people in these countries began to form democracies.

<u>B</u> *Squelch* means   A. to encourage.   B. to hold back.   C. to release.

9 venerate
(vĕn′ər-āt′)
-verb

- The Tlingit Indians **venerate** the wolf and the raven, and their totem poles illustrate stories in praise of these animals.
- The guests at our dean's retirement banquet made it clear that they **venerated** her; when she entered the room, everyone rose.

<u>B</u> *Venerate* means   A. to pity.   B. to honor.   C. to remember.

10 zealot
(zĕl′ət)
-noun

- Annie, a **zealot** about health, runs a hundred miles a week and never lets a grain of sugar touch her lips.
- The Crusaders were Christian **zealots** during the Middle Ages who left their homes and families and went off to try to capture the Holy Land.

<u>A</u> *Zealot* means   A. an extremist.   B. an observer.   C. a doubter.

Matching Words with Definitions

Following are definitions of the ten words. Clearly write or print each word next to its definition. The sentences above and on the previous page will help you decide on the meaning of each word.

1. _____*instigate*_____ To bring about by moving others to action; stir up

2. _____*rudimentary*_____ Fundamental; necessary to learn first

3. _____*resilient*_____ Able to recover quickly from harm, illness, or misfortune

4. _____*collaborate*_____ To work together on a project; cooperate in an effort

5. _____*zealot*_____ A person totally devoted to a purpose or cause

6. _____*squelch*_____ To silence or suppress; crush

7. _____*venerate*_____ To respect deeply; revere

8. _____*despondent*_____ Downhearted; hopeless; overwhelmed with sadness

9. _____*retrospect*_____ Reviewing the past; considering past events

10. _____*scoff*_____ To make fun of; mock; refuse to take seriously

CAUTION: Do not go any further until you are sure the above answers are correct. Then you can use the definitions to help you in the following practices. Your goal is eventually to know the words well enough so that you don't need to check the definitions at all.

Sentence Check 1

Using the answer line provided, complete each item below with the correct word from the box. Use each word once.

A. collaborate	B. despondent	C. instigate	D. resilient	E. retrospect
F. rudimentary	G. scoff	H. squelch	I. venerate	J. zealot

rudimentary   1. My ability to speak Spanish is ___, but I can at least manage to ask directions or order a meal.

despondent   2. Jaime was ___ over the death of his dog, his companion for fourteen years.

instigate   3. The novel *Uncle Tom's Cabin*, which exposed the horrors of slavery, helped to ___ the American Civil War.

zealot   4. Dawn is a ___ about banning nuclear weapons. She has walked for miles in protest marches and stood in the rain for hours during demonstrations.

venerate   5. Mother Teresa, who devoted her life to helping the poor, is ___(e)d by some people as a twentieth-century saint.

scoff   6. The Cord, in the 1920s, was the first car with front-wheel drive, but in those days most people considered the idea ridiculous and ___(e)d at it.

collaborate   7. Marie and Pierre Curie ___(e)d on important scientific experiments involving radioactivity.

squelch   8. Kim's parents nagged her so hard about practicing the piano that they finally ___(e)d any interest she might have had in music.

retrospect   9. Since I'd like to be a photographer, I can see, in ___, that I would have gained valuable experience if I'd taken pictures for the school newspaper.

resilient   10. Athletes need to be ___. After a defeat, an individual or a team must be able to come back and fight for victory the next time.

NOTE: Now check your answers to these items by turning to page 177. Going over the answers carefully will help you prepare for the next two practices, for which answers are not given.

Sentence Check 2

Using the answer lines provided, complete each item below with **two** words from the box. Use each word once.

rudimentary   1–2. Even though their knowledge of carpentry was only ____, the boys ___(e)d
collaborate   on building a treasure chest.

scoff   3–4. "Everyone gets ___(e)d at now and then," Lynn said. "You just have to be
resilient   ___ enough to bounce back after a facetious° remark."

venerate   5–6. Many people who ___(e)d Dr. Martin Luther King, Jr., were ___ when he
despondent   was killed, but then courageously vowed to carry on his work.

_____instigate_____
_____retrospect_____
7–8. At the time of the American Revolution, many people viewed those who ___(e)d the rebellion as troublemakers. In ___, however, we view them as heroes.

_____squelch_____
_____zealot_____
9–10. Being illiterate until the age of 20 didn't ___ George Washington Carver's spirit. He went on to become a great botanist—and a ___ about using peanuts, from which he made such products as ink, shampoo, and linoleum.

Final Check: *Hardly a Loser*

Here is a final opportunity for you to strengthen your knowledge of the ten words. First read the following selection carefully. Then fill in each blank with a word from the box at the top of the previous page. (Context clues will help you figure out which word goes in which blank.) Use each word once.

Tom seemed to be a loser born into a long line of losers. His great-grandfather, condemned to death during the Revolutionary War for siding with the British, had fled to Canada. Tom's father, wanted for arrest after he helped (1)_____instigate_____ a plot to overthrow the Canadian government, had fled back to the United States.

Tom never received even the most (2)_____rudimentary_____ formal education. During his mere three months of schooling, he stayed at the bottom of his class. The teacher (3)_____scoff_____(e)d at him, telling him that he was hopelessly stupid.

Tom's first job, selling papers and candy on a train, ended when he accidentally set the baggage car on fire. His second, as a telegraph operator, ended when he was caught sleeping on the job. At 22, he was jobless, penniless, and living in a cellar. Obviously, Tom's youth had not provided the optimum° foundation for success.

Tom, however, didn't allow his situation to be a detriment° or to (4)_____squelch_____ his hopes. Instead of becoming (5)_____despondent_____, he was (6)_____resilient_____ enough to recover from his misfortunes and find another job. He managed, in fact, to save enough money to open a workshop, where he (7)_____collaborate_____(e)d with an electrical engineer in designing and then selling machines. A (8)_____zealot_____ when it came to solving mechanical puzzles, Tom worked nearly nonstop, sleeping only about four hours each night.

By the time he was in his 80s, Tom was credited with over a thousand inventions, including the phonograph, light bulb, and motion picture camera. He was also very famous—so much so that he was (9)_____venerate_____(e)d nationwide as the greatest living American.

In (10)_____retrospect_____, Thomas Alva Edison wasn't such a loser after all.

Scores   Sentence Check 2 _____%   Final Check _____%

Enter your scores above and in the **Vocabulary Performance Chart** on the inside back cover of the book.

ambiguous	inane
dissident	juxtapose
embellish	lethargy
fritter	sporadic
inadvertent	subsidize

Ten Words in Context

In the space provided, write the letter of the meaning closest to that of each **boldfaced** word. Use the context of the sentences to help you figure out each word's meaning.

1 ambiguous
(ăm-bĭg′yoo-əs)
-adjective

● The portrait known as the "Mona Lisa" is famous for the woman's **ambiguous** expression. Is she smiling or not?

● Omar left an **ambiguous** message on my answering machine: "Meet me at twelve o'clock." I couldn't tell whether he meant noon or midnight.

A *Ambiguous* means   A. unclear.   B. unintentional.   C. unpleasant.

2 dissident
(dĭs′ə-dənt)
-noun

● Some **dissidents** in the Catholic church favor such changes as allowing women to be priests and allowing priests to marry.

● In a dictatorship, **dissidents** are not tolerated. People who speak out against the government may be imprisoned or even executed.

A *Dissident* means   A. a rebel.   B. a dishonest person.   C. a foolish person.

3 embellish
(ĕm-bĕl′ĭsh)
-verb

● Lauren **embellished** the door of her room with postcards from her friends and photos of her cats.

● The cover of the biology textbook was **embellished** with a pattern of colorful seashells.

B *Embellish* means   A. to hide.   B. to decorate.   C. to damage.

4 fritter
(frĭt′ər)
-verb

● I thought my little sister would **fritter** away her entire allowance on M&M's, but instead of wasting her money, she put it in her piggy bank.

● Vince **fritters** away both his time and his money playing game after game in video arcades.

C *Fritter away* means   A. to earn.   B. to count.   C. to waste.

5 inadvertent
(ĭn′-ăd-vûr′tnt)
-adjective

● Alexander Fleming's discovery of penicillin was **inadvertent**. He forgot to cover a dish of bacteria, and some mold got into it. The next day, Fleming found that the mold had killed the bacteria.

● The final draft of Nancy's paper was shorter than the previous version, but this was **inadvertent**. She had accidentally deleted an entire page without realizing it.

C *Inadvertent* means   A. not required.   B. not finished.   C. not intended.

6 inane
(ĭn-ān′)
-adjective

● The conversation at the party was **inane**, consisting mainly of foolish comments about whose clothes were the most "awesome."

● Television programming is often so **inane** that TV has been described as "bubble gum for the mind."

A *Inane* means   A. silly.   B. interesting.   C. shocking.

7 juxtapose
(jŭks′tə-pōz′)
-*verb*

- The photograph dramatically **juxtaposed** white birch trees and a dark gray sky.
- Dottie spread her new dress out on her bed and then **juxtaposed** all her scarves and jackets to it to see which combination would look best.

B *Juxtapose* means   A. to cover up.   B. to put side by side.   C. to replace.

8 lethargy
(lĕth′ər-jē)
-*noun*

- Although Wendy seemed to recover from the flu, her **lethargy** persisted. She felt exhausted for weeks.
- With the hot weather, **lethargy** descended upon the class. The students had trouble staying awake, and even the instructor gazed dreamily out the window.

A *Lethargy* means   A. weariness.   B. hopelessness.   C. foolishness.

9 sporadic
(spə-răd′ĭk)
-*adjective*

- It rained continuously until noon. After that, there were only **sporadic** showers.
- Dave makes **sporadic** attempts to give up smoking, but his occasional efforts have been halfhearted.

B *Sporadic* means   A. steady.   B. irregular.   C. long.

10 subsidize
(sŭb′sə-dīz)
-*verb*

- During college, many students are **subsidized** by their parents, while others rely on grants or loans.
- Public television is **subsidized** by various grants and by individual and community donations.

A *Subsidize* means   A. to pay for.   B. to advertise.   C. to criticize.

Matching Words with Definitions

Following are definitions of the ten words. Clearly write or print each word next to its definition. The sentences above and on the previous page will help you decide on the meaning of each word.

1. _____juxtapose_____ To place close together, especially in order to compare or contrast

2. _____lethargy_____ A great lack of energy; inactivity due to laziness; sluggishness

3. _____ambiguous_____ Able to be interpreted in more than one way; not clear

4. _____inane_____ Without sense or meaning; foolish

5. _____dissident_____ A person opposed to established ideas or beliefs, especially in politics or religion

6. _____embellish_____ To decorate; beautify by adding details

7. _____subsidize_____ To support financially; provide a grant or contribution

8. _____fritter_____ To spend or waste a little at a time

9. _____inadvertent_____ Unintentional; accidental

10. _____sporadic_____ Happening now and then; occasional

CAUTION: Do not go any further until you are sure the above answers are correct. Then you can use the definitions to help you in the following practices. Your goal is eventually to know the words well enough so that you don't need to check the definitions at all.

Sentence Check 1

Using the answer line provided, complete each item below with the correct word from the box. Use each word once.

A. **ambiguous**	B. **dissident**	C. **embellish**	D. **fritter**	E. **inadvertent**
F. **inane**	G. **juxtapose**	H. **lethargy**	I. **sporadic**	J. **subsidize**

lethargy   1. Instead of refreshing me, an afternoon nap only deepens my ___; I wake up even sleepier than I was before.

sporadic   2. I get news of Darren only now and then, in ___ letters from him or his mother.

subsidize   3. A research grant will ___ Belinda's study of common fears among the elderly.

inadvertent   4. My recent trip to Newark was ___. I wanted to go to New York City, but I got on the wrong train.

fritter   5. Tracy has learned the hard way not to ___ away her time and affection on friends who don't really care about her.

embellish   6. My little brother has ___(e)d his bedroom ceiling with stars arranged like several of the constellations.

juxtapose   7. In plays and movies, good and evil characters are often ___(e)d. This contrast makes the good ones seem even better and the bad ones seem even worse.

dissident   8. When student ___s led a protest against China's communist leaders in 1989, some students were killed by government troops.

ambiguous   9. Checking a job applicant's references, the personnel manager was puzzled by one ___ comment: "You will be lucky if you can get her to work for you."

inane   10. Steve Martin was poking fun at ___ ideas for products when he said, "I got a fur sink, an electric dog polisher, a gasoline-powered turtleneck sweater—and, of course, I bought some dumb stuff too."

NOTE: Now check your answers to these items by turning to page 177. Going over the answers carefully will help you prepare for the next two practices, for which answers are not given.

Sentence Check 2

Using the answer lines provided, complete each item below with **two** words from the box. Use each word once.

lethargy
sporadic   1–2. "Spring fever" isn't really a detriment° to health, but it often includes ___: people just want to sleep. Also, attention to work is interrupted off and on by a(n) ___ need to daydream.

juxtapose
dissident   3–4. On the cover of the news magazine, two pictures were ___(e)d: those of a young ___ and the elderly ruler he was opposing.

subsidize
embellish   5–6. Local businesses ___(e)d our club's Christmas party for the homeless, so we were able to afford a special meal as well as decorations to ___ the room.

_____ fritter

_____ inane

_____ ambiguous

_____ inadvertent

7–8. Why do you want to ___ away your money week after week on tickets for silly movies that all the critics agree are ___?

9–10. This week's episode of one television serial had a(n) ___ ending: we don't know whether one of the characters survives his heart attack or dies. In retrospect°, I don't think this was ___. I believe the producers want to keep us guessing so we'll tune in again next week.

Final Check: *Grandfather at the Art Museum*

Here is a final opportunity for you to strengthen your knowledge of the ten words. First read the following selection carefully. Then fill in each blank with a word from the box at the top of the previous page. (Context clues will help you figure out which word goes in which blank.) Use each word once.

Last Saturday, my grandfather and I spent some time in the modern section of an art museum. Our visit was completely (1)_____ inadvertent _____. We'd come to see a show of nature photographs and wandered into the wrong room. Instead of leaving, Grandfather just stood there, staring at the paintings. His idea of worthwhile art is the soft-focus photography on greeting cards, and here was an exhibit of angry paintings by political (2)_____ dissident _____s.

In one painting, an empty plate and a plate that was piled high with food had been (3)_____ juxtapose _____(e)d on a table; the tablecloth was an American flag. Around this painting was an ornate golden frame (4)_____ embellish _____(e)d with tiny plastic models of hot dogs, apple pies, and other typical American foods. There was nothing (5)_____ ambiguous _____ about the message—it was crystal-clear. The artist was saying that some people in this country don't have enough to eat. After a few moments of stunned silence, my grandfather jolted the sleepy-looking guard out of his (6)_____ lethargy _____ by shouting, "Garbage! What is this garbage?"

When we learned that two major corporations had collaborated° to (7)_____ subsidize _____ this exhibit and even owned some of the art works, Grandfather was outraged. "How dare they (8)_____ fritter _____ away their money on one piece of unpatriotic trash after another while people are starving?" I started to say that the painting itself was a protest against starvation, but Grandfather just scoffed° at me. "Don't be (9)_____ inane _____," he said, squelching° my attempt to explain the painting. "Let's get out of here." So we did.

On the way home, Grandfather stared out the car window. He was silent except for (10)_____ sporadic _____ sputterings of "Garbage!" and "Incredible!"

Scores   Sentence Check 2 _____%   Final Check _____%

berate	maudlin
estrange	regress
euphoric	relinquish
impetuous	ubiquitous
infallible	zenith

Ten Words in Context

In the space provided, write the letter of the meaning closest to that of each **boldfaced** word. Use the context of the sentences to help you figure out each word's meaning.

1 berate
(bǐ-rāt′)
-verb

● Nick's mother often **berates** him. And when she isn't yelling at him, she ignores him.

● Vanessa can accept reasonable criticism, but she was upset when her boss **berated** her loudly in front of everyone else in the office.

_C_ *Berate* means   A. to disappoint.   B. to neglect.   C. to scold angrily.

2 estrange
(ě-strānj′)
-verb

● My cousin's recent moodiness has **estranged** some of his old friends.

● After his divorce, Gavin didn't want to **estrange** his children, so he called and visited them often.

_B_ *Estrange* means   A. to frighten.   B. to drive away.   C. to dislike.

3 euphoric
(yōō-fôr′ĭk)
-adjective

● I was **euphoric** when I received my grades. To my amazement and joy, they were all A's and B's.

● Nikki is **euphoric** today, and it's easy to see why she's in such high spirits. She's just gotten the lead role in our school's production of *Beauty and the Beast*.

_A_ *Euphoric* means   A. very happy.   B. boastful.   C. sentimental.

4 impetuous
(ĭm-pĕch′ōō-əs)
-adjective

● Whenever I make an **impetuous** purchase, I end up being dissatisfied: the shoes aren't comfortable, the shirt is the wrong color, the jacket costs too much. From now on, I intend to think more carefully before I buy.

● Children tend to be **impetuous** and often don't think about the consequences of their actions. For instance, they'll throw snowballs at passing cars without worrying about possibly causing an accident.

_A_ *Impetuous* means   A. impulsive.   B. considerate.   C. imaginative.

5 infallible
(ĭn-făl′ə-bəl)
-adjective

● Computers aren't **infallible**. If you put the wrong data into a computer, you'll get wrong answers.

● A sign over my sister's desk reads, "I'm **infallible**. I never make misteaks."

_A_ *Infallible* means   A. perfect.   B. imperfect.   C. everywhere.

6 maudlin
(môd′lĭn)
-adjective

● The verses in greeting cards are often far too sentimental. I prefer humor to such **maudlin** messages.

● The authors of **maudlin** soap operas must feel that they haven't done their job unless viewers are crying by the end of each show.

_C_ *Maudlin* means   A. short.   B. comical.   C. overly emotional.

7 regress
(rĭ-grĕs′)
-verb

● When his baby sister was born, seven-year-old Jeremy **regressed** for a while and began sucking his thumb again.

● Adolescents under stress sometimes **regress** to childish ways: dependency, temper tantrums, and silliness.

__A__ *Regress* means   A. to go backward.   B. to reach a high point.   C. to act hastily.

8 relinquish
(rĭ-lĭng′kwĭsh)
-verb

● No beer is allowed in the "family area" of the stadium, so fans must **relinquish** their six-packs at the gate before they take their seats.

● Donna had to **relinquish** her share in the beach house because she couldn't afford it anymore.

__B__ *Relinquish* means   A. to buy.   B. to give up.   C. to enjoy.

9 ubiquitous
(yo͞o-bĭk′wə-təs)
-adjective

● Mites are **ubiquitous**. They live on top of Mt. Everest, in the depths of the ocean, at the South Pole, and even around the roots of your hairs.

● We postponed our plan to drive home on Sunday because a dense fog was **ubiquitous**. It covered the entire town.

__C__ *Ubiquitous* means   A. scarce.   B. newly discovered.   C. found everywhere.

10 zenith
(zē′nĭth)
-noun

● Florence reached the **zenith** of her career when she became president of Ace Products.

● At age 50, my uncle is afraid that he has already **passed** the zenith of his life; but at age 52, my father thinks the best is yet to come.

__C__ *Zenith* means   A. an end.   B. an earlier condition.   C. the highest point.

Matching Words with Definitions

Following are definitions of the ten words. Clearly write or print each word next to its definition. The sentences above and on the previous page will help you decide on the meaning of each word.

1. _____relinquish_____   To surrender (something); give (something) up

2. _____impetuous_____   Done or acting in a hurry, with little thought; impulsive

3. _____maudlin_____   Tearfully sentimental; overly emotional

4. _____berate_____   To criticize or scold harshly

5. _____ubiquitous_____   Existing or seeming to exist everywhere at the same time

6. _____zenith_____   The highest point or condition; peak

7. _____estrange_____   To make unsympathetic or unfriendly; alienate

8. _____infallible_____   Not capable of error or failure; unable to make a mistake

9. _____euphoric_____   Overjoyed; having an intense feeling of well-being

10. _____regress_____   To return to an earlier, generally worse, condition or behavior

CAUTION: Do not go any further until you are sure the above answers are correct. Then you can use the definitions to help you in the following practices. Your goal is eventually to know the words well enough so that you don't need to check the definitions at all.

Sentence Check 1

Using the answer line provided, complete each item below with the correct word from the box. Use each word once.

A. berate	B. estrange	C. euphoric	D. impetuous	E. infallible
F. maudlin	G. regress	H. relinquish	I. ubiquitous	J. zenith

___regress___ 1. People in bombed-out, war-torn cities sometimes ___ to more primitive ways of life.

___zenith___ 2. To many people, Mozart's works represent the ___ of eighteenth-century music.

___euphoric___ 3. Mei Lin was ___ when the college that was her first choice accepted her.

___relinquish___ 4. When Dad lost his job, he had to ___ his identification card, his employee parking permit, and the key to his desk.

___estrange___ 5. Kay used to be friendly, but since her promotion, she has become so cold that she has ___(e)d former coworkers.

___infallible___ 6. "I don't expect you to be ___," the boss said, "but I don't want you to make the same mistakes over and over."

___berate___ 7. "I know I was late," Liz said, "but you could have pointed it out quietly. You didn't have to ___ me."

___ubiquitous___ 8. In our neighborhood, litter is ___—the sidewalks are ankle-deep in trash. We need a cleanup campaign.

___maudlin___ 9. Uncle Antonio becomes ___ when he talks about his dear old mother in Italy. Tears also come to the eyes of all who listen.

___impetuous___ 10. Joyce isn't usually ___, but last week she had a sudden urge to try out her nephew's skateboard. Everyone in the office has already signed the cast on her broken wrist.

NOTE: Now check your answers to these items by turning to page 177. Going over the answers carefully will help you prepare for the next two practices, for which answers are not given.

Sentence Check 2

Using the answer lines provided, complete each item below with **two** words from the box. Use each word once.

___infallible___
___relinquish___ 1–2. If people were ___, we could ___ our erasers, our correction tape or fluid, and the "delete" key.

___impetuous___
___berate___ 3–4. I'm trying to be less ___, but I still sometimes act on impulse. Later, in retrospect°, I always ___ myself for not using better judgment.

___ubiquitous___
___maudlin___ 5–6. Since my father died, reminders of him seem ___. I know I'm being ___, but everywhere I look, I see something that makes me cry.

_____ *estrange* _____

_____ *regress* _____

7–8. Patrick ___(e)d his wife when he wasted their money on gambling and ostentatious° clothes. Since their separation, their young daughter has ___(e)d to infantile behavior.

_____ *zenith* _____

_____ *euphoric* _____

9–10. Our neighborhood basketball team reached its ___ when it won the citywide championship. The local businesses that had subsidized° the team were delighted, and the players themselves were ___.

Final Check: *My Brother's Mental Illness*

Here is a final opportunity for you to strengthen your knowledge of the ten words. First read the following selection carefully. Then fill in each blank with a word from the box at the top of the previous page. (Context clues will help you figure out which word goes in which blank.) Use each word once.

My brother Gary is mentally ill. At first my parents thought it was their fault, but now we know that his illness has much more to do with his body chemistry than with anything they did.

Gary's illness involves extreme mood swings. For weeks, he'll be (1)_____ *euphoric* _____, feeling that the world is great and that he's at the (2)_____ *zenith* _____ of life. He may even view himself as (3)_____ *infallible* _____ and get angry if anyone even suggests he has made a mistake. Sometimes, too, he becomes a(n) (4)_____ *impetuous* _____ shopper, spending thousands of dollars on whatever appeals to him. When we ask him to (5)_____ *relinquish* _____ the expensive things he's bought so that we can return them, he refuses, saying he wants to "live like a king." At such times, Gary has to go to the hospital.

Gary's "highs," however, are nothing compared with his "lows." At first, he is simply (6)_____ *maudlin* _____. He may sit in the living room all evening, talking and crying about his former girlfriends, our dead grandmother, or childhood hurts. Misfortune and horror, he says, are (7)_____ *ubiquitous* _____ in his life—there's nowhere he can go to avoid them. Within days, he is very despondent° and so overcome with lethargy° that he can't even get out of bed. Shutting out everyone around him, he (8)_____ *estrange* _____s his family and friends. Then he (9)_____ *berate* _____(e)s himself for all the faults he feels he has. Finally, he tries to kill himself. Again, he must go to the hospital.

When Gary takes his medicine, he does very well. He is charming, gregarious°, bright, and full of life. But when he feels good, he soon stops taking his medicine and begins to (10)_____ *regress* _____. Then we know he is headed for another severe mood swing.

I love my brother dearly, but living with him is like being on a roller coaster. For all of our sakes, I wish we could help him more.

Scores   Sentence Check 2 _____%   Final Check _____%

Enter your scores above and in the **Vocabulary Performance Chart** on the inside back cover of the book.

charlatan	hoist
corroborate	illicit
disseminate	irrevocable
diverge	precipitate
dormant	proliferation

Ten Words in Context

In the space provided, write the letter of the meaning closest to that of each **boldfaced** word. Use the context of the sentences to help you figure out each word's meaning.

1 charlatan
(shär'lə-tən)
-noun

- My grandmother once bought a "magnetic box" from a **charlatan** who assured her that it would cure her arthritis. Of course, the box was worthless.
- In the days of the Wild West, **charlatans** sold "snake oil" as a remedy for everything from baldness to insanity.

C *Charlatan* means A. an investor. B. an expert. C. a con artist.

2 corroborate
(kə-rŏb'ə-rāt')
-verb

- You claim you were at a soccer game when the crime was committed. Can anyone **corroborate** your story?
- Sid says he saw a flying saucer in the park, but no one else in the area has come forward to **corroborate** his account.

B *Corroborate* means A. to question. B. to support. C. to understand.

3 disseminate
(dĭs-sĕm'ə-nāt')
-verb

- Campaign workers went all over the city to **disseminate** pamphlets and flyers about their candidate.
- What would be the best way to **disseminate** information about the next school board meeting? It's important for all parents to attend.

A *Disseminate* means A. to spread. B. to conceal. C. to improve.

4 diverge
(dĭ-vûrj')
-verb

- The brothers' paths **diverged** greatly. One became a famous lawyer, and the other ended up in jail for armed robbery.
- In a well-known poem, Robert Frost uses a branching path as a symbol of life's decisions: "Two roads **diverged** in a wood, and I—I took the one less traveled by."

A *Diverge* means A. to separate. B. to unite. C. to disappear.

5 dormant
(dôr'mənt)
-adjective

- Many insects lay eggs that remain **dormant** all winter and do not hatch until spring, in the warmer weather.
- A visit to Puerto Rico reawakened Anita's **dormant** interest in Spanish, the language of her childhood.

A *Dormant* means A. not active. B. irreversible. C. growing.

6 hoist
(hoist)
-verb

- Let's go over to the construction site and watch the crane **hoist** the beams into place for the new skyscraper.
- So far, attempts to **hoist** the wreckage of the jetliner from the ocean floor have been unsuccessful.

C *Hoist* means A. to follow. B. to display. C. to raise.

7 illicit
(ĭl-lĭs′ĭt)
-adjective

- Years of **illicit** activities resulted in Gene's being sentenced to serve a life term in prison.
- Ted's business is **illicit**: he drives an unlicensed passenger van along a route that's supposed to be used only by city buses.

_B_ *Illicit* means   A. fake.   B. unlawful.   C. unprofitable.

8 irrevocable
(ĭr-rĕv′ə-kə-bəl)
-adjective

- Layla would like to break off her engagement to Ahmed, but she feels that her promise to marry him is **irrevocable**.
- Giving a child up for adoption has become a subject of debate. Should the mother be allowed to change her mind, or should her decision be **irrevocable**?

_A_ *Irrevocable* means   A. not reversible.   B. mistaken.   C. not certain.

9 precipitate
(prē-sĭp′ə-tāt′)
-verb

- Mark's search for a larger house was **precipitated** by his marriage to a woman with four children.
- The discovery that Elliot had been setting fires **precipitated** his parents' decision to send him to a child psychologist.

_A_ *Precipitate* means   A. to bring on.   B. to prevent.   C. to permit.

10 proliferation
(prō-lĭf′ər-ā′shən)
-noun

- Hana's doctors hope that chemotherapy will halt the **proliferation** of cancer cells in her body.
- The **proliferation** of dandelions in my yard is too much for me to handle. They're growing faster than I can destroy them.

_C_ *Proliferation* means   A. damage.   B. a shortage.   C. a rapid increase.

Matching Words with Definitions

Following are definitions of the ten words. Clearly write or print each word next to its definition. The sentences above and on the previous page will help you decide on the meaning of each word.

1. _dormant_   Inactive; alive but not actively growing, as if asleep

2. _disseminate_   To spread or scatter widely; distribute

3. _irrevocable_   Not able to be canceled or undone; irreversible

4. _proliferation_   A rapid spread or increase

5. _corroborate_   To confirm; strengthen with further evidence; provide proof of

6. _precipitate_   To cause to happen quickly, suddenly, or sooner than expected

7. _hoist_   To lift, especially with some mechanical means, like a cable

8. _charlatan_   A fake; a person who falsely claims to have some special skill or knowledge

9. _diverge_   To branch off in different directions from the same starting point; to become different

10. _illicit_   Illegal

CAUTION: Do not go any further until you are sure the above answers are correct. Then you can use the definitions to help you in the following practices. Your goal is eventually to know the words well enough so that you don't need to check the definitions at all.

Sentence Check 1

Using the answer line provided, complete each item below with the correct word from the box. Use each word once.

A. **charlatan**	B. **corroborate**	C. **disseminate**	D. **diverge**	E. **dormant**
F. **hoist**	G. **illicit**	H. **irrevocable**	I. **precipitate**	J. **proliferation**

diverge   1. Children's lives often ___ from the paths their parents planned for them.

charlatan   2. The "natural healer" was a ___. He knew nothing about healing—natural or otherwise.

irrevocable   3. I thought your vow to quit smoking was ___, but you've broken it already.

dormant   4. When I visited the art museum, my ___ creative instinct awakened. Now I've signed up for a course in sculpture.

precipitate   5. Rafael's growth of four inches over the summer ___(e)d a shopping trip for new clothes.

illicit   6. In our city, the police department has special units to investigate ___ activities such as gambling and drug use.

hoist   7. The stone slabs are too heavy for us to move, so we're bringing in a forklift to ___ them onto the walkway.

disseminate   8. The environmental group ___(e)d leaflets about the oil spill, describing the damage and urging people to boycott the oil company.

corroborate   9. I'm afraid I can't ___ Todd's claim that he's never had problems with schoolwork. The fact is that he's failed several courses.

proliferation   10. Sadly, the ___ of homeless dogs and cats has become so great that about seventeen million of them are killed in U.S. animal shelters each year.

NOTE: Now check your answers to these items by turning to page 177. Going over the answers carefully will help you prepare for the next two practices, for which answers are not given.

Sentence Check 2

Using the answer lines provided, complete each item below with **two** words from the box. Use each word once.

corroborate
diverge   1–2. The map ___s my belief that just before the lake, the highway ___s into two roads, which go off in opposite directions.

dormant
illicit   3–4. Rocky was briefly involved in a gang. Then his ___ conscience woke up, and he realized he really didn't want to engage in ___ activities.

hoist
irrevocable   5–6. When the movers tried to ___ our piano to a second-floor window, a cable broke, and the piano crashed onto the sidewalk. We know the damage was inadvertent°, but our decision to sue the moving company for negligence is ___.

_____disseminate_____

_____precipitate_____

_____proliferation_____

_____charlatan_____

7–8. Employees were ordered not to ___ any information about the fire at the factory; the news might scare off stockholders and ___ bankruptcy.

9–10. After a retirement community was built in Morristown, there was a ___ of ___s in the area, peddling "miracle" cures for all kinds of ills—some of which were not only useless but actually a detriment° to health.

Final Check: *A Get-Rich-Quick Scam*

Here is a final opportunity for you to strengthen your knowledge of the ten words. First read the following selection carefully. Then fill in each blank with a word from the box at the top of the previous page. (Context clues will help you figure out which word goes in which blank.) Use each word once.

It's said that "there's a sucker born every minute." In retrospect°, after the events of last summer, I think most of them must live in my hometown, Glenville. I, along with nearly everyone else in town, was taken in by a (1)_____charlatan_____—a swindler who made us believe he could help us get rich overnight.

This con artist, whose name was Chester Turner, supposedly came into town to open a real estate office. After buying up lots of cheap land, he hinted to some of the town's leading citizens that there would soon be an incredible (2)_____proliferation_____ of people wanting to buy land in Glenville. Naturally, those who received this interesting information promptly (3)_____disseminate_____(e)d it throughout town, and soon we were all talking about it. When people questioned Turner about the value of town land, he would hint that there was oil in Glenville by asking, "What if there were energy lying (4)_____dormant_____ under the ground in the area, just waiting to spurt out?"

An oil find, we all agreed, would (5)_____precipitate_____ a huge increase in land prices. Our suspicions about oil seemed to be (6)_____corroborate_____(e)d by some "oil company executives" overheard talking in the local diner. According to their waitress, they would soon have cranes (7)_____hoist_____ the oil derricks so they could begin pumping out millions of gallons of the precious liquid. Soon people were pounding on Turner's door, begging him to sell them land in Glenville.

After Turner left town with our money, we realized that he and his "oil men" had collaborated° to swindle us. We began to hear rumors that all of them had been arrested for carrying out (8)_____illicit_____ activities in another state. Although we had all been of one mind when Turner was around, our views now (9)_____diverge_____(e)d. Most of us just kissed our money goodbye, though we berated° ourselves for trusting Turner. Some people, however, clung to the belief that they could somehow get Turner to give their money back. They couldn't accept the fact that the loss of their money was (10)_____irrevocable_____.

Scores	Sentence Check 2 _____%	Final Check _____%

ante-, anti-	extra-
chron, chrono-	ject
-cide	liber, liver
de-	vit, viv
dorm	voc, vok

Ten Word Parts in Context

Common word parts—also known as *prefixes, suffixes*, and *roots*—are used in forming many words in English. Figure out the meanings of the following ten word parts by looking *closely* and *carefully* at the context in which they appear. Then, in the space provided, write the letter of the meaning closest to that of each word part.

1 ante-, anti-

● Before you enter Tyrone's living room, you pass through a small **anteroom**, where guests can leave their coats.

● A clever saying warns us not to **anticipate** trouble before it happens: "Worrying casts tomorrow's clouds over today's sunshine."

<u>C</u> The word part *ante-* or *anti-* means

A. after.   B. free.   C. before.

2 chron, chrono-

● An acute illness is short and usually severe. By contrast, a **chronic** illness lasts a long period of time.

● A resumé should list jobs in reverse **chronological** order—that is, the most recent job should be listed first.

<u>A</u> The word part *chron* or *chrono-* means

A. time.   B. outside.   C. alive.

3 -cide

● Do the **pesticides** used in farming kill only pests? Or are they also harmful to humans?

● **Genocide** isn't simply the murder of a number of people. It's the intentional killing of a particular racial, cultural, or political group.

<u>B</u> The word part *-cide* means

A. alive.   B. kill.   C. freedom.

4 de-

● When the two trains ran into each other, one was **derailed**, but the other stayed on the tracks.

● A good kitchen fan can **deodorize** the room by drawing away strong cooking odors, such as those of onion and garlic.

<u>C</u> The word part *de-* means

A. voice.   B. preceding.   C. removal.

5 dorm

● The volcano has been **dormant** for years, but it may awaken and erupt soon.

● The **dormouse**, or "sleeping mouse," got its name because it hibernates through the winter.

<u>C</u> The word part *dorm* means

A. lively.   B. separation.   C. sleep.

6 extra-

● Chang studies hard for his classes, but he's also involved in **extracurricular** activities, including soccer and chess.

● **Extrasensory** perception, or ESP, is the ability to receive information in ways that do not involve the physical senses.

<u>C</u> The word part *extra-* means

A. enclosed.   B. throw.   C. outside.

7 ject

- The pilot **ejected** from the plane shortly before the crash. Fortunately, his parachute opened in time to save his life.
- The farther away a **projector** is, the larger the picture it throws onto the screen.

A The word part *ject* means   A. throw.   B. keep.   C. call.

8 liber, liver

- Freddy is very **liberal** with advice. He constantly tells all his relatives and friends how they should run their lives.
- According to the Bible, Moses **delivered** the people of Israel from slavery in Egypt.

B The word part *liber* or *liver* means   A. alive.   B. free.   C. outside.

9 vit, viv

- My elderly aunt still has great **vitality**: she works in a bakery part-time and walks two or three miles every day.
- People who **survive** a disaster sometimes feel guilty because they lived through it, while others died.

A The word part *vit* or *viv* means   A. life.   B. separation.   C. death.

10 voc, vok

- My father is extremely **vocal** in his disapproval of text-messaging. He always yells at me, "If you want to talk to someone, *use the phone!*"
- The man on trial for robbery **invoked** his Fifth Amendment rights, saying he would not give any information that could be held against him.

B The word part *voc* or *vok* means   A. memory.   B. voice.   C. time.

Matching Word Parts with Definitions

Following are definitions of the ten word parts. Clearly write or print each word part next to its definition. The sentences above and on the previous page will help you decide on the meaning of each word part.

1. _____vit, viv_____ Life, lively

2. _____extra-_____ Outside, beyond

3. _____chron, chrono-_____ Time

4. _____liber, liver_____ Free, freedom

5. _____de-_____ Away, separation, removal

6. _____ante-, anti-_____ Before, preceding

7. _____voc, vok_____ Voice, call

8. _____dorm_____ Sleep

9. _____ject_____ Throw, toss

10. _____-cide_____ Kill, killing, killer

CAUTION: Do not go any further until you are sure the above answers are correct. Then you can use the definitions to help you in the following practices. Your goal is eventually to know the word parts well enough so that you don't need to check the definitions at all.

Sentence Check 1

Using the answer line provided, complete each *italicized* word below with the correct word part from the box. Use each word part once.

A. ante-, anti-	B. chron	C. cide	D. de-	E. dorm
F. extra-	G. ject	H. liber	I. vit, viv	J. voc, vok

_____antipasto_____ 1. At the Italian restaurant, we had a(n) (. . . *pasto*) ___ of olives, cheeses, and other appetizers before the main dish.

_____revived_____ 2. I was very tired when I got home from work, but a short nap (*re . . . ed*) ___ me.

_____injection_____ 3. The veterinarian asked Rosa to hold her cat firmly while he gave it an (*in . . . ion*) ___ to protect it from rabies.

_____defrosting_____ 4. A microwave oven is perfect for (. . . *frosting*) ___ frozen foods in a hurry.

_____dormitories_____ 5. The conference was held at a college campus, so participants could sleep in the (. . . *itories*) ___ instead of going to hotels.

_____extraordinary_____ 6. In a crisis, people sometimes perform (. . . *ordinary*) ___ feats of strength, like lifting an automobile off a crash victim.

_____liberated_____ 7. Modern inventions have (. . . *ated*) ___ us from many household chores. For instance, the dryer frees us from having to hang laundry on a clothesline.

_____Regicide_____ 8. (*Regi . . .*) ___ means "the killing of a king." A famous instance is Charles I of England, who was beheaded in 1649.

_____vocabulary_____ 9. Leah has an amazing (. . . *abulary*) ___ for a two-year-old. She was just telling me the difference between "Mr. Crocodile" and "Mr. Alligator."

_____anachronism_____ 10. An (*ana . . . ism*) ___ is someone or something that seems to belong to an earlier time and is out of place in the present. San Francisco's cable cars are an example.

NOTE: Now check your answers to these items by turning to page 177. Going over the answers carefully will help you prepare for the next two practices, for which answers are not given.

Sentence Check 2

Using the answer line provided, complete each *italicized* word in the sentences below with the correct word part from the box. Use each word part once.

_____vocation_____
_____vivid_____
1–2. Angela chose medicine as her (. . . *ation*) ___ because when she was twelve years old, she had a(n) (. . . *id*) ___ dream that convinced her she had been "called" to heal people.

_____homicide_____
_____chronic_____
3–4. Many people believe that (*homi . . .*) ___ will remain a(n) (. . . *ic*) ___ problem in American society until our ubiquitous° handguns are made illegal. So long as guns can be obtained almost anywhere, people will be tempted to use them.

_____dormers_____   5–6. The attic bedroom has three windows, called (. . . *ers*) ___. They're set at an
_____detached_____   angle to the roof, so they look as if they are partly (. . . *tached*) ___ from the
                           rest of the house.

_____liberty_____   7–8. The queen's closest advisers were at (. . . *ty*) ___ to enter the throne room
_____antechamber_____   freely. All others had to wait in the (. . . *chamber*) ___ before they were
                           allowed to see her.

extraterrestrials 9–10. In science fiction stories, (. . . *terrestrials*) ___ such as E.T. are often able to
_____projecting_____   communicate by (*pro . . . ing*) ___ their thoughts into Earth people's minds.
                           Real scientists, however, scoff° at this idea, thinking such communication
                           impossible.

Final Check: *Holiday Blues*

Here is a final opportunity for you to strengthen your knowledge of the ten word parts. First read the following selection carefully. Then complete each *italicized* word in the parentheses below with a word parts from the box at the top of the previous page. (Context clues will help you figure out which word part goes in which blank.) Use each word part once.

Tensions and sadness greatly (. . . *tract*) (1)_____detract_____ from many people's enjoyment of the winter holidays. For those who are (. . . *ically*) (2)_____chronically_____ depressed, the holiday season can intensify the problem.

For one thing, holidays are extra work. When juxtaposed° with a person's existing job, school, or family obligations, such additional tasks as shopping for gifts or baking trays of Christmas cookies may precipitate° a feeling of hopelessness. Also, the (. . . *ordinary*) (3)_____extraordinary_____ expectations that many have for the holidays often (*e . . . e*) (4)_____evoke_____ sad feelings. For instance, (. . . *cipation*) (5)_____anticipation_____ of the traditional family gatherings may awaken (. . . *ant*) (6)_____dormant_____ feelings of disappointment that one's family is not as warm or close as it "should" be. In the hopes of (*in . . . ing*) (7)_____injecting_____ more happiness into the season or of (*re . . . alizing*) (8)_____revitalizing_____ family relationships, people may fritter° away paycheck after paycheck on extravagant, ostentatious° gifts meant to impress their relatives. The financial burden then adds to the holiday problems.

Not everyone is resilient° enough to bear all this pressure. In fact, (*sui . . .*) (9)_____suicide_____ rates increase around the holidays. Some despondent° people, however, wisely seek counseling in hopes of (. . . *ating*) (10)_____liberating_____ themselves from the holiday blues.

Scores   Sentence Check 2 _____%   Final Check _____%

Enter your scores above and in the **Vocabulary Performance Chart** on the inside back cover of the book.

The box at the right lists twenty-five words from Unit One. Using the clues at the bottom of the page, fill in these words to complete the puzzle that follows.

Word box:
berate
charlatan
despondent
dexterous
dissident
diverge
dormant
embellish
facetious
fritter
hoist
illicit
impetuous
inane
lethargy
maudlin
optimum
regress
resilient
scoff
scrupulous
squelch
ubiquitous
venerate
vicarious

ACROSS

1. To decorate; beautify by adding details
5. A fake; a person who falsely claims to have some special skill or knowledge
6. Careful about moral standards; conscientious
8. Best possible; most desirable
10. Illegal
11. Without sense or meaning; foolish
13. Downhearted; hopeless
16. To branch off in different directions
18. To return to an earlier, usually worse, condition or behavior
21. Humorous; playful or joking
22. To silence or suppress; crush
23. Skillful in using the hands or body

DOWN

2. To criticize or scold harshly
3. To lift, especially with some mechanical means
4. Tearfully sentimental; over-emotional
7. Existing or seeming to exist everywhere at the same time
9. A great lack of energy; inactivity due to laziness
10. Done or acting in a hurry, with little thought; impulsive
12. To respect deeply; revere
14. Inactive; alive but not actively growing, as if asleep
15. To spend or waste bit by bit
16. A person opposed to established ideas or beliefs
17. Experienced through the imagination
19. Able to recover quickly from harm, illness, or misfortune
20. To make fun of

PART A

Choose the word that best completes each item and write it in the space provided.

corroborate   1. Because I had witnessed the accident, one driver asked me to ___ his claim that the other driver had gone through a red light.

     A. collaborate   B. estrange   C. corroborate   D. juxtapose

venerate   2. Asians tend to ___ the elderly, but in America, age does not necessarily bring respect.

     A. precipitate   B. venerate   C. juxtapose   D. squelch

instigates   3. If Bart's parents leave him alone with his sister for even thirty seconds, he ___ a fight with her.

     A. subsidizes   B. collaborates   C. instigates   D. hoists

diverges   4. When driving to Melissa's house, go left at the fork in the road, the point where the road ___ into two.

     A. berates   B. scoffs   C. diverges   D. precipitates

proliferation   5. Overcrowding in early factories provided an ideal environment for the ___ of bacteria, resulting in epidemics of tuberculosis.

     A. proliferation   B. detriment   C. discretion   D. retrospect

sensory   6. Our brains interpret our ___ impressions for us. For instance, the images of things we look at must go to the brain so we can actually "see" them.

     A. inadvertent   B. scrupulous   C. sensory   D. resilient

facetious   7. I thought the handyman was being ___ when he said he had to cut a bigger hole in my wall in order to fix the little hole, but that's exactly what he did.

     A. dexterous   B. facetious   C. ubiquitous   D. maudlin

squelch   8. I tried to ___ the laugh rising in my throat, but seeing the boss looking all over his desk for the glasses he had pushed up on his head was too funny.

     A. squelch   B. venerate   C. berate   D. juxtapose

scrupulous   9. Grandfather was known for being ___. Once he spent twenty-five cents for the trolley in order to go back to a store and return the extra nickel that he had received in change.

     A. illicit   B. scrupulous   C. dormant   D. vicarious

dormant   10. The nineteenth-century French writer Alfred de Musset said, "Know that there is often hidden in us a(n) ___ poet, always young and alive." It is up to us to awaken that creative part of ourselves.

     A. inane   B. facetious   C. illicit   D. dormant

(Continues on next page)

PART B

On the answer line, write the letter of the choice that best completes each item.

___A___ 11. At a party, a **gregarious** person is likely to
    A. be part of a lively group of people.
    B. leave early.
    C. sit and talk with just one person all evening.
    D. begin an argument over something silly.

___A___ 12. You can consider an event in **retrospect** only
    A. after the event has occurred.
    B. before the event happens.
    C. if the event is a happy one.
    D. while the event is actually happening.

___C___ 13. Valerie received an unexpected inheritance of $1,000. She **frittered** it away by
    A. giving it to her parents to pay household bills.
    B. making a down payment on a car.
    C. spending it on clothing and lottery tickets.
    D. putting it into her college savings fund.

___B___ 14. A **resilient** person who gets the flu
    A. will probably need a long time to recover.
    B. is soon able to resume her normal activities.
    C. complains endlessly about her misfortune.
    D. becomes afraid she'll catch something else.

___B___ 15. Some people become downright **maudlin** at weddings. For instance, when my sister got married, Uncle Arthur
    A. refused to kiss the bride.
    B. hugged her and sobbed, "You're leaving us!"
    C. seemed quiet and depressed.
    D. laughed, told jokes, and danced up a storm.

___A___ 16. Your brother has just announced that he plans to be President someday. You **scoff** at him, saying,
    A. "Right. And I'm going to be the Queen of England."
    B. "That'd be pretty hard, but I bet you could do it."
    C. "Tell me why you are interested in doing that."
    D. "It's cool that you're aiming so high."

___D___ 17. An essay called "How To **Estrange** Your Friends" might suggest
    A. inviting friends to your house to watch videos, eat pizza, and hang out.
    B. offering to teach friends a sport or skill that you're good at.
    C. noticing when friends are feeling depressed and sending them a card or a little gift.
    D. borrowing friends' money and not repaying it.

___D___ 18. You would most likely become **despondent** if
    A. it's a beautiful sunny day, your work is all done, and you've got money in your pocket.
    B. your boss has asked to see you, and you don't know if you're going to be fired or promoted.
    C. the restaurant you went to for lunch was out of your favorite kind of pie.
    D. your best friend is moving away, you've lost your job, and your car has broken down.

___A___ 19. Gene **embellished** his car by
    A. adding fancy hubcaps and a two-tone paint job.
    B. changing the oil at least every three thousand miles.
    C. not getting rid of soda cans and fast-food wrappers.
    D. never having it serviced and letting the engine burn up.

___C___ 20. Keith is known for being **impetuous**. Last week, he
    A. signed up to become a foster parent after thinking about it for several months.
    B. received the "Most Dependable Employee" award at his workplace.
    C. suddenly decided to drive across six states to visit a childhood friend, without even checking to see if the friend was at home.
    D. refused to lend his mother the money she needed to have some emergency dental work done.

Score   (Number correct) _____ x 5 = _____ %

PART A

Complete each item with a word from the box. Use each word once.

A. ambiguous	B. charlatan	C. euphoric	D. infallible	E. irrevocable
F. juxtapose	G. lethargy	H. regress	I. relinquish	J. subsidize
K. vicarious	L. zealot	M. zenith		

_____zenith_____ 1. Some people who reach the ___ of their careers find that "it's lonely at the top."

_____juxtapose_____ 2. To provide contrast, the photographer ___(e)d the men in their dark suits and the women in their pale dresses.

_____lethargy_____ 3. After a big picnic meal in the warm sun, a(n) ___ came over me, so I took a nap under a maple tree.

_____relinquish_____ 4. "If you don't maintain a B average," said the coach, "you ___ your right to be on this team."

_____vicarious_____ 5. Literature and drama allow us to experience problems in a(n) ___ way, giving us painless opportunities to shape our real-life views.

_____subsidize_____ 6. Public TV stations hold fund drives to encourage their viewers to help ___ the costs of their programs.

_____euphoric_____ 7. Kaylin's family was ___ when she arrived home, alive and well, three hours late. She had missed her plane, the one that had crashed.

_____infallible_____ 8. Jason sounds so sure of himself that he gives people the impression he is ___. But he makes mistakes too, just like the rest of us.

_____irrevocable_____ 9. The state trooper warned my brother, "Your driver's license is not ___. If you get one more speeding ticket, you will lose your license for a year."

_____charlatan_____ 10. Mrs. Angelo was shocked to learn that the "doctor" she had been seeing for three years was a(n) ___. In reality, he had attended medical school for only two semesters.

_____ambiguous_____ 11. When my older sister asked whether she and her seven kids could visit us for a week, my mother's response was so ___ that I'm not sure if she said yes or no.

_____regress_____ 12. The Bradleys won't go on vacation until their new puppy is fully trained. They're afraid that if he stays at the kennel for a week, he will ___ and start ruining the rugs again.

_____zealot_____ 13. After her first husband died from alcohol-related causes, Carry Nation became an anti-drinking ___. One year, as she traveled around the country, campaigning against alcohol, she destroyed twenty saloons with a hatchet.

(Continues on next page)

PART B

Write **C** if the italicized word is used **correctly**. Write **I** if the word is used **incorrectly**.

__I__ 14. Meeting my brother in the cafeteria at lunchtime was *inadvertent*. We had arranged the night before to meet for lunch.

__C__ 15. Rumors that the bank was losing money *precipitated* a panic. Hundreds of depositors demanded their savings.

__I__ 16. My aunt and uncle are rich but *ostentatious*. Judging by their modest possessions, you'd never know how much money they really have.

__C__ 17. Use *discretion* about where to consult with your doctor. If you run into him or her at church or the supermarket, it's not appropriate to ask about your warts or athlete's foot.

__C__ 18. Earth happens to be a place where oxygen is *ubiquitous*, making the planet suitable for many forms of life.

__I__ 19. During my childhood, we made *sporadic* visits to my grandparents' house. In fact, we went to see them every Sunday afternoon.

PART C

On the answer line, write the letter of the word that is the **synonym** of the boldfaced word.

Example: __A__ **dissident**   A. rebel   B. supporter   C. inhabitant

__A__ 20. **berate**   A. scold   B. invite   C. praise

__C__ 21. **rudimentary**   A. foolish   B. advanced   C. elementary

__C__ 22. **detriment**   A. advantage   B. contradiction C. obstacle

PART D

On the answer line, write the letter of the word that is the **antonym** of the boldfaced word.

Example: __B__ **dissident**   A. rebel   B. supporter   C. inhabitant

__B__ 23. **inane**   A. inexpensive B. sensible   C. silly

__C__ 24. **dexterous**   A. skillful   B. spiritual   C. clumsy

__B__ 25. **illicit**   A. usual   B. lawful   C. illegal

Score   (Number correct) _____   x 4 = _____%

Each item below starts with a pair of words in CAPITAL LETTERS. For each item, figure out the relationship between these two words. Then decide which of the choices (A, B, C, or D) expresses a similar relationship. Write the letter of your choice on the answer line.

D   1. DETRIMENT : ADVANTAGE ::
   A. help : assistance   C. determination : persistence
   B. work : digging   D. forgetting : remembering

A   2. DEXTEROUS : BRAIN SURGEON ::
   A. strong : weightlifter   C. honest : bank robber
   B. young : violinist   D. neat : mathematician

B   3. GREGARIOUS : UNSOCIABLE ::
   A. ambitious : hardworking   C. jealous : possessive
   B. enormous : tiny   D. famous : rich

A   4. OPTIMUM : GOOD ::
   A. worst : bad   C. careful : careless
   B. best : worse   D. high : low

C   5. COLLABORATE : TEAMMATES ::
   A. fight : pacifists   C. compete : rivals
   B. watch : listen   D. bark : cats

D   6. DESPONDENT : HOPELESS ::
   A. sensible : careless   C. generous : donation
   B. popular : friendless   D. fortunate : lucky

B   7. RUDIMENTARY : JELL-O ::
   A. outdated : pudding   C. expensive : donut
   B. advanced : wedding cake D. simple : French pastry

B   8. ZEALOT : SPORTS FAN ::
   A. musician : biologist   C. scientist : wrestler
   B. athlete : runner   D. writer : reader

A   9. AMBIGUOUS : MISUNDERSTAND ::
   A. funny : laugh   C. boring : enjoy
   B. doubtful : agree   D. clear : disagree

D   10. DISSIDENT : SUPPORT ::
   A. customer : pay   C. actor : comedy
   B. soprano : sing   D. leader : follow

(Continues on next page)

__B__ 11. EMBELLISH : COLORED LIGHTS ::
  A. exercise : armchair
  B. destroy : dynamite
  C. eat : nails
  D. sign : scissors

__A__ 12. INANE : SENSELESS ::
  A. injured : hurt
  B. pleasing : flower
  C. flawed : perfect
  D. audible : odorless

__D__ 13. BERATE : NAUGHTY CHILD ::
  A. comfort : lottery winner
  B. congratulate : grieving widow
  C. obey : prisoner
  D. praise : hardworking student

__C__ 14. EUPHORIC : SCHOLARSHIP WINNER ::
  A. calm : bride
  B. angry : puppy
  C. frightened : hostage
  D. surprised : instructor

__A__ 15. IMPETUOUS : CAUTIOUS ::
  A. passionate : unemotional
  B. quiet : handsome
  C. cheerful : encouraging
  D. shy : timid

__D__ 16. UBIQUITOUS : AIR ::
  A. rare : cellular phone
  B. ferocious : giraffe
  C. playful : insect
  D. sparkling : diamond

__C__ 17. DISSEMINATE : LEAFLETS ::
  A. hear : photographs
  B. color : size
  C. plant : seeds
  D. buy : sell

__C__ 18. IRREVOCABLE : DEATH ::
  A. new : history
  B. unlikely : race
  C. shiny : mirror
  D. freezing : sun

__A__ 19. HOIST : CRANE ::
  A. cut : knife
  B. fly : cane
  C. read : pen
  D. saw : hammer

__D__ 20. ILLICIT : LEGAL ::
  A. sun : star
  B. warm : hot
  C. cool : ice
  D. loud : quiet

Score   (Number correct) _____ x 5 = _____%

Enter your scores above and in the **Vocabulary Performance Chart** on the inside back cover of the book.

PART A

Listed in the left-hand column below are ten common word parts, followed by words in which the parts are used. In each blank, write in the letter of the correct definition on the right.

Word Parts	Examples	Definitions
H 1. **ante-, anti-**	anteroom, anticipate	A. Time
A 2. **chron-, chrono-**	chronic, chronological	B. Voice, call
E 3. **-cide**	pesticide, genocide	C. Away, separation, removal
C 4. **de-**	derail, deodorize	D. Life, lively
I 5. **dorm**	dormant, dormouse	E. Kill, killing, killer
J 6. **extra-**	extracurricular, extrasensory	F. Free, freedom
G 7. **ject**	eject, projector	G. Throw, toss
F 8. **liber, liver**	liberal, deliver	H. Before, preceding
D 9. **viv, vit**	vitality, survive	I. Sleep
B 10. **voc, vok**	vocal, invoke	J. Outside, beyond

PART B

Using the answer line provided, complete each *italicized* word in the sentences below with the correct word part from the box. Not every word part will be used.

A. **ante-**	B. **chron**	C. **-cide**	D. **de-**	E. **dorm**
F. **extra-**	G. **ject**	H. **liver**	I. **vit**	J. **vok**

_____dormitory_____ 11. A passenger train's (. . . *itory*) ___ car has sleeping facilities for the train's crew.

_____synchronized_____ 12. The chorus line was so wonderfully (*syn . . . ized*) ___—the dancers kept perfect time, seeming to move as one person.

_____vitamin_____ 13. In the refining process, white rice and white bread lose much of their (. . . *amin*) ___ content. For this reason, they are less nutritious than brown rice and whole-wheat bread.

_____project_____ 14. Ventriloquists must be able to (*pro . . .*) ___ their voices while keeping their lips closed. This act of "throwing the voice" creates the illusion that the words are being spoken by someone else—usually, a puppet sitting on the performer's lap.

_____deplane_____ 15. Airplane passengers used to be let off outdoors. Now they usually (. . . *plane*) ___ onto a ramp that leads directly into the terminal.

(Continues on next page)

PART C

Use your knowledge of word parts to determine the meaning of the **boldfaced** words. On the answer line, write the letter of each meaning.

___B___ 16. He **antedated** his check to the IRS.

       A. dated correctly   B. dated earlier than the actual date   C. wrote too late

___A___ 17. A new **bactericide** was being developed in the laboratory.

       A. something that destroys bacteria   B. a picture of bacteria   C. a dish of bacteria

___C___ 18. That textbook is filled with **extraneous** information.

       A. information that is timely   B. information that no longer applies   C. information beyond what students need to know

___C___ 19. My friend Kareem would like to **liberate** all the animals in the zoo.

       A. adopt   B. kill   C. set free

___A___ 20. The singer always **vocalized** before a concert.

       A. exercised her voice   B. took a nap   C. moved around on stage

Score   (Number correct) _____ x 5 = _____%

Enter your scores above and in the **Vocabulary Performance Chart** on the inside back cover of the book.

Unit Two

equivocate	propensity
fortuitous	reprehensible
impeccable	sham
liaison	solace
predisposed	solicitous

Ten Words in Context

In the space provided, write the letter of the meaning closest to that of each **boldfaced** word. Use the context of the sentences to help you figure out each word's meaning.

1 equivocate
(ē-kwĭv′ə-kāt′)
-verb

● Bob can't get his boss to say whether or not he intends to give him a raise. When Bob asks him, he **equivocates**, saying, "You've been doing good work, Bob."

● Lonnell doesn't want to come right out and tell Tiffany he doesn't love her. If she asks, he **equivocates** by telling her something like "You know how I feel."

B *Equivocate* means   A. to be blunt.   B. to be unclear.   C. to deny.

2 fortuitous
(fôr-tōō′ə-təs)
-adjective

● The birth of triplets wasn't entirely **fortuitous**. The mother had taken a fertility drug, which often causes multiple births.

● It was strictly **fortuitous** that Vince found his missing class notes. They happened to drop out of his dictionary when it fell to the floor.

A *Fortuitous* means   A. accidental.   B. predictable.   C. overdue.

3 impeccable
(ĭm-pĕk′ə-bəl)
-adjective

● My aunt always looks stylish but never overdressed. Her taste in clothes is **impeccable**.

● When she auditioned for the play, Julie gave an **impeccable** performance. She read the lines perfectly and got the part.

A *Impeccable* means   A. flawless.   B. deceptive.   C. faulty.

4 liaison
(lē-ā′zŏn′)
-noun

● The president of the Student Council acts as a **liaison** between the students and the administration.

● Because she is bilingual, Elena often serves as a **liaison** between the Spanish- and English-speaking personnel in her office.

C *Liaison* means   A. a follower.   B. a caregiver.   C. a link.

5 predisposed
(prē′dĭs-pōzd′)
-adjective

● Terry didn't want to move in the first place, so she was **predisposed** to hate the new apartment.

● As a Brad Pitt fan, I'm **predisposed** to enjoy any movie he stars in.

B *Predisposed* means   A. unlikely.   B. likely.   C. pretending.

6 propensity
(prə-pĕn′sĭ-tē)
-noun

● Because Ivan has a **propensity** to gain weight, he watches what he eats.

● Cheryl is aware of her **propensity** to blab, so she warns her friends not to tell her anything they wouldn't want repeated.

B *Propensity* means   A. a coincidence.   B. an inclination.   C. a concern.

7 reprehensible
(rĕp′rĭ-hĕn′sə-bəl)
-adjective

- The Riordans never discipline their son. No matter how **reprehensible** his behavior is, they just say, "Kids will be kids."
- The company's failure to clean up the oil spill was **reprehensible** and drew harsh criticism.

A *Reprehensible* means   A. shameful.   B. misleading.   C. uncertain.

8 sham
(shăm)
-noun

- Karen's apparent affection for Raul is a **sham**. He's rich, and she cares only about his money.
- When the city inspectors came, the restaurant kitchen was sparkling. However, such cleanliness was a **sham**—the place is usually filthy.

A *Sham* means   A. something false.   B. something confusing.   C. something accidental.

9 solace
(sŏl′ĭs)
-noun

- After a family quarrel, Tamara finds **solace** in the privacy and quiet of her own room.
- Whenever I'm upset and need **solace**, I call my friend Lisa. Talking to her always makes me feel better.

C *Solace* means   A. excitement.   B. perfection.   C. relief.

10 solicitous
(sə-lĭs′ĭ-təs)
-adjective

- The waiter was overly **solicitous**. He kept interrupting our conversation to ask, "Is everything all right here?"
- **Solicitous** toward her elderly neighbor, Marie calls every day to see how he is feeling and if he needs anything.

B *Solicitous* means   A. distant.   B. attentive.   C. patient.

Matching Words with Definitions

Following are definitions of the ten words. Clearly write or print each word next to its definition. The sentences above and on the previous page will help you decide on the meaning of each word.

1. ___propensity___ A natural preference or tendency

2. ___reprehensible___ Deserving of blame, criticism, or disapproval

3. ___fortuitous___ Happening by chance, by accident, or at random; lucky

4. ___solace___ Comfort in sorrow or misfortune; consolation

5. ___liaison___ A person who serves as a connection between individuals or groups; a go-between

6. ___equivocate___ To be deliberately vague in order to mislead

7. ___impeccable___ Faultless; perfect

8. ___solicitous___ Showing or expressing concern, care, or attention

9. ___predisposed___ Tending toward or open to something beforehand

10. ___sham___ A pretense or counterfeit; something meant to deceive

CAUTION: Do not go any further until you are sure the above answers are correct. Then you can use the definitions to help you in the following practices. Your goal is eventually to know the words well enough so that you don't need to check the definitions at all.

Sentence Check 1

Using the answer line provided, complete each item below with the correct word from the box. Use each word once.

A. equivocate	B. fortuitous	C. impeccable	D. liaison	E. predisposed
F. propensity	G. reprehensible	H. sham	I. solace	J. solicitous

_____solace_____ 1. When my grandmother died, I found ___ in the thought that she had lived a long, happy life.

_____impeccable_____ 2. Jan writes at least three drafts of every paper so that the final result will be ___. She wants each assignment she turns in to be perfect.

_____predisposed_____ 3. The boss is in a rotten mood today, so he's not ___ to tolerate any mistakes.

_____solicitous_____ 4. My brother and I are both grown up, but Mom is still ___ about our health. She says, "You'll always be my babies."

_____reprehensible_____ 5. Many people consider child abuse such a(n) ___ crime that they think the penalties should be as harsh as possible.

_____sham_____ 6. The "going-out-of-business" sale was a ___. A year later, the store was still open.

_____propensity_____ 7. It's hard to believe that Stacy, with her ___ for flashy clothes and nightlife, has become a missionary.

_____fortuitous_____ 8. Unexpectedly, I ran into a former neighbor who had just started her own business. The ___ meeting led to a summer job offer for me.

_____liaison_____ 9. For several months, Olive acted as a ___ between her divorced parents, but she finally insisted that they deal with each other directly.

_____equivocate_____ 10. The job candidate ___(e)d when he said he'd been "working out West." Actually, he'd been a ski bum for three years.

NOTE: Now check your answers to these items by turning to page 177. Going over the answers carefully will help you prepare for the next two practices, for which answers are not given.

Sentence Check 2

Using the answer lines provided, complete each item below with **two** words from the box. Use each word once.

_____propensity_____
_____equivocate_____

1–2. When Shirley said she was sick of Len's ___ to flirt with other women, he ___(e)d by making an ambiguous° statement: "I promise you'll never catch me flirting again."

_____solace_____
_____liaison_____

3–4. The woman wasn't permitted to visit her husband, a political prisoner, so it gave her some ___ to have a minister act as a ___ between them.

_____predisposed_____
_____solicitous_____

5–6. Even before I met my father's nurse, I was ___ to like her, because I had heard how ___ she was toward him.

_____ fortuitous _____
_____ reprehensible _____

7–8. It was strictly ___ that no one was killed when the chemical plant exploded. The explosion, however, was no matter of chance, but the result of ___ carelessness on the part of an employee.

_____ impeccable _____
_____ sham _____

9–10. The artist was in the illicit° business of making copies of paintings, then selling them as originals. His work was so ___ that even museum owners didn't realize the paintings were ___s.

Final Check: *A Phony Friend*

Here is a final opportunity for you to strengthen your knowledge of the ten words. First read the following selection carefully. Then fill in each blank with a word from the box at the top of the previous page. (Context clues will help you figure out which word goes in which blank.) Use each word once.

When my grandfather, Henry Altman, died, he left me a large sum of money. This was very surprising because he and my father had become estranged° years before, after a quarrel, and the old man had never even seen me. I was sad that he had died before we could meet.

Soon after the news of my inheritance, a young man named Seth showed up to offer me his sympathy. Seth said he had been a friend of my grandfather's and that when the old man had become ill, he'd asked Seth to act as a (1)_____ liaison _____ between himself and the granddaughter he'd never met. "It's too late for Henry," said Seth, "but I think he'd want me to offer you my friendship. In his later years, he regretted his earlier (2)_____ propensity _____ to quarrel with his family."

Believing that Seth had been my grandfather's friend made me (3)_____ predisposed _____ to like him, and it gave me (4)_____ solace _____ to speak to someone who had known my grandfather. Still, I was puzzled because Seth wasn't able to give me much information. For example, when I asked some questions about Grandfather's second wife, Seth seemed to (5)_____ equivocate _____, saying, "All I can say is that she was quite a woman." On the other hand, Seth appeared genuinely (6)_____ solicitous _____ about my welfare, and his manners were (7)_____ impeccable _____. I had never met anyone so perfectly polite.

I really didn't know what to make of him until, one day, I had a(n) (8)_____ fortuitous _____ meeting with an old school friend I hadn't seen in years. When I described Seth, my friend looked startled and said, "I know that guy. He's a phony, a charlatan°—a complete (9) _____ sham _____. He's after the money, and I bet he never even knew your grandfather."

When I checked, my friend's story was corroborated° by reports of how Seth had tricked several other women out of their inheritances. The next time he called, I told him I knew about his (10)_____ reprehensible _____ behavior and would notify the police if he ever tried to contact me again.

Scores   Sentence Check 2 _____%   Final Check _____%

Enter your scores above and in the **Vocabulary Performance Chart** on the inside back cover of the book.

attrition	oblivious
circumvent	reticent
cohesive	robust
grievous	sanction
inundate	vociferous

Ten Words in Context

In the space provided, write the letter of the meaning closest to that of each **boldfaced** word. Use the context of the sentences to help you figure out each word's meaning.

1 attrition
(ə-trĭsh′ən)
-noun

- Sports teams are constantly looking for new talent to replace players lost through **attrition**—those who retire, quit because of injuries, and so on.
- Colleges try not to have a high rate of **attrition**. They want students to stay until graduation, rather than drop out early.

B *Attrition* means   A. an increase in numbers.   B. a natural loss of individuals.   C. ill health.

2 circumvent
(sŭr′kəm-vĕnt′)
-verb

- If we take this roundabout route, we can **circumvent** the rush-hour traffic and get home early.
- I had to swerve to the right to **circumvent** a huge pothole.

A *Circumvent* means   A. to avoid.   B. to meet head-on.   C. to make smaller.

3 cohesive
(kō-hē′sĭv)
-adjective

- For a **cohesive** pie dough, one that doesn't fall apart, be sure to add enough liquid.
- A family needs to be **cohesive**—to stay together even when stresses and strains threaten to tear it apart.

A *Cohesive* means   A. connected.   B. popular.   C. large.

4 grievous
(grēv′əs)
-adjective

- The death of a beloved pet is a **grievous** loss for a child.
- The assassination of a great leader, such as Mahatma Gandhi or Martin Luther King, Jr., often does **grievous** harm to a society.

C *Grievous* means   A. preventable.   B. unavoidable.   C. terrible.

5 inundate
(ĭn′ŭn-dāt′)
-verb

- During the heavy rains, the river overflowed and **inundated** the fields, destroying all the crops.
- After his brief announcement at the beginning of the press conference, the President was **inundated** with questions from reporters.

A *Inundate* means   A. to flood.   B. to strengthen.   C. to go around.

6 oblivious
(ə-blĭv′ē-əs)
-adjective

- The driver continued into the intersection, apparently **oblivious** to the fact that the light had turned red.
- It's easy to spot two people in love. They are the ones who, **oblivious** to everyone else present, see only each other.

B *Oblivious to* means   A. angry about.   B. not noticing.   C. overwhelmed by.

7 reticent
(rĕt′ĭ-sənt)
-adjective

- Lamar is very **reticent** about his first marriage; he never talks about his former wife or what led to their divorce.
- It's odd that many people who love to gossip about someone else are so **reticent** about their own lives.

B *Reticent* means   A. dishonest.   B. quiet.   C. unaware.

8 robust
(rō-bŭst′)
-adjective

- Once an energetic, **robust** man, Mr. Rand has been considerably weakened by illness.
- A number of weightlifters who were previously **robust** have ruined their health and vigor by taking steroids.

C *Robust* means   A. very noisy.   B. sickly.   C. strong and well.

9 sanction
(săngk′shən)
-verb

- By greeting the dictator with extreme courtesy and fanfare, the ambassador seemed to **sanction** his policies.
- Many people whose children attend religious schools would like the government to **sanction** the use of public funds to help pay for their education.

A *Sanction* means   A. to grant approval of.   B. to criticize severely.   C. to remember.

10 vociferous
(vō-sĭf′ər-əs)
-adjective

- When male loons sense that their territory is being invaded, they give **vociferous** cries of challenge.
- The principal became angry and **vociferous**, shouting at students who tried to sneak out of the fire drill.

C *Vociferous* means   A. distant.   B. mild.   C. loud.

Matching Words with Definitions

Following are definitions of the ten words. Clearly write or print each word next to its definition. The sentences above and on the previous page will help you decide on the meaning of each word.

1. _____sanction_____   To authorize, allow, or approve

2. _____inundate_____   To cover, as by flooding; overwhelm with a large number or amount

3. _____circumvent_____   To avoid by going around or as if by going around; to escape from, prevent, or stop through cleverness

4. _____reticent_____   Quiet or uncommunicative; reluctant to speak out

5. _____robust_____   Healthy and strong; vigorous

6. _____cohesive_____   Sticking or holding together; unified

7. _____vociferous_____   Noisy; expressing feelings loudly and intensely

8. _____attrition_____   A gradual natural decrease in number; becoming fewer in number

9. _____grievous_____   Causing grief or pain; very serious or severe

10. _____oblivious_____   Unaware; failing to notice

CAUTION: Do not go any further until you are sure the above answers are correct. Then you can use the definitions to help you in the following practices. Your goal is eventually to know the words well enough so that you don't need to check the definitions at all.

Sentence Check 1

Using the answer line provided, complete each item below with the correct word from the box. Use each word once.

A. attrition	B. circumvent	C. cohesive	D. grievous	E. inundate
F. oblivious	G. reticent	H. robust	I. sanction	J. vociferous

oblivious   1. The chatty, slow-moving clerk at the checkout counter seemed ___ to the fact that the line of impatient customers was growing longer and longer.

vociferous   2. A quiet, polite discussion may be better than a(n) ___ argument, but some people get more satisfaction out of yelling and shouting.

sanction   3. In many places, the law doesn't ___ gambling—but the officials don't do much to stop it, either.

robust   4. A half-hour of aerobic exercise every other day will help you stay ___.

circumvent   5. People sometimes do odd things to ___ regulations. In New York, when saloons were illegal, one owner called his place "O'Neal's Baloon."

cohesive   6. If you want your essay to be ___, stick to your point.

grievous   7. Alzheimer's disease is a disaster for the patient and a(n) ___ burden for the family.

inundate   8. Some days we're ___(e)d with junk e-mail—it can take an hour to delete all the unwanted messages.

attrition   9. The cutting down of the rain forests has caused a dangerous rate of ___ among species that live in those forests.

reticent   10. Some people who could benefit from counseling avoid seeing a therapist because they prefer to be ___ about private matters.

NOTE: Now check your answers to these items by turning to page 177. Going over the answers carefully will help you prepare for the next two practices, for which answers are not given.

Sentence Check 2

Using the answer lines provided, complete each item below with **two** words from the box. Use each word once.

inundate
 oblivious   1–2. Craig is ___(e)d with bills, but he continues to fritter° away his money. He's ___ to his financial problems.

sanction
 attrition   3–4. The company doesn't ___ the policy of laying off workers. It believes that the optimum° way to reduce the staff is by ___: employees who quit or retire simply aren't replaced.

grievous
 reticent   5–6. Child abuse is a(n) ___ crime, but children are often ___ about it. Their silence may prevent them from collaborating° with the police or the courts to bring the abusers to justice.

_____robust_____   7–8. Although my brother was ___ enough to meet the army's standards for
_____circumvent_____   enlisting, his eyesight was too poor. He tried to ___ this problem by
memorizing the eye chart.

_____vociferous_____   9–10. The teacher of the "Cooking for Health" class was ___ about avoiding egg
_____cohesive_____   yolks. "You don't need yolks for a(n) ___ batter!" he shouted. "The whites
will hold it together."

Final Check: *Coco the Gorilla*

Here is a final opportunity for you to strengthen your knowledge of the ten words. First read the following
selection carefully. Then fill in each blank with a word from the box at the top of the previous page.
(Context clues will help you figure out which word goes in which blank.) Use each word once.

Illegal killings of gorillas are reducing their numbers far faster than
would be expected from normal (1)_____attrition_____. Here is
the story of one gorilla family.

Carrying spears and knives, hunters entered an African game
preserve, where it was unlawful to kill or capture wildlife. When they
spotted a young male gorilla, they closed in. Ten adult gorillas, members
of a(n) (2)_____cohesive_____ family group, attempted
to shield the infant. The men quickly killed all the adult gorillas. As if
(3)_____oblivious_____ to the infant's screams, the men strapped
his hands and feet to bamboo poles with wire, then carried him down
the mountain on which he'd been born.

After several weeks, Dian Fossey, an American studying gorillas in
the wild, learned that the young gorilla had been taken to park officials.
She found him in a cage so small that he had no room to stand or turn.
He was clearly frightened and nearly dead—thirsty, starving, and with infected wounds at his ankles and
wrists. Fossey could hardly believe that the officials could (4)_____sanction_____ such reprehensible°
cruelty.

When Fossey demanded an explanation from the park's chief official, he seemed (5)_____reticent_____
about the animal. Finally, however, he admitted that he had made an illicit° deal with a German zoo. In
return for a new car, he had arranged for the gorilla's capture. Fossey was (6)_____vociferous_____ in
insisting that the infant be released into her care. The official agreed on the condition that the infant be
shipped to the zoo as soon as his health returned.

For several months, Fossey cared for the infant, now named Coco, who would cling to her for
solace°. When he became more (7)_____robust_____, he began to romp and explore. In
an effort to (8)_____circumvent_____ the agreement to send Coco to the zoo, Fossey
(9)_____inundate_____(e)d government officials with letters, begging them to step in and arrange
for him to be returned to the wild. In the end, though, the little gorilla was taken away from her—a(n)
(10)_____grievous_____ hardship for both of them. Gorillas can live into their 50s, but Coco died in
the zoo at the age of 12.

Scores	Sentence Check 2 _____%	Final Check _____%

Enter your scores above and in the **Vocabulary Performance Chart** on the inside back cover of the book.

bolster	relegate
depreciate	replete
indiscriminate	sedentary
inquisitive	tenet
nebulous	terse

Ten Words in Context

In the space provided, write the letter of the meaning closest to that of each **boldfaced** word. Use the context of the sentences to help you figure out each word's meaning.

1 bolster
(bōl′stər)
-*verb*

● The front porch was sagging, so we had to **bolster** it with cinder blocks until it could be repaired.
● When Yoko was in the hospital, visits from friends **bolstered** her spirits.

<u>C</u> *Bolster* means   A. to reach.   B. to replace.   C. to support.

2 depreciate
(dĭ-prē′shē-āt′)
-*verb*

● As soon as you drive a new car off the lot, it **depreciates**; it's immediately worth less than you paid for it.
● The property **depreciated** when the city built a sewage plant nearby.

<u>B</u> *Depreciate* means   A. to become better.   B. to become less valuable.   C. to become definite.

3 indiscriminate
(ĭn′dĭ-skrĭm′ĭ-nĭt)
-*adjective*

● Some people end up hopelessly in debt because of **indiscriminate** spending, so be selective about what and how much you buy.
● I confess to an **indiscriminate** love of chocolate. I don't distinguish between plain old Hershey bars and fancy imported chocolates—I adore them all.

<u>C</u> *Indiscriminate* means   A. healthy.   B. unenthusiastic.   C. not selective.

4 inquisitive
(ĭn-kwĭz′ə-tĭv)
-*adjective*

● **Inquisitive** students usually do better than those who are less curious and less eager to learn.
● Small children are naturally **inquisitive**. They wonder about the world around them, and they are constantly asking "Why?"

<u>C</u> *Inquisitive* means   A. hard-working.   B. particular.   C. questioning.

5 nebulous
(nĕb′yə-ləs)
-*adjective*

● When I ask Leonard what he wants for his birthday, he never gives me any specific ideas. He just gives a **nebulous** answer like "Oh, something I can use."
● "A good essay cannot be **nebulous**," the English instructor explained. "It must contain sharp, precise details."

<u>A</u> *Nebulous* means   A. indefinite.   B. long.   C. specific.

6 relegate
(rĕl′ə-gāt′)
-*verb*

● At family gatherings, we kids were always **relegated** to the kitchen table, while the adults ate in the dining room.
● When we have overnight guests, my parents give them my room and **relegate** me to a cot in the attic.

<u>A</u> *Relegate* means   A. to send.   B. to punish.   C. to reward.

7 replete
(rĭ-plēt′)
-adjective

● The show was **replete** with dazzling effects, including gorgeous scenery, glittering costumes, dramatic lighting, and thrilling music.

● The book of household hints got an excellent review. "It's **replete** with good advice," the critic wrote. "Every homeowner should purchase a copy."

B   *Replete* means   A. replaced.   B. filled.   C. followed.

8 sedentary
(sĕd′n-tĕr′ē)
-adjective

● People in **sedentary** occupations, such as bus drivers and writers, need to make a special effort to exercise.

● My older sister's lifestyle is so **sedentary** that the longest walk she ever takes is from her living-room couch to the front seat of her car.

C   *Sedentary* means   A. involving much walking.   B. involving stress.   C. involving much sitting.

9 tenet
(tĕn′ĭt)
-noun

● One of the basic **tenets** of democracy is freedom of speech.

● This world might be a paradise if everyone lived by such **tenets** as "Never cause suffering."

A   *Tenet* means   A. a principle.   B. a ritual.   C. a prediction.

10 terse
(tûrs)
-adjective

● I was hurt by Roberto's **terse** response to my invitation. All he said was "No thanks."

● A British humor magazine once gave this **terse** advice to people about to marry: "Don't."

C   *Terse* means   A. dishonest.   B. unclear.   C. short.

Matching Words with Definitions

Following are definitions of the ten words. Clearly write or print each word next to its definition. The sentences above and on the previous page will help you decide on the meaning of each word.

1. _____depreciate_____   To fall or decrease in value or price; to lower the value of

2. _____indiscriminate_____   Not chosen carefully; not based on careful selection

3. _____sedentary_____   Marked by much sitting; requiring or taking little exercise

4. _____tenet_____   A belief or principle held to be true by an individual or group

5. _____terse_____   Brief and clear; effectively concise

6. _____bolster_____   To hold up, strengthen, or reinforce; support with a rigid object

7. _____inquisitive_____   Curious; eager to learn

8. _____replete_____   Plentifully supplied; well-filled

9. _____nebulous_____   Vague; unclear

10. _____relegate_____   To assign to a less important or less satisfying position, place, or condition

CAUTION: Do not go any further until you are sure the above answers are correct. Then you can use the definitions to help you in the following practices. Your goal is eventually to know the words well enough so that you don't need to check the definitions at all.

Sentence Check 1

Using the answer line provided, complete each item below with the correct word from the box. Use each word once.

A. bolster	B. depreciate	C. indiscriminate	D. inquisitive	E. nebulous
F. relegate	G. replete	H. sedentary	I. tenet	J. terse

_____terse_____ 1. John considers Arlene rude because her comments are usually ___, but I prefer her brief, clear answers to his long-winded ones.

_____indiscriminate_____ 2. Phan's TV viewing is ___. He just watches whatever happens to be on.

_____bolster_____ 3. When a sofa leg broke, we ___(e)d that end of the sofa with a pile of books.

_____depreciate_____ 4. Houses and antiques often increase in value as they get older, but most other things, like cars, computers, and appliances, tend to ___.

_____tenet_____ 5. A large sign in the boys' treehouse stated their club's main ___: "No Girls or Snakes Allowed!!!"

_____replete_____ 6. The refrigerator was ___ with all kinds of marvelous foods for the party.

_____relegate_____ 7. The catcher worried that unless he started playing better, he'd be ___(e)d to the minor leagues.

_____nebulous_____ 8. Before this semester, my thoughts about a career were ___, but now I have a much clearer idea of what work I want to do.

_____sedentary_____ 9. When we were children, my active sister was always playing tag or jumping rope. I was more ___, preferring to spend hour after hour just sitting and reading.

_____inquisitive_____ 10. The book *Answers to 1,001 Interesting Questions* sounds like the perfect gift for a(n) ___ person.

NOTE: Now check your answers to these items by turning to page 178. Going over the answers carefully will help you prepare for the next two practices, for which answers are not given.

Sentence Check 2

Using the answer lines provided, complete each item below with **two** words from the box. Use each word once.

_____depreciate_____
_____nebulous_____
1–2. When my parents bought their new house, they asked the real estate agent whether it was likely to increase in value or ___. The agent gave this ___ answer: "It's always hard to tell about these things."

_____relegate_____
_____sedentary_____
3–4. Dad was a construction worker, but as soon as he reached 60—though he was as robust° as ever—his company ___(e)d him to a(n) ___ desk job.

_____inquisitive_____
_____bolster_____
5–6. The guides at the Leaning Tower of Pisa are inundated° with questions from ___ travelers: "Why is it leaning?" "How far is it leaning?" "Is it being ___(e)d to keep it from falling any further?"

_____ replete

_____ tenet

7–8. Folk wisdom is ___ with contradictory sayings and ___s. It's fun to juxtapose° pairs such as "He who hesitates is lost" and "Look before you leap."

_____ terse

_____ indiscriminate

9–10. Stan is not exactly a(n) ___ speaker, which is why he's earned the nickname "Motor Mouth." What's more, his conversation is totally ___; he uses no discretion° but just says anything that comes to mind.

Final Check: *Our Annual Garage Sale*

Here is a final opportunity for you to strengthen your knowledge of the ten words. First read the following selection carefully. Then fill in each blank with a word from the box at the top of the previous page. (Context clues will help you figure out which word goes in which blank.) Use each word once.

It's almost September—time for our annual garage sale. Since we hate to relinquish° anything we've spent money on, we have a large supply of unwanted items. They keep piling up in the basement, which is now so full that we've had to (1)_____ relegate _____ some of the collection to the garage. Though the sale is a lot of work, the sight of all those piles and boxes (2)_____ bolster _____s our determination to go through with it.

This proliferation° of stuff has left us with a huge number of possessions for sale, from tools and spools to baskets and gaskets. This year, for example, we have an old bike that some zealot° for exercise might buy and a soft chair and footstool for a more (3)_____ sedentary _____ customer. Our ad states our main (4)_____ tenet _____: "Something for everyone!" Maybe that's a bit (5)_____ nebulous _____, but we don't want to be specific. We just want to disseminate° the general idea that our sale will be (6)_____ replete _____ with treasures.

Last year, one customer took a quick look and departed with the (7)_____ terse _____ comment "Nothing but junk." However, most people seem to take a completely (8)_____ indiscriminate _____ approach to shopping. They're predisposed° to spend their money on anything that's a bargain, even if it isn't in optimum° condition—such as rusty baking pans and broken lamps. Then there are the (9)_____ inquisitive _____ shoppers who want us to tell them every detail about every item: How old is it? What did we pay for it? Will it increase in value, or will it (10)_____ depreciate _____?

Friends have foolishly asked us where in the world we get all this junk to sell year after year—an inane° question, because the answer is simple. We shop at garage sales.

Scores   Sentence Check 2 _____ %   Final Check _____ %

autonomy	recourse
bureaucratic	reiterate
mandate	tantamount
ostracize	tenacious
raucous	utopia

Ten Words in Context

In the space provided, write the letter of the meaning closest to that of each **boldfaced** word. Use the context of the sentences to help you figure out each word's meaning.

1 autonomy
(ô-tŏn′ə-mē)
-noun

● In 1776, the American colonists, tired of being ruled by England, fought for their **autonomy**.

● Children as young as age two begin to want some **autonomy**. The term "terrible twos" reflects their struggle for independence.

B *Autonomy* means   A. assistance.   B. freedom from control.   C. self-sacrifice.

2 bureaucratic
(byo̅o̅r′ə-krăt′ĭk)
-adjective

● **Bureaucratic** organizations can become so bogged down in regulations that almost no work gets done.

● "This family is more **bureaucratic** than the federal government!" Mac complained to his parents. "You have rules for everything."

A *Bureaucratic* means   A. over-regulated.   B. old-fashioned.   C. independent.

3 mandate
(man′dāt′)
-noun

● All the union members voted for the strike, giving their leaders a clear **mandate**.

● The senator received so many letters supporting his position on gun control that he felt he had the **mandate** of the people.

C *Mandate* means   A. a criticism.   B. a delay.   C. official permission.

4 ostracize
(ŏs′trə-sīz′)
-verb

● Children who look or act "different" are often **ostracized** by their classmates. No one will play with them or even talk to them.

● When Selena married a man twenty years younger than herself, she was **ostracized** by the entire family. No one would have anything to do with her.

A *Ostracize* means   A. to reject.   B. to feel sorry for.   C. to control.

5 raucous
(rô′kəs)
-adjective

● The audience at the rock concert was so **raucous** that we feared the noise and commotion would lead to violence.

● At the horror movie, the audience's behavior became **raucous**. Everyone was shouting at the characters on the screen and pretending to shriek with fright.

B *Raucous* means   A. persistent.   B. disorderly.   C. angry.

6 recourse
(rē′kôrs′)
-noun

● "Unless you pay your bill," the company threatened, "we'll have no **recourse** but to sue you."

● "We'll try treating you with medication," the doctor explained. "If that isn't effective, the only **recourse** will be surgery."

A *Recourse* means   A. a choice.   B. a problem.   C. a question.

7 reiterate
(rē-ĭt'ə-rāt')
-*verb*

- The agency director stated, "I have said this before, but let me **reiterate**: Unless we receive the funds to hire more staff, the children of this city will continue to suffer."
- I hate it when a speaker **reiterates** the same point over and over, as if the listeners weren't paying attention or were just too stupid to understand.

A *Reiterate* means   A. to repeat.   B. to forget.   C. to exclude.

8 tantamount
(tănt'ə-mount')
-*adjective*

- Charging three dollars for a cup of coffee is **tantamount** to robbery.
- My mother's refusal to let me have the car was **tantamount** to forbidding me to go to the beach.

B *Tantamount to* means   A. the result of.   B. just like.   C. independent of.

9 tenacious
(tə-nā'shəs)
-*adjective*

- The cat's grip on the tree limb was **tenacious**, but we weren't sure how long she could keep hanging on so firmly.
- My aunt's **tenacious** determination to recover may have pulled her through her illness.

A *Tenacious* means   A. grasping strongly.   B. weak and ineffective.   C. slowly shrinking.

10 utopia
(yoō-tō'pē-ə)
-*noun*

- In 1888, Edward Bellamy wrote about a **utopia** where everyone would have a comfortable income, work only until the age of 45, and then enjoy leisure.
- Everyone has a different idea of **utopia**. A situation that seems perfect to me might make you miserable.

C *Utopia* means   A. a city.   B. a self-government.   C. a paradise.

Matching Words with Definitions

Following are definitions of the ten words. Clearly write or print each word next to its definition. The sentences above and on the previous page will help you decide on the meaning of each word.

1. _____utopia_____ An ideal or perfect place or state; a place achieving social or political perfection

2. _____raucous_____ Noisy and disorderly; boisterous

3. _____recourse_____ A source of help, security, or strength; something to turn to; option

4. _____bureaucratic_____ Insisting on strict rules and routine, often to the point of hindering effectiveness

5. _____reiterate_____ To state again or repeatedly

6. _____autonomy_____ Independence; self-government

7. _____mandate_____ A group's expressed wishes; clear signal to act; vote of confidence

8. _____ostracize_____ To expel or exclude from a group; shun

9. _____tantamount_____ Equal in effect or value; the same as

10. _____tenacious_____ Holding firmly; persistent; stubborn

CAUTION: Do not go any further until you are sure the above answers are correct. Then you can use the definitions to help you in the following practices. Your goal is eventually to know the words well enough so that you don't need to check the definitions at all.

Sentence Check 1

Using the answer line provided, complete each item below with the correct word from the box. Use each word once.

A. autonomy	B. bureaucratic	C. mandate	D. ostracize	E. raucous
F. recourse	G. reiterate	H. tantamount	I. tenacious	J. utopia

__autonomy__   1. I'd love a job with a great deal of ___. I want to set my own hours, work at home whenever I like, and make many decisions on my own.

__ostracize__   2. In high school, Felipe was ___(e)d because of his political views, but in college he found many people who shared his opinions.

__reiterate__   3. When you write a letter of complaint, begin by stating what you want the company to do about the problem. Then ___ this request at the end.

__tantamount__   4. Our local supermarket is so expensive that shopping there is ___ to throwing our money away.

__raucous__   5. The children on the school bus were so ___ that the driver got a headache from all the noise.

__tenacious__   6. Helen's smoking was a ___ habit; she wasn't able to give it up until she watched her brother die of lung cancer.

__utopia__   7. Idealists have sometimes tried to establish ___s, but these communities have always failed. I wonder if it is possible to achieve perfection.

__bureaucratic__   8. While most college instructors are flexible, some are very ___, allowing no exceptions to the rules regardless of the circumstances.

__mandate__   9. In a landslide election, the voters' ___ is clear. If the vote has been close, though, it's difficult to tell what "the people" really want.

__recourse__   10. In the past, workers often had no ___ when employers discriminated against them. Today, however, they can seek help from the Equal Employment Opportunity Commission.

NOTE: Now check your answers to these items by turning to page 178. Going over the answers carefully will help you prepare for the next two practices, for which answers are not given.

Sentence Check 2

Using the answer lines provided, complete each item below with **two** words from the box. Use each word once.

__utopia__
__autonomy__   1–2. One concept of a(n) ___ is a society in which each individual maintains his or her ___ yet collaborates° with others to achieve the good for all.

__bureaucratic__
__reiterate__   3–4. "My company is so ___," Nick complained, "that we are buried in paperwork. Sometimes we have to ___ the same information on five different forms."

__mandate__
__recourse__   5–6. If elected officials ignore the ___ of the people, citizens always have the ___ of voting those officials out of office.

_____tenacious_____   7–8. Our neighbor has a ___ belief in superstitions. For instance, she insists that
_____tantamount_____   our owning a black cat is ___ to asking for grievous° misfortune.

_____ostracize_____   9–10. The kids' basketball league ___(e)d one team because of the reprehensible°
_____raucous_____   behavior of its players. They engaged in ___ horseplay on the court,
                                  instigated° fights, and constantly tried to circumvent° the rules. Now the
                                  other teams refuse to play them.

Final Check: *A Debate on School Uniforms*

Here is a final opportunity for you to strengthen your knowledge of the ten words. First read the following selection carefully. Then fill in each blank with a word from the box at the top of the previous page. (Context clues will help you figure out which word goes in which blank.) Use each word once.

At Monday's student council meeting, the officers debated about whether or not students should be required to wear uniforms.

Barbara, president of the senior class, stated that as an elected representative of the students, she wouldn't vote to change the dress code without a clear (1)_____mandate_____ from the students calling for such a change. "Personally," she said, "I think that forcing people to wear certain clothing robs them of their (2)_____autonomy_____. What is school supposed to teach us, if not the ability to think and act independently? Besides," she added, "the school administration is (3)_____bureaucratic_____ enough. We don't need any more rules and regulations."

Rashid, vice-president of the junior class, disagreed. "The current situation in our school is (4)_____tantamount_____ to a three-ring circus," he said. "Some students compete to see who can look most outrageous. Some of the outfits show so much skin that they belong on a beach. Other kids are such snobs about their ostentatious° designer clothes that they (5)_____ostracize_____ kids who can't afford to keep up with them. I'm not saying that uniforms would change the school into a(n) (6)_____utopia_____. No place is perfect. I just think that if we want school to be more fair, our best (7)_____recourse_____ is a strict dress code."

At that, several students burst into (8)_____raucous_____ disagreement, yelling and pounding on their desks. After several minutes of vociferous° chaos, the meeting came to order, and Barbara was called on again.

(9)_____Tenacious_____ in her opinion, she insisted, "I understand what you're saying, Rashid, but I want to (10)_____reiterate_____ a point I made earlier. Uniforms do away with one aspect of personal choice, and one of my tenets° is that personal choice is precious."

Scores   Sentence Check 2 _____%   Final Check _____%

Enter your scores above and in the **Vocabulary Performance Chart** on the inside back cover of the book.

clandestine	indigenous
contingency	liability
egocentric	prolific
exonerate	reinstate
incongruous	superfluous

Ten Words in Context

In the space provided, write the letter of the meaning closest to that of each **boldfaced** word. Use the context of the sentences to help you figure out each word's meaning.

1 clandestine
(klăn-děs′tĭn)
-*adjective*

- In a **clandestine** meeting in an alley, Steve sold his employer's valuable anti-aging formula to a competitor.
- The famous "Underground Railroad" was not an actual railroad; it was a **clandestine** network that took escaped slaves to safety in the years before the Civil War.

_C_ *Clandestine* means   A. popular.   B. unnecessary.   C. secret.

2 contingency
(kən-tĭn′jən-sē)
-*noun*

- Faye thought her company might transfer her to another city. With that **contingency** in mind, she decided to rent a house rather than buy one.
- We believe in providing for every **contingency**. We have a list of emergency phone numbers, a first-aid kit, and a box of candles in case of a power failure.

_A_ *Contingency* means   A. a possibility.   B. an advantage.   C. a desire.

3 egocentric
(ē′gō-sĕn′trĭk)
-*adjective*

- Denise is completely **egocentric**. Whatever event takes place, she thinks only of how it will affect her personally.
- "We've talked enough about me," said the **egocentric** author to a friend. "Now let's talk about you. What do you think of my new book?"

_A_ *Egocentric* means   A. selfish.   B. considerate.   C. self-educated.

4 exonerate
(ĕg-zŏn′ər-āt′)
-*verb*

- Saul was suspected of shoplifting, but he was **exonerated** when the hidden camera's photos clearly showed another man taking handfuls of DVDs from a rack and stuffing them into his backpack.
- Politicians accused of illegal activities always seem to say the same thing: that they'll be **exonerated** when all the facts are known.

_C_ *Exonerate* means   A. to be harmed.   B. to be found guilty.   C. to be found not guilty.

5 incongruous
(ĭn-kŏng′grō͞o-əs)
-*adjective*

- The cuckoo lays eggs in other birds' nests. This practice can result in the **incongruous** sight of one large cuckoo chick among several tiny baby robins.
- It wasn't really **incongruous** for a former general to join the peace movement. He had seen the horrors of war.

_A_ *Incongruous* means   A. contradictory.   B. unnecessary.   C. not noticeable.

6 indigenous
(ĭn-dĭj′ə-nəs)
-*adjective*

- Kangaroos are **indigenous** only to Australia. They have never been found living anywhere else in the world.
- Corn was not **indigenous** to Europe, so Europeans had never seen or heard of it until their explorers first reached the New World and found it growing there.

_B_ *Indigenous* means   A. important.   B. native.   C. welcomed.

7 liability
(lī′ə-bĭl′ə-tē)
-noun

- My shyness with strangers would be a **liability** in any job that involved meeting the public, such as sales.
- When Juanita returned to school at age 40, she was afraid her age would be a **liability**. Instead, she found that it gave her an advantage over younger students.

B *Liability* means   A. an asset.   B. a handicap.   C. a necessity.

8 prolific
(prō-lĭf′ĭk)
-adjective

- Rabbits deserve their reputation for being **prolific**. A female rabbit can produce three families each summer.
- Haydn was a **prolific** composer. He wrote, among many other musical works, 104 symphonies.

A *Prolific* means   A. creating abundantly.   B. working secretly.   C. important.

9 reinstate
(rē′ĭn-stāt′)
-verb

- Michiko left work for a year to stay home with her new baby. When she returned, she was relieved and happy to be **reinstated** in her former job.
- The college had canceled the course in folklore, but the demand was so great that the class had to be **reinstated**.

C *Reinstate* means   A. to recognize.   B. to appreciate.   C. to put back.

10 superfluous
(soŏ-pûr′floō-əs)
-adjective

- In the phrase "rich millionaire," the word *rich* is **superfluous**. All millionaires are rich.
- Lately, business at the store has been so slow that the three clerks have almost nothing to do. Two of them seem **superfluous**.

A *Superfluous* means   A. unnecessary.   B. ordinary.   C. required.

Matching Words with Definitions

Following are definitions of the ten words. Clearly write or print each word next to its definition. The sentences above and on the previous page will help you decide on the meaning of each word.

1. _____liability_____ Something that acts as a disadvantage; a drawback

2. _____clandestine_____ Done in secret; kept hidden

3. _____incongruous_____ Out of place; having parts that are not in harmony or that are inconsistent

4. _____contingency_____ A possible future event that must be prepared for or guarded against; possibility

5. _____indigenous_____ Living, growing, or produced naturally in a particular place; native

6. _____superfluous_____ Beyond what is needed, wanted, or useful; extra

7. _____prolific_____ Producing many works, results, or offspring; fertile

8. _____exonerate_____ To clear of an accusation or charge; prove innocent

9. _____egocentric_____ Self-centered; seeing everything in terms of oneself

10. _____reinstate_____ To restore to a previous position or condition; bring back into being or use

CAUTION: Do not go any further until you are sure the above answers are correct. Then you can use the definitions to help you in the following practices. Your goal is eventually to know the words well enough so that you don't need to check the definitions at all.

Sentence Check 1

Using the answer line provided, complete each item below with the correct word from the box. Use each word once.

A. clandestine	B. contingency	C. egocentric	D. exonerate	E. incongruous
F. indigenous	G. liability	H. prolific	I. reinstate	J. superfluous

incongruous   1. Agnes is only five feet tall, but her boyfriend is six-foot-four. They make a(n) ___-looking couple.

reinstate   2. Sharon and Eli have ___(e)d a Jewish family tradition they hadn't observed for years: lighting candles on the Sabbath.

liability   3. Bad handwriting isn't a serious ___ in an age of computers.

indigenous   4. Gardens in the desert usually feature ___ plants, such as cactus. Native plants thrive in dry heat and need little watering.

contingency   5. Although our city has never been struck by an earthquake, it has emergency plans for just such a ___.

exonerate   6. Two students were blamed for starting the fire in the physics lab, but they were ___(e)d when it was found that the cause was faulty electrical equipment.

prolific   7. Flies are amazingly ___. Within a five-month breeding period, one female can produce thousands of offspring.

clandestine   8. Because a submarine is able to hide under water, it can be very useful in ___ operations.

superfluous   9. "Your writing is too wordy," the teacher had written on my paper. "Eliminate all those ___ words and phrases."

egocentric   10. Nancy is so ___ that when I told her my car had been stolen, her only reaction was, "Does this mean you can't drive me to work tomorrow?"

NOTE: Now check your answers to these items by turning to page 178. Going over the answers carefully will help you prepare for the next two practices, for which answers are not given.

Sentence Check 2

Using the answer lines provided, complete each item below with **two** words from the box. Use each word once.

incongruous
indigenous   1–2. People who spend Christmas in Florida often find the decorations ___. Santa Clauses, sleighs, reindeer, and fir trees somehow seem ___ to the North and look odd juxtaposed° with palm trees and tropical flowers.

exonerate
reinstate   3–4. When a million dollars mysteriously vanished, the company decided to fire its accountant. But he was ___(e)d and ___(e)d in his position when the cause was discovered to be a computer malfunction.

prolific
superfluous   5–6. The ___ author has just had her fiftieth novel published. Although she has written numerous books, her writing style remains tight, with no ___ words.

_____egocentric_____

_____liability_____

7–8. The foreman is so ___ that he has become a ___ to the company. Concerned only with his own needs, he's oblivious° to the needs of the workers.

_____clandestine_____

_____contingency_____

9–10. The ship's captain seemed to be losing his mental balance. Fearing that he might become completely insane, the crew held a(n) ___ meeting to discuss what to do in that ___.

Final Check: *My Large Family*

Here is a final opportunity for you to strengthen your knowledge of the ten words. First read the following selection carefully. Then fill in each blank with a word from the box at the top of the previous page. (Context clues will help you figure out which word goes in which blank.) Use each word once.

For many years I didn't realize that my family was larger than normal. That's because enormous families somehow seemed (1)_____indigenous_____ to our neighborhood. I don't know what made people on our block so (2)_____prolific_____, but the Harrisons, who lived on one side of us, had nine kids; and the Montoyas, on the other side, had twelve. When Mom said she was going to have her eleventh child, the ten of us wondered if another baby wasn't (3)_____superfluous_____: one more than necessary. Still, I think we enjoyed one another as much as any family I know. Naturally, we had our battles, but though they were sometimes intense, they never lasted long, and it didn't take much to (4)_____reinstate_____ yourself in a brother's or a sister's good graces. If nothing else worked, you could always (5)_____exonerate_____ yourself by blaming whatever had happened on another sibling who wasn't home at the moment. Also, we learned to cooperate. When you have to get along with so many different people, you learn not to be (6)_____egocentric_____. A self-centered person wouldn't have lasted ten minutes in my home.

Of course, there were times when the size of our family was a (7)_____liability_____. With all those people around, any kind of (8)_____clandestine_____ activity was just about impossible—there was simply no place to hide and no way to keep a secret. Our numbers could be a detriment°, as well. Once, a new neighbor, not realizing how many of us there were, offered to take us all for ice cream. With amusement, he watched the (9)_____incongruous_____ sight of nine children and one toddler trying to squeeze into an ordinary passenger car. Although he obviously hadn't been prepared for such a (10)_____contingency_____, it didn't squelch° his plans. He just grinned and said, "Okay, we'll go in shifts."

Scores	Sentence Check 2 _____ %	Final Check _____ %

Enter your scores above and in the **Vocabulary Performance Chart** on the inside back cover of the book.

a-, an-	pan-
bibl-, biblio-	prim, prime
fid	rect
-ism	sym-, syn-
nov	ver

Ten Word Parts in Context

Figure out the meanings of the following ten word parts by looking *closely* and *carefully* at the context in which they appear. Then, in the space provided, write the letter of the meaning closest to that of each word part.

1 a-, an-

- Harold is completely **apolitical**. He never votes and never even seems to know who the candidates are.
- Aspirin is an **analgesic**, or painkiller. If you take it, you will soon be without pain.

_B_ The word part *a-* or *an-* means

   A. true.   B. without.   C. new.

2 bibl-, biblio-

- The first book printed from movable type was the Gutenberg **Bible**.
- Mr. Steffen was a noted **bibliophile**, so when his collection of books was sold, many other book lovers crowded the auction room.

_A_ The word part *bibl-* or *biblio-* means

   A. book.   B. religious doctrine.   C. belief.

3 fid

- People think of dogs as trusty companions. This is reflected in the traditional name for a dog, "**Fido**," which means "faithful one."
- From the viewpoint of a particular religion, an **infidel** is a person who does not believe in that faith.

_B_ The word part *fid* means

   A. first.   B. loyalty.   C. real.

4 -ism

- **Totalitarianism** is a system of government in which a dictator rules and the state controls every aspect of people's lives.
- William Penn came to America in the 1600s to establish the principles of his religion, **Quakerism**.

_A_ The word part *-ism* means

   A. a set of beliefs.   B. a lack of something.   C. a rank.

5 nov

- People are always trying to sell us something new. One year the **novelty** was in-line skates, and the next year it was scooters.
- Anya is an **innovative** cook, always thinking of creative, unusual combinations, like sweet potatoes and oranges.

_B_ The word part *nov* means

   A. important.   B. original.   C. realistic.

6 pan-

- As the name implies, the **Pan-American** Games involve athletes from all the Americas—North America, Central America, and South America.
- Some people turn to drugs in hopes of finding a **panacea**, a remedy for all the problems in their lives.

_C_ The word part *pan-* means

   A. new.   B. true.   C. entire.

7 prim, prime

- When you go deep into a forest, you can imagine yourself back in **primeval** times, long before humans appeared on the scene.
- "**Prime**" beef is the highest-quality cut. Unfortunately, it's also highest in fat and in price.

A The word part *prim* or *prime* means
A. first.   B. true.   C. entire.

8 rect

- The pool, a large **rectangle**, was surrounded by bushes in rows as straight as the sides of the pool itself.
- We sometimes learn best by trying something new, making a mistake, and then figuring out how to **rectify** the error.

C The word part *rect* means
A. real.   B. recent.   C. straight.

9 sym-, syn-

- A **syndrome** is a collection of symptoms that normally accompany a particular disease.
- We'd better **synchronize** our watches before the race starts. Let's set them all right now, at exactly 1:46.

B The word part *sym-* or *syn-* means
A. truth.   B. together.   C. faith.

10 ver

- I thought Jesse was lying about having seen a UFO, but when neighbors showed up, they **verified** his story.
- A **verdict** should be an honest statement of how members of the jury have judged a case.

C The word part *ver* means
A. together.   B. orderly.   C. true.

Matching Word Parts with Definitions

Following are definitions of the ten word parts. Clearly write or print each word part next to its definition. The sentences above and on the previous page will help you decide on the meaning of each word part.

1. -ism Doctrine, system, practice of
2. fid Trust, faith, loyalty
3. rect Straight, right
4. a-, an- Without, lacking, not
5. prim, prime First (in order or importance)
6. ver True, real
7. sym-, syn- With, together
8. nov New, original, fresh
9. pan- All
10. bibl-, biblio- Book

CAUTION: Do not go any further until you are sure the above answers are correct. Then you can use the definitions to help you in the following practices. Your goal is eventually to know the word parts well enough so that you don't need to check the definitions at all.

Sentence Check 1

Using the answer line provided, complete each *italicized* word below with the correct word part from the box. Use each word part once.

A. a-, an-	**B. bibl-, biblio-**	**C. fid**	**D. -ism**	**E. nov**
F. pan-	**G. prim, prime**	**H. rect**	**I. sym-, syn-**	**J. ver**

confident _____ 1. Vicki has gotten an A on every paper and test in her biology class, so she is (*con . . . ent*) ___ that she'll get an A for the course.

very _____ 2. I don't know how the magician did it, but he held up the (. . . *y*) ___ card I was thinking of.

panorama _____ 3. From the top of the mountain, Tarik was able to take pictures of a breathtaking (. . . *orama*) ___. The entire valley was spread out before him.

primary _____ 4. The (. . . *ary*) ___ grades are generally considered to be kindergarten and first grade.

direct _____ 5. When people say "as the crow flies," they mean in a straight line, a (*di . . .*) ___ route from one place to another.

bibliotherapy _____ 6. Psychologists often use (. . . *therapy*) ___ to help troubled children. When children read books about others in similar situations, they may be able to work through their own problems.

Synonyms _____ 7. (. . . *onyms*) ___ are words with the same meaning. But even words that are very close in meaning may suggest different things—for example, *break* and *shatter*.

Hinduism _____ 8. (*Hindu . . .*) ___ includes a principle called reincarnation: the belief that when we die, our souls return to earth to exist in new bodies.

anonymous _____ 9. When she received the (. . . *onymous*) ___ note from "an admirer," Jenny was eager to know who had sent it.

renovate _____ 10. Ted and Sara are trying to decide if it's worthwhile trying to (*re . . . ate*) ___ their rickety old farmhouse, or if it would make more sense just to tear it down and build a new one.

NOTE: Now check your answers to these items by turning to page 178. Going over the answers carefully will help you prepare for the next two practices, for which answers are not given.

Sentence Check 2

Using the answer line provided, complete each *italicized* word in the sentences below with the correct word part from the box. Use each word part once.

primary _____
pantheism _____ 1–2. The (. . . *ary*) ___ principle of (. . . *theism*) ___ is that God is the entire universe and all things and beings within it. In other words, God is ubiquitous°.

Nazism _____
bibliography _____ 3–4. When they collaborated° on a term paper about (*Naz . . .*) ___, Eddie and Dina compiled a long (. . . *graphy*) ___ of books dealing with Hitler, the Nazis, and World War II.

_____symphony_____   5–6. A (. . . *phony*) ___ orchestra consists of about a hundred musicians. If that
_____direction_____   many people are going to play together as a cohesive° unit, they must follow
                              the (*di . . . ion*) ___ of the conductor.

_____amoral_____   7–8. Animals are said to be (. . . *moral*) ___, having no concept of right or wrong,
_____verified_____   but that isn't always (. . . *ified*) ___ by their behavior. For instance, a dog
                              may slink around guiltily after chewing on the rug.

_____innovative_____   9–10. My uncle thinks he is on the verge of developing an (*in . . . ative*) ___ gadget
_____confiding_____   that will make a fortune. To keep his idea from being stolen, he is (*con . . . ing*)
                               ___ in only a few people he really trusts.

Final Check: *Alex's Search*

Here is a final opportunity for you to strengthen your knowledge of the ten word parts. First read the
following selection carefully. Then complete each *italicized* word in the parentheses below with a word
part from the box at the top of the previous page. (Context clues will help you figure out which word part
goes in which blank.) Use each word part once.

Although Alex was brought up in a traditional Catholic
household, he himself never truly adopted (*Catholic . . .*)
(1)_____Catholicism_____ as his faith, but set off
on a search for his own religious beliefs. He read the entire
(. . . *e*) (2)_____Bible_____ thoroughly and visited
many places where people gather together to worship—
churches, (. . . *agogues*) (3)_____synagogues_____,
mosques, and temples—but he was not attracted by
the tenets° of any particular organized religion. Finally, Alex
developed what he thought was a completely (. . . *el*)
(4)_____novel_____ idea: that God exists in all of
nature: in trees, rivers, mountains, and even stones. As
he learned more about the beliefs of early humans and
more (. . . *itive*) (5)_____primitive_____ societies,
though, he discovered that this concept—(. . . *theism*)
(6)_____pantheism_____—was not really new and
had existed for a long time and in many places.

All this estranged° Alex from his parents, who felt that
his idea was tantamount° to (. . . *theism*) (7)_____atheism_____, the same as saying there is no God
at all. They saw him as an (*in . . . el*) (8)_____infidel_____ who had abandoned the faith of his own
people, and they begged him to (. . . *ify*) (9)_____rectify_____ this grievous° error and return to
the Catholic church. Alex, however, argued that since no one could (. . . *ify*) (10)_____verify_____
religious principles scientifically, people should accept the fact that some beliefs may differ from their own.

| Scores | Sentence Check 2 _____% | Final Check _____% |

Enter your scores above and in the **Vocabulary Performance Chart** on the inside back cover of the book.

The box at the right lists twenty-five words from Unit Two. Using the clues at the bottom of the page, fill in these words to complete the puzzle that follows.

Word list:
attrition
bolster
egocentric
equivocate
exonerate
inquisitive
inundate
liability
liaison
ostracize
prolific
raucous
recourse
reinstate
reiterate
replete
reticent
robust
sham
solace
solicitous
tenet
terse
utopia
vociferous

(Crossword grid with completed answers: VOCIFEROUS, ATTRITION, SOLICITOUS, LIABILITY, REPLETE, BOLSTER, INQUISITIVE, REINSTATE, SOLACE, UTOPIA, EGOCENTRIC, EXONERATE, RETICENT, and others.)

ACROSS

2. Expressing feelings loudly
4. A gradual natural decrease in number; becoming fewer
6. Showing or expressing concern, care, or attention
7. Something that acts as a disadvantage; drawback
8. Plentifully supplied
10. To hold up, strengthen, or reinforce
11. Curious; eager to learn
18. To restore to a previous position or condition
19. Comfort in sorrow or misfortune; consolation
21. An ideal or perfect place or state
23. Self-centered; seeing everything in terms of oneself
24. To clear of an accusation or charge; prove innocent
25. Quiet or uncommunicative; reluctant to speak out

DOWN

1. Healthy and strong; vigorous
3. To be deliberately vague in order to mislead
5. A person who serves as a connection between individuals or groups
9. Producing many works, results, or offspring; fertile
12. A pretense or counterfeit; something meant to deceive
13. Brief and clear
14. To expel or exclude
15. Noisy and disorderly
16. To state again or repeatedly
17. A source of help, security, or strength; something to turn to
20. To cover, as by flooding; overwhelm with a large number or amount
22. A belief or principle held to be true by an individual or group

PART A

Choose the word that best completes each item and write it in the space provided.

propensity   1. When he's caught in a tight spot, Peter has an unfortunate ___ to lie. As a result, few people trust him anymore.

      A. utopia   B. propensity   C. attrition   D. contingency

cohesive   2. My friends and I are a ___ group. We stick together through good times and bad.

      A. prolific   B. bureaucratic   C. cohesive   D. terse

liability   3. In almost any job, being unable to read is a definite ___.

      A. recourse   B. mandate   C. tenet   D. liability

robust   4. Toshio seems so ___ today that it's hard to believe he was close to death only two months ago.

      A. robust   B. terse   C. indigenous   D. superfluous

equivocated   5. When I asked my father if he liked my new dress, he ___, saying, "That green is a terrific color."

      A. inundated   B. equivocated   C. ostracized   D. depreciated

tenacious   6. At age 10, my cousin still has a ___ belief in Santa Claus. She becomes upset at any suggestion that he doesn't exist.

      A. sedentary   B. tenacious   C. tantamount   D. nebulous

reiterated   7. The math teacher ___ his explanation of the problem several times because his students were having difficulty understanding it.

      A. depreciated   B. reiterated   C. exonerated   D. circumvented

clandestine   8. Because of the ___ nature of drug dealing, it is very difficult to stop. Most of the transactions take place on dark street corners or behind closed doors.

      A. terse   B. clandestine   C. solicitous   D. fortuitous

sanction   9. The managers at Brian's company refused to ___ the early-retirement plan proposed by the union because they felt the plan would cost too much.

      A. ostracize   B. sanction   C. inundate   D. circumvent

replete   10. A modern American wedding is ___ with customs originally intended to ensure the couple's fertility, including having a wedding cake, throwing rice, and tying shoes to the back of the car.

      A. tantamount   B. inquisitive   C. replete   D. grievous

(Continues on next page)

PART B

On the answer line, write the letter of the choice that best completes each item.

___D___ 11. Tamika is interested only in **sedentary** jobs, such as
    A. digging ditches.   C. teaching physical-education classes.
    B. working in a busy sporting-goods store.   D. sitting at a desk answering an office phone.

___C___ 12. Some people wanted the fired teacher to be **reinstated** because she
    A. didn't deserve her pension.   C. was an excellent teacher.
    B. had already started working at a new job.   D. had allowed cheating in her classroom.

___A___ 13. Which of the following phrases contains a **superfluous** word?
    A. "A big huge whale."   C. "A frisky young dog."
    B. "A small red chicken."   D. "A beautiful black cat."

___A___ 14. Lilian is extremely **reticent** about her private life. As a result, I
    A. know almost nothing about it.   C. really get tired of her bragging.
    B. know every detail of her private life.   D. worry that she trusts the wrong people.

___D___ 15. A meeting in my neighbor's apartment was so **raucous** that
    A. I didn't know it was taking place.   C. everyone was very pleased.
    B. she had to borrow some chairs from me.   D. the noise kept me awake for hours.

___D___ 16. Which of the following is an example of **attrition**?
    A. The number of students enrolled in the algebra class remained the same all semester.
    B. The population in our town has increased so much we've had to build a second school.
    C. In January we had a single pair of mice; by December we had 55 adults and babies.
    D. The 50-year class reunion attracted 47 graduates, while the 60-year reunion of that same class attracted 41 graduates.

___D___ 17. Because the new morning talk show was not attracting a large audience, it was **relegated** to
    A. 9 p.m., when it could compete with the most popular shows.
    B. a new host with a more sparkling personality.
    C. a reality series featuring a new kind of danger every week.
    D. 1:30 a.m., when few people would be watching.

___B___ 18. I considered it **tantamount** to lying when a coworker
    A. caught our boss telling a lie.
    B. remained silent when another worker was accused of his error.
    C. refused to tell a lie, no matter what the consequences were.
    D. criticized others for lying.

___C___ 19. Which of the following people was **solicitous** to the sick man?
    A. His boss, who threatened to fire him if he didn't get back to work.
    B. His daughter, who whined, "But you promised to take me to the mall today."
    C. His wife, who made him chicken soup and brought him aspirin.
    D. His little boy, who bounced up and down on his bed yelling "Get up, Daddy!"

___A___ 20. One way to give children **autonomy** is to
    A. stand back and let them make their own decisions—and their own mistakes.
    B. watch them every minute and punish them if they do anything wrong.
    C. put them on a schedule that includes time for schoolwork, sports, and enrichment activities.
    D. praise them when they get good grades and display their artwork on the refrigerator.

Score   (Number correct) _____ x 5 = _____%

Enter your scores above and in the **Vocabulary Performance Chart** on the inside back cover of the book.

PART A

Complete each item with a word from the box. Use each word once.

A. **circumvent**	B. **exonerate**	C. **grievous**	D. **inundate**	E. **mandate**
F. **oblivious**	G. **predisposed**	H. **prolific**	I. **sham**	J. **solace**
K. **tenet**	L. **utopia**	M. **vociferous**		

_____ utopia _____   1. I hate mornings. My idea of a(n) ___ would be a world in which no job or class began before noon.

_____ mandate _____   2. The local election made the voters' ___ clear: Build more neighborhood parks.

_____ grievous _____   3. People who ignore their elderly parents do them a(n) ___ wrong.

_____ circumvent _____   4. We tried to ___ the construction area by taking the other highway, but that road was being repaired too.

_____ tenet _____   5. The main ___ of the "Girls Are Great" club is that girls can do anything boys can do.

_____ exonerate _____   6. Gerry was accused of stealing a wallet but was ___(e)d when the wallet was found in another student's locker.

_____ predisposed _____   7. Because his father and grandfather both had heart disease, my cousin worries that he may be ___ to the same disorder.

_____ oblivious _____   8. Susan signed in and began work, ___ to the fact that she had forgotten to change from her bedroom slippers into her shoes.

_____ solace _____   9. When their young daughter died last year, the Bakers found ___ with a support group of other parents who had also lost a child.

_____ inundate _____   10. After telling a reader to say goodbye to her boyfriend, the newspaper advice columnist was ___(e)d with thousands of letters saying she was wrong.

_____ vociferous _____   11. When three-year-old Ginger doesn't get what she wants, her protests are so ___ that you can hear her all over the neighborhood.

_____ sham _____   12. The invitation we sent my parents to attend a friend's birthday party was a(n) ___. We were actually giving a surprise party in honor of their anniversary.

_____ prolific _____   13. According to _Guinness World Records_, the most ___ woman on record is a Russian peasant who lived in the early 1700s. She gave birth to sixty-nine children—sixteen pairs of twins, seven sets of triplets, and four sets of quadruplets.

(Continues on next page)

PART B

Write **C** if the italicized word is used **correctly**. Write **I** if the word is used **incorrectly**.

___I___ 14. Sally's appearance was *impeccable*. Even her fingernails were dirty.

___I___ 15. Some people invest in art and antiques, hoping that their investments will eventually *depreciate*.

___I___ 16. When Clarence arrived at camp, he was immediately *ostracized* by the other campers. He was thrilled to be so warmly welcomed.

___C___ 17. After getting no satisfaction at the car dealership, Mom decided that her best *recourse* would be to contact the president of the company.

___C___ 18. As a *liaison* between the hospital staff and patients' families, Jon provides information about patients' conditions in language their families can understand.

___C___ 19. My cousin is so *egocentric* that when the family got together for his sister's graduation, he assumed the gathering was in honor of his new job as manager of a fast-food restaurant.

PART C

On the answer line, write the letter of the word that is the **synonym** of the boldfaced word.

Example: ___A___ **robust**   A. healthy   B. dangerous   C. weak

___C___ 20. **reprehensible**   A. forbidden   B. admirable   C. blameworthy

___C___ 21. **nebulous**   A. clear   B. large   C. vague

___B___ 22. **indigenous**   A. angry   B. native   C. foreign

PART D

On the answer line, write the letter of the word that is the **antonym** of the boldfaced word.

Example: ___C___ **robust**   A. healthy   B. dangerous   C. weak

___B___ 23. **inquisitive**   A. excited   B. bored   C. curious

___C___ 24. **incongruous**   A. inconsistent   B. complete   C. suitable

___A___ 25. **terse**   A. wordy   B. relaxed   C. brief

Score   (Number correct) _____   x 4 = _____ %

Each item below starts with a pair of words in CAPITAL LETTERS. For each item, figure out the relationship between these two words. Then decide which of the choices (A, B, C, or D) expresses a similar relationship. Write the letter of your choice on the answer line.

_C_   1. FORTUITOUS : BY CHANCE ::
         A. anonymous : by name   C. commonplace : familiar
         B. blessed : unlucky   D. automated : by hand

_B_   2. REPREHENSIBLE : MURDER ::
         A. enjoyable : sickness   C. impossible : fact
         B. praiseworthy : good deed   D. terrible : kindness

_A_   3. SHAM : DISGUISE ::
         A. plan : blueprint   C. framework : building
         B. smile : frown   D. mask : face

_B_   4. SOLICITOUS : UNCARING ::
         A. sole : only   C. solar : system
         B. satisfying : displeasing   D. solitary : alone

_D_   5. CIRCUMVENT : GO AROUND ::
         A. circulate : stop   C. bridge : go back
         B. tunnel : go over   D. depart : go away

_C_   6. OBLIVIOUS : AWARE ::
         A. obvious : clear   C. optional : required
         B. insulting : disrespectful   D. unclear : vague

_D_   7. RETICENT : SILENT ::
         A. evil : ugly   C. helpful : nurse
         B. lighthearted : gloomy   D. well-known : famous

_B_   8. VOCIFEROUS : PROTESTORS ::
         A. violent : pacifists   C. virtuous : criminals
         B. brave : heroes   D. victorious : losers

_C_   9. BOLSTER : WEAKEN ::
         A. heal : cure   C. build : destroy
         B. scrub : clean   D. search : hope

_D_   10. INDISCRIMINATE : SELECTIVE ::
         A. indistinct : vague   C. content : satisfied
         B. injurious : harmful   D. intolerant : open-minded

(Continues on next page)

_C_ 11. SEDENTARY : RECEPTIONIST ::
A. healthy : plumber   C. dangerous : firefighter
B. hammer : carpenter   D. unskilled : nuclear physicist

_A_ 12. TENET : RELIGION ::
A. custom : culture   C. law : friendship
B. hobby : workplace   D. foreign policy : day-care center

_D_ 13. AUTONOMY : PRISONER ::
A. wealth : billionaire   C. victory : country
B. information : newspaper   D. expertise : beginner

_A_ 14. BUREAUCRATIC : CORPORATION ::
A. educational : museum   C. predictable : surprise
B. peaceful : riot   D. damp : famine

_B_ 15. RAUCOUS : SOCCER FANS ::
A. delicate : boxers   C. soothing : rock musicians
B. competitive : political candidates   D. powerless : police

_C_ 16. UTOPIA : IMPERFECT ::
A. wedding : happy   C. attack : peaceful
B. situation comedy : new   D. lecture : educational

_D_ 17. CONTINGENCY : PREPARE ::
A. accident : happen   C. mistake : intend
B. car : repair   D. goal : aim

_A_ 18. EXONERATE : EVIDENCE ::
A. pollute : chemicals   C. write : essay
B. bake : cake   D. sleep : energy

_C_ 19. INCONGRUOUS : BLUE APPLE ::
A. unbearable : comfortable   C. inedible : granite
B. inferior : first-class   D. impossible : somersault

_B_ 20. PROLIFIC : OFFSPRING ::
A. deceptive : truth   C. children : parents
B. imaginative : ideas   D. teacher : students

Score   (Number correct) _____ x 5 = _____%

Enter your scores above and in the **Vocabulary Performance Chart** on the inside back cover of the book.

PART A

Listed in the left-hand column below are ten common word parts, followed by words in which the parts are used. In each blank, write in the letter of the correct definition on the right.

Word Parts		Examples	Definitions
_C_	1. **a-, an-**	apolitical, analgesic	A. First (in order or importance)
_H_	2. **bibl-, biblio-**	Bible, bibliophile	B. All
_G_	3. **fid**	Fido, infidel	C. Without, lacking, not
_F_	4. **-ism**	totalitarianism, Quakerism	D. New, original, fresh
_D_	5. **nov**	novelty, innovative	E. Straight, right
_B_	6. **pan**	Pan-American, panacea	F. Doctrine, system, practice of
_A_	7. **prim, prime**	primeval, prime	G. Trust, faith, loyalty
_E_	8. **rect**	rectangle, rectify	H. Book
_J_	9. **sym-, syn-**	symptom, synchronize	I. True, real
_I_	10. **ver**	verify, verdict	J. With, together

PART B

Using the answer line provided, complete each *italicized* word in the sentences below with the correct word part from the box. Not every word part will be used.

A. **an-**	B. **biblio-**	C. **fid**	D. **-ism**	E. **nov**
F. **pan-**	G. **prime**	H. **rect**	I. **syn-**	J. **ver**

bibliophile   11. My uncle, a(n) (. . . *phile*) ___, collects rare and beautiful books.

Buddhism   12. Zen (*Buddh* . . .) ___ stresses meditation and self-reliance.

Anorexia   13. (. . . *orexia*) "___" means "a lack of appetite for food."

Pan   14. The (. . . -*American*) ___ Highway runs from Alaska to Chile, linking all the Americas.

synthesis   15. Musical comedies are a(n) (. . . *thesis*) ___ of several arts, bringing together dancing, singing, and acting.

(Continues on next page)

PART C

Use your knowledge of word parts to determine the meaning of the **boldfaced** words. On the answer line, write the letter of each meaning.

_B_ 16. Ramona was a **novice** at carpentry.

    A. an expert   B. a beginner   C. a worker

_A_ 17. The book is an outdated **primer** on chemistry.

    A. a first book   B. an argument   C. a workbook

_A_ 18. The church teaches **rectitude**.

    A. righteousness   B. patience   C. the masses

_C_ 19. The jurors doubted the **veracity** of the defense attorney's witness.

    A. memory   B. intentions   C. honesty

_C_ 20. The President's wife is his best friend and **confidante**.

    A. an admirer   B. the mother of his children   C. a person one trusts enough to tell secrets to

Score   (Number correct) _____ x 5 = _____%

Unit Three

advocate	impede
antipathy	inclusive
emancipate	jurisdiction
idiosyncrasy	precarious
imminent	preposterous

Ten Words in Context

In the space provided, write the letter of the meaning closest to that of each **boldfaced** word. Use the context of the sentences to help you figure out each word's meaning.

1 advocate
(ăd′və-kāt′)
-verb

- One author was refused permission to give a speech on campus because he **advocates** violence as a means of social reform.
- Some gardeners consider chemicals and pesticides harmful; instead, they **advocate** using "organic" methods of growing fruits and vegetables.

__B__ *Advocate* means   A. to oppose.   B. to promote.   C. to understand.

2 antipathy
(ăn-tĭ′pə-thē)
-noun

- Malik's parents didn't understand why he hated school until they found that the reason for his **antipathy** was poor eyesight: he couldn't see the chalkboard.
- I can't believe that my sister is going to marry Frank. Just a few months ago, she showed complete **antipathy** toward him.

__A__ *Antipathy* means   A. a strong dislike.   B. a lack of concern.   C. a preference.

3 emancipate
(ē-măn′sĭ-pāt′)
-verb

- The salesman promised that his amazing machine—a vacuum cleaner, floor polisher, and carpet shampooer in one—would **emancipate** us from hours of backbreaking housework.
- When the Allies entered Germany at the end of World War II, they **emancipated** many foreigners and political prisoners who had been used as slave laborers in German industries.

__C__ *Emancipate* means   A. to encourage.   B. to administer justice.   C. to free.

4 idiosyncrasy
(ĭd′ē-ō-sĭng′krə-sē)
-noun

- My uncle asks very personal questions, but please don't be offended—it's just an **idiosyncrasy** of his. He doesn't realize how odd it seems to others.
- For as long as I've known Cara, she's had the unusual **idiosyncrasy** of dressing only in black.

__A__ *Idiosyncrasy* means   A. a personal habit.   B. a dangerous habit.   C. a selfish habit.

5 imminent
(ĭm′ə-nənt)
-adjective

- We canceled the picnic because a thunderstorm seemed **imminent**.
- As word spread that the king's death was **imminent**, the people began to gather at the palace gates. They wanted to be nearby when he died.

__C__ *Imminent* means   A. over.   B. delayed.   C. likely to occur soon.

6 impede
(ĭm-pēd′)
-verb

- Muddy roads **impeded** the progress of the trucks bringing food to the refugees.
- The construction work at the mall **impeded** shoppers, who had to step around piles of planks, cables, crates, tools, and sacks of cement.

__B__ *Impede* means   A. to oppress.   B. to slow down.   C. to include.

7 inclusive
(ĭn-klōō′sĭv)
-adjective

- The cost of the vacation package was **inclusive**, covering our airfare and all hotels, meals, and tours.
- The newspaper's coverage of the trial was **inclusive**; every day, it printed a word-for-word transcript of the courtroom proceedings.

A _Inclusive_ means   A. complete.   B. lacking something.   C. about to start.

8 jurisdiction
(jŏŏr′ĭs-dĭk′shən)
-noun

- Shakespeare's theater, the Globe, was built across the river from London. Officials had forbidden theaters in London, but the other side of the river was beyond their **jurisdiction**.
- The United States has no **jurisdiction** over foreign embassies on American soil; those embassies are under the authority of their own governments.

C _Jurisdiction_ means   A. advice.   B. beliefs.   C. control.

9 precarious
(prē-kâr′ē-əs)
-adjective

- The icy roads made travel **precarious**.
- The old, worn-out electrical wiring in the building puts all the residents in a **precarious** position. At any moment, it could fail, causing a fire.

A _Precarious_ means   A. unsafe.   B. illegal.   C. unusual.

10 preposterous
(prē-pŏs′tər-əs)
-adjective

- Louis always comes up with **preposterous** get-rich-quick schemes. Now he wants to open a doughnut shop in Antarctica.
- The discovery of x-rays in 1895 was followed by some **preposterous** ideas and fears. For example, merchants in England sold "x-ray-proof" underwear.

C _Preposterous_ means   A. risky.   B. exciting.   C. ridiculous.

Matching Words with Definitions

Following are definitions of the ten words. Clearly write or print each word next to its definition. The sentences above and on the previous page will help you decide on the meaning of each word.

1. _impede_ — To delay or slow; get in the way of

2. _inclusive_ — Including much or everything; broad or complete in coverage

3. _advocate_ — To speak or write in favor of; support

4. _jurisdiction_ — The authority to administer justice; power; range or extent of authority

5. _antipathy_ — A strong dislike or distaste; hatred

6. _emancipate_ — To set free from slavery, captivity, or oppression

7. _preposterous_ — Contrary to nature or reason and thus laughable; absurd

8. _idiosyncrasy_ — A personal peculiarity; quirk

9. _precarious_ — Dangerous; risky; dangerously uncertain

10. _imminent_ — About to happen

CAUTION: Do not go any further until you are sure the above answers are correct. Then you can use the definitions to help you in the following practices. Your goal is eventually to know the words well enough so that you don't need to check the definitions at all.

Sentence Check 1

Using the answer line provided, complete each item below with the correct word from the box. Use each word once.

A. advocate	B. antipathy	C. emancipate	D. idiosyncrasy	E. imminent
F. impede	G. inclusive	H. jurisdiction	I. precarious	J. preposterous

_____precarious_____ 1. For someone allergic to insect bites, beekeeping would be a(n) ___ occupation.

_____advocate_____ 2. Nutritionists today ___ a diet low in fats and high in fiber.

_____inclusive_____ 3. The caterer's services were really ___: food, wine, flowers, decorations, coat check, music, and master of ceremonies.

_____imminent_____ 4. When the jury's verdict was ___, the lawyers, reporters, and spectators immediately returned to the courtroom.

_____impede_____ 5. I swore that nothing would keep me from getting to Gloria's wedding on time, but I was ___(e)d by a traffic jam.

_____emancipate_____ 6. One aim of today's women's groups is to ___ women from job and wage discrimination.

_____jurisdiction_____ 7. Since the bank robbery had involved crossing state lines, the federal government had ___ in the case.

_____antipathy_____ 8. Burt has a(n) ___ for everything that isn't "100 percent American." He thinks it makes him a patriot, but I think a dislike of foreigners or foreign ways shows ignorance.

_____preposterous_____ 9. When the little boy said there was a frog in his glass of milk, everyone laughed at his ___ idea—until he showed us the frog.

_____idiosyncrasy_____ 10. Tamiko always takes off her shoes before entering the house. Ralph thought this was just a(n) ___ of hers, but he later learned that it's a Japanese custom.

NOTE: Now check your answers to these items by turning to page 178. Going over the answers carefully will help you prepare for the next two practices, for which answers are not given.

Sentence Check 2

Using the answer lines provided, complete each item below with **two** words from the box. Use each word once.

_____advocate_____
_____inclusive_____ 1–2. One member of the school board ___s a more ___ high-school curriculum, with courses in subjects such as parenting and preserving the environment as well as the more traditional academic subjects.

_____idiosyncrasy_____
_____impede_____ 3–4. Chet refuses to use a cell phone. For most people, this ___ would certainly ___ their attempts to have a social life, but Chet isn't very gregarious° anyway.

_____precarious_____
_____imminent_____ 5–6. Being outdoors in an electrical storm is a(n) ___ situation. When a storm is ___, the optimum° strategy is to go indoors and stay there.

_____emancipate_____

_____jurisdiction_____

7–8. During the Civil War, President Lincoln's administration could not actually ___ the slaves because his government had no ___ in the South.

_____antipathy_____

_____preposterous_____

9–10. Ellen's ___ toward Jack is based on her ___ but tenacious° belief that in a former life, Jack robbed her family of its life's savings.

Final Check: *Ann's Love of Animals*

Here is a final opportunity for you to strengthen your knowledge of the ten words. First read the following selection carefully. Then fill in each blank with a word from the box at the top of the previous page. (Context clues will help you figure out which word goes in which blank.) Use each word once.

Perhaps more than anyone else I know, Ann cares about animals. Her affection for them is all-(1)_____inclusive_____, extending even to animals others find less appealing, such as rats, which she keeps as pets. Because she loves animals, Ann hates to see them caged. She objects to anything that (2)_____impede_____s any creature's movements. This explains a(n) (3)_____idiosyncrasy_____ of hers: she lets her pet white rats run freely throughout her apartment.

Ann's view of cages has also led to a strong (4)_____antipathy_____ toward zoos. If Ann had (5)_____jurisdiction_____ over all the zoos in the world, she would make them illegal and (6)_____emancipate_____ all the animals from their captivity. Many people will argue that zoos protect animals, but Ann scoffs° at this idea, saying it's (7)_____preposterous_____ because animals often die when they are being trapped for zoos or shipped to zoos. She believes that the most (8)_____precarious_____ life in the wild is preferable to the safest life in captivity. In addition, Ann says, some zoos inadvertently° cause grievous° harm to animals by purchasing them from dealers who have obtained the animals illegally. The zoo officials don't want animals to be harmed, but accepting them from corrupt sources encourages illicit° trapping and killing.

Of course, Ann realizes that her utopia°—a society without cages or zoos, with animals permitted to stay in their native habitats—is far from (9)_____imminent_____. Nevertheless, her spirit has not been squelched°, and she continues to (10)_____advocate_____ freeing the animals in the hope that someday zoos will close their gates forever.

| Scores | Sentence Check 2 _____% | Final Check _____% |

Enter your scores above and in the **Vocabulary Performance Chart** on the inside back cover of the book.

austere	metamorphosis
esoteric	notorious
facsimile	perfunctory
grotesque	provocative
mesmerize	travesty

Ten Words in Context

In the space provided, write the letter of the meaning closest to that of each **boldfaced** word. Use the context of the sentences to help you figure out each word's meaning.

1 austere
(ô-stîr')
-adjective

● Ms. Stone's appearance was **austere**. She wore plain, dark-colored clothing with no jewelry, and she never used makeup.

● The walls in Mario's den are white and nearly bare, and his white furniture has simple lines. This **austere** decor gives the room a pleasantly calm mood.

__B__ *Austere* means ____ A. very ugly. ____ B. very plain. ____ C. very youthful.

2 esoteric
(ĕs'ə-tĕr'ĭk)
-adjective

● The instruction manuals that come with computer software often use such **esoteric** terms that they seem to be written in a foreign language.

● The poetry of Ezra Pound, filled with references to ancient Greek culture, is too **esoteric** for most readers.

__A__ *Esoteric* means ____ A. difficult to understand. ____ B. shallow. ____ C. unfavorable.

3 facsimile
(făk-sĭm'ə-lē)
-noun

● When a **facsimile** of an old Sears-Roebuck catalog was published recently, it became a bestseller. People enjoyed seeing what was for sale a century ago.

● The word *fax* is short for **facsimile**. With a fax machine, you can send a precise image of a document across the country electronically in seconds.

__C__ *Facsimile* means ____ A. an original. ____ B. a distorted version. ____ C. an accurate copy.

4 grotesque
(grō-tĕsk')
-adjective

● Most people found the movie character E.T. adorable, but I thought the little alien was **grotesque**, with its weird combination of babyish features and old, wrinkled skin.

● The clown made **grotesque** faces, squinting his eyes, pulling down the corners of his mouth, and sticking out his tongue.

__A__ *Grotesque* means ____ A. strange-looking. ____ B. hard to understand. ____ C. charming.

5 mesmerize
(mĕz'mə-rīz')
-verb

● The intense eyes of the woman in the photograph **mesmerized** me. I couldn't take my eyes off the picture.

● When driving at night, you can become **mesmerized** by the lines on the road or by other cars' headlights or taillights. To avoid a hypnotic state, keep your eyes moving from front to side to rearview mirror.

__B__ *Mesmerize* means ____ A. to amuse. ____ B. to fascinate. ____ C. to distort.

6 metamorphosis
(mĕt'ə-môr'fĕ-sĭs)
-noun

● A caterpillar's transformation into a butterfly is a well-known example of **metamorphosis**.

● In Franz Kafka's famous story "The **Metamorphosis**," a man wakes up on his thirtieth birthday to discover that he has turned into an enormous insect.

__A__ *Metamorphosis* means ____ A. a change in form. ____ B. a disaster. ____ C. a scientific theory.

7 notorious
(nō-tôr′ē-əs)
-adjective

A *Notorious* means

- Batman and Robin matched wits with the Joker and the Penguin, who were **notorious** for their evil deeds.
- The local diner is **notorious** for bitter coffee, soggy vegetables, limp salads, and mystery meat.

A. regarded negatively.   B. regarded with curiosity.   C. ignored.

8 perfunctory
(pər-fŭnk′tə-rē)
-adjective

A *Perfunctory* means

- The doctor's examination was **perfunctory**. He seemed to be just going through the motions without taking any interest in the patient.
- Most of the candidates were passionate on the subject of nuclear weapons, but one spoke in a very **perfunctory** way, apparently bored with the topic.

A. uninterested.   B. enthusiastic.   C. exaggerated.

9 provocative
(prō-vŏk′ə-tĭv)
-adjective

C *Provocative* means

- "A good essay is **provocative**," said our English instructor. "It gets the reader interested and attentive, starting with the very first paragraph."
- To arouse the viewers' curiosity, the television ad began with a **provocative** image: a spaceship landing on a baseball field, at home plate.

A. predictable.   B. difficult to understand.   C. attention-getting.

10 travesty
(trăv′ĭs-tē)
-noun

A *Travesty* means

- The fraternity skit, a **travesty** of college life, exaggerated and ridiculed many campus activities.
- The musical-comedy version of *Hamlet* was a **travesty**. The critics and audience agreed that it made a mockery of Shakespeare's profound tragedy.

A. a joking, disrespectful imitation.   B. an exact copy.   C. a simple version.

Matching Words with Definitions

Following are definitions of the ten words. Clearly write or print each word next to its definition. The sentences above and on the previous page will help you decide on the meaning of each word.

1. _____mesmerize_____ To hypnotize or fascinate; hold spellbound

2. _____metamorphosis_____ A great or complete change; transformation

3. _____travesty_____ A crude, exaggerated, or ridiculous representation; mockery

4. _____perfunctory_____ Done only as a routine, with little care or interest; performed with no interest or enthusiasm

5. _____notorious_____ Known widely but unfavorably; having a bad reputation

6. _____provocative_____ Tending to arouse interest or curiosity

7. _____facsimile_____ An exact copy or reproduction

8. _____esoteric_____ Intended for or understood by only a certain group; beyond the understanding of most people

9. _____austere_____ Without decoration or luxury; severely simple

10. _____grotesque_____ Distorted or strikingly inconsistent in shape, appearance, or manner

CAUTION: Do not go any further until you are sure the above answers are correct. Then you can use the definitions to help you in the following practices. Your goal is eventually to know the words well enough so that you don't need to check the definitions at all.

Sentence Check 1

Using the answer line provided, complete each item below with the correct word from the box. Use each word once.

A. austere	B. esoteric	C. facsimile	D. grotesque	E. mesmerize
F. metamorphosis	G. notorious	H. perfunctory	I. provocative	J. travesty

__travesty__ 1. The trial was a ___ of justice because several of the jurors had been bribed.

__notorious__ 2. King Henry VIII of England was ___ not only for getting married six times, but also for having two of his wives executed.

__provocative__ 3. To capture readers' attention, an author sometimes begins an article with a(n) ___ question, such as, "Which do you think is more dangerous, climbing stairs or parachuting out of an airplane?"

__grotesque__ 4. In some modern paintings, human figures are distorted into such ___ shapes that it's hard to recognize facial features and body parts.

__facsimile__ 5. Lining the music school's hallway are framed ___s of handwritten pages of music by great composers.

__esoteric__ 6. Legal documents are usually worded in such ___ language that most people need a lawyer to translate the "legalese" into plain English.

__mesmerize__ 7. As I stood looking at the grandfather clock, I became ___(e)d by the shiny pendulum that swung back and forth, back and forth, back and forth.

__perfunctory__ 8. Usually the therapist showed great interest in her patients, but today she was too worried about her own family to give more than ___ responses.

__austere__ 9. My sister's dormitory room is rather ___, with cement-block walls and bare floors, but she's made it less stark by hanging colorful posters and adding bright bedspreads and cushions.

__Metamorphosis__ 10. The magician David Copperfield does a trick called "___." One person is chained and locked in a box. When the box is opened, that person is gone, and someone else is chained there instead.

NOTE: Now check your answers to these items by turning to page 178. Going over the answers carefully will help you prepare for the next two practices, for which answers are not given.

Sentence Check 2

Using the answer lines provided, complete each item below with **two** words from the box. Use each word once.

__grotesque__
__travesty__ 1–2. The political cartoon showed the judge as a(n) ___ figure, with a huge belly and a gaping mouth. To me it's unfair—a ___ of journalistic ethics.

__notorious__
__austere__ 3–4. The cat burglar in the film, ___ for stealing expensive jewelry, committed all his robberies wearing a(n) ___ outfit: a black T-shirt, plain black pants, black shoes, and black gloves.

_____provocative_____   5–6. The novel has a(n) ___ opening scene, in which a young woman and her
_____mesmerize_____   parrot sneak out of a house on a ladder. The novel goes on to ___ the reader
                                       with one spellbinding episode after another.

_____perfunctory_____   7–8. Former principals had made only ___ efforts to rid the school of drugs, but
_____metamorphosis_____   the new principal, supported by a mandate° from the parents' association,
                                       attacked the problem head-on. As a result, the school has undergone a ___
                                       from "hooked" to "clean."

_____facsimile_____   9–10. At the jewelers' convention, ___s of several famous gems were on display.
_____esoteric_____   I enjoyed seeing them, but I didn't understand the accompanying ___
                                       explanation of the technical methods used to produce the copies.

Final Check: *A Costume Party*

Here is a final opportunity for you to strengthen your knowledge of the ten words. First read the following selection carefully. Then fill in each blank with a word from the box at the top of the previous page. (Context clues will help you figure out which word goes in which blank.) Use each word once.

On the afternoon of a friend's New Year's Eve costume party, I made only a(n) (1)_____perfunctory_____ effort to put a costume together. Unenthusiastic about spending much time on this, I wanted to create something as simple and rudimentary° as possible, even if the effect would be rather (2)_____austere_____. I decided on a ghost costume—just a plain sheet with eyeholes cut out. Since all my sheets are green, I had to be the ghost of a frog.

The party began for me with a (3)_____provocative_____ encounter: the door was opened by Julia Roberts, smiling flirtatiously and clutching her Best Actress Oscar—or at least an excellent (4)_____facsimile_____ of it. Then, when I went inside, the first men I saw were two (5)_____notorious_____ pirates, Blackbeard and Captain Hook. I listened in on their conversation, expecting to be (6)_____mesmerize_____(e)d by fascinating tales of cut-throat adventures; instead, I heard only the (7)_____esoteric_____ language of two math majors.

Giving up any hope of understanding their remarks, I looked around for my own friends. But their (8)_____metamorphosis_____ from ordinary people to famous or odd people was so complete that I couldn't recognize anyone. Most of the costumes were in good taste. One, though, struck me as a (9)_____travesty_____: a person dressed as Abraham Lincoln—a President I venerate° for his character and leadership—was wearing a bull's-eye target, in crude mockery of President Lincoln's assassination. Another person looked frighteningly (10)_____grotesque_____, with a mouth twisted to one side and three eyes, all of different sizes.

In the course of the evening, I also met Cleopatra, Shakespeare, and Snoopy, among others. I may never again spend time at a gathering replete° with so many celebrities.

| Scores | Sentence Check 2 _____% | Final Check _____% |

Enter your scores above and in the **Vocabulary Performance Chart** on the inside back cover of the book.

connoisseur	lucid
conspiracy	plight
contrite	superficially
distraught	symmetrical
germane	verbose

Ten Words in Context

In the space provided, write the letter of the meaning closest to that of each **boldfaced** word. Use the context of the sentences to help you figure out each word's meaning.

1 connoisseur
(kŏn′ə-sûr′)
-noun

● My sister is a **connoisseur** of Southern novels. She's read dozens of them, and she knows all about the authors and their different styles.

● Curtis has broad knowledge of French wines—where they are made, when they are at their best, and exactly how each one tastes. He's a true **connoisseur**.

B *Connoisseur* means A. a doubter. B. an authority. C. a leader.

2 conspiracy
(kən-spĭr′ə-sē)
-noun

● The **conspiracy** to overthrow the government was started by two of the premier's own advisors.

● Although only Lee Harvey Oswald was arrested for the assassination of President Kennedy, many believe there was a **conspiracy** to kill the President.

A *Conspiracy* means A. a plot. B. an idea. C. an announcement.

3 contrite
(kən-trīt′)
-adjective

● Dolores was especially **contrite** about tearing her sister's dress because she'd borrowed it without permission.

● Judges are often more lenient with offenders who truly regret their crimes. A criminal who seems genuinely **contrite** may get a shorter sentence.

C *Contrite* means A. angry. B. confused. C. sorry.

4 distraught
(dĭ-strôt′)
-adjective

● The parents of the little girl who wandered off in the crowded mall were **distraught** until she was found.

● As the snowstorm got worse and worse and his wife still hadn't arrived home from work, Jeff became increasingly **distraught**.

A *Distraught* means A. upset. B. busy. C. forgetful.

5 germane
(jər-mān′)
-adjective

● Stacy went to the law library to look up information that might be **germane** to her client's case.

● It bothered Christine when her new boss asked if she had a boyfriend. That information certainly wasn't **germane** to her work.

B *Germane* means A. damaging. B. related. C. foreign.

6 lucid
(loo′sĭd)
-adjective

● I usually find computer manuals horribly unclear, but this one is **lucid**.

● The scientist's explanation of global warming was so **lucid** that the entire audience was able to grasp it.

A *Lucid* means A. easy to understand. B. repetitious. C. fair to both sides.

7 plight
(plīt)
-noun

- The **plight** of the homeless can be somewhat relieved by decent shelters.
- There were reports of a cave-in at the mine, but it was too soon to know much about the **plight** of the trapped miners.

C *Plight* means   A. a delayed situation.   B. an unlikely situation.   C. an unfortunate situation.

8 superficially
(soō′pər-físh′əl-lē)
-adverb

- Nina spent a full week studying for the exam. Joyce, however, reviewed **superficially**, flipping through the pages of her textbook an hour before the test.
- This morning, the mechanic was short of time and inspected my car only **superficially**. He said he'd check it thoroughly later and then give me an estimate.

B *Superficially* means   A. thoroughly.   B. slightly.   C. daily.

9 symmetrical
(sĭ-mĕt′rĭ-kəl)
-adjective

- The children's sandcastle was **symmetrical**, with a wall on each side and a tower and flag at each end.
- No one's face is perfectly **symmetrical**. For example, one eye is usually slightly higher than the other, and the left and right sides of the mouth differ.

C *Symmetrical* means   A. unique.   B. beautiful.   C. balanced.

10 verbose
(vər-bōs′)
-adjective

- The **verbose** senator said, "At this point in time, we have an urgent and important need for more monetary funds to declare unconditional war on drugs and combat this evil and harmful situation." The reporter wrote, "The senator said we urgently need more money to fight drugs."
- Gabe is the most **verbose** person I know. He always uses ten words when one would do.

B *Verbose* means   A. loud.   B. wordy.   C. self-important.

Matching Words with Definitions

Following are definitions of the ten words. Clearly write or print each word next to its definition. The sentences above and on the previous page will help you decide on the meaning of each word.

1. _____distraught_____   Very troubled; distressed

2. _____verbose_____   Using or containing too many words

3. _____superficially_____   In an on-the-surface manner; not thoroughly

4. _____germane_____   Having to do with the issue at hand; relevant

5. _____lucid_____   Clearly expressed; easily understood

6. _____contrite_____   Truly sorry for having done wrong; repentant

7. _____symmetrical_____   Well proportioned; balanced; the same on both sides

8. _____connoisseur_____   An expert in fine art or in matters of taste

9. _____plight_____   A situation marked by difficulty, hardship, or misfortune

10. _____conspiracy_____   A secret plot by two or more people, especially for a harmful or illegal purpose

CAUTION: Do not go any further until you are sure the above answers are correct. Then you can use the definitions to help you in the following practices. Your goal is eventually to know the words well enough so that you don't need to check the definitions at all.

Sentence Check 1

Using the answer line provided, complete each item below with the correct word from the box. Use each word once.

A. connoisseur	B. conspiracy	C. contrite	D. distraught	E. germane
F. lucid	G. plight	H. superficially	I. symmetrical	J. verbose

contrite 1. Claire was truly sorry for having started the argument with Sal. To show how ___ she felt, she e-mailed him an apology.

plight 2. Everyone is greatly concerned about the ___ of the hostages. We're not even certain they're still alive.

symmetrical 3. The garden is ___, with the same flowers and shrubs, arranged in the same pattern, on each side of a central path.

connoisseur 4. A ___ of Asian art told me that my Chinese vase is very old, quite rare, and valuable.

verbose 5. In writing, it is actually easier to be ___ than to make the effort to cut out the unnecessary words.

conspiracy 6. During the Revolutionary War, Benedict Arnold, an American officer, was involved in a ___ to help the British win.

germane 7. The teacher and the other students became irritated when Susan kept asking questions that weren't ___ to the class discussion.

distraught 8. My parents had expected my sister home by ten o'clock. By the time she finally walked in at two in the morning, they were very ___.

lucid 9. Ved's teacher was so pleased with his clear explanation of a difficult theory that she wrote on his paper, "Wonderfully ___!"

superficially 10. Whenever Miki tries to buy a new dress, her husband is only ___ interested. If she shows him one and asks his opinion, all he says is, "It's fine. Let's buy it and get out of here."

NOTE: Now check your answers to these items by turning to page 178. Going over the answers carefully will help you prepare for the next two practices, for which answers are not given.

Sentence Check 2

Using the answer lines provided, complete each item below with **two** words from the box. Use each word once.

distraught
conspiracy 1–2. In the horror movie, the heroine becomes more and more ___ as she realizes that her husband and friends are involved in a ___ against her.

connoisseur
superficially 3–4. Ms. Lewis is a ___ of Native American crafts. She can identify the tribe of the artist after examining a necklace or piece of pottery only ___.

contrite
plight 5–6. The drunk driver is ___ about causing the accident, but his regret won't give Marsha solace° or ease her ___. She is permanently disabled.

_____germane_____   7–8. The professor said, "It seems ___ to our discussion of the Age of Reason to
_____symmetrical_____   mention that ___ architecture was typical. Balance was valued—both in art
                                 and in the individual."

_____verbose_____   9–10. Using too many superfluous° words can make something more difficult to
_____lucid_____   understand. Thus if the essay had not been so ___, it would have been more
                               ___.

Final Check: *The Missing Painting*

Here is a final opportunity for you to strengthen your knowledge of the ten words. First read the following
selection carefully. Then fill in each blank with a word from the box at the top of the previous page.
(Context clues will help you figure out which word goes in which blank.) Use each word once.

It wasn't until noon that Daniel Cobb noticed that the painting
was missing. He immediately became (1)_____distraught_____. As a
(2)_____connoisseur_____ of art, he was well aware of the enormous
value of the painting—and this was a grievous° loss. He was so upset
that when he phoned the police, he could not think or talk clearly
enough to give a (3)_____lucid_____ description of his unfortunate
(4)_____plight_____. Instead, he found himself rambling
so much that he was afraid the police would think he was just a
(5)_____verbose_____ old fool.

Nevertheless, the police soon arrived at Cobb's home, which was
magnificent—a fine old mansion in a (6)_____symmetrical_____
style, with a row of columns on each side of the front door. Leading the
police to the room from which the painting had been taken, Cobb began
to explain. "Last night," he said, "my wife and I gave a dinner party for art
experts. We showed them our entire collection. I remember that they gave the missing painting special
attention. At least, a few of them seemed to look at it more than just (7)_____superficially_____. I can
only assume that we are the victims of a (8)_____conspiracy_____. Our guests must have plotted a
clandestine° action: to sneak into the house during the night and take the painting."

As Cobb finished speaking, his wife entered the room, having just returned from town. She was clearly
alarmed by the presence of the police. After Cobb quickly reiterated° his story, however, she started to
laugh. "Today's Monday," she finally said.

"I hardly see how that's (9)_____germane_____ to our problem!" her husband responded.

"Remember, we told the Leeworth Art Association it could exhibit the painting today, for its annual
show. That's where I've been. I took the painting there early this morning."

Cobb looked embarrassed but relieved that his guests had been exonerated° by his wife's story.
"Accept my sincere apology for having bothered you. I am most (10)_____contrite_____," he said
to the police officers. "Please stay and have some lunch."

Scores	Sentence Check 2 _____%	Final Check _____%

Enter your scores above and in the **Vocabulary Performance Chart** on the inside back cover of the book.

adept	presumptuous
encompass	sordid
entrepreneur	standardize
eradicate	stint
homogeneous	stringent

Ten Words in Context

In the space provided, write the letter of the meaning closest to that of each **boldfaced** word. Use the context of the sentences to help you figure out each word's meaning.

1 adept
(ə-dĕpt′)
-*adjective*

- People enjoy visiting my parents, who are **adept** at making guests feel welcome and at home.
- Justin is an **adept** liar. He always looks so innocent and sincere that everyone believes his lies.

<u>A</u> *Adept* means   A. skillful.   B. profitable.   C. awkward.

2 encompass
(ĕn-kŭm′pəs)
-*verb*

- Our history teacher's broad knowledge of the subject **encompasses** details of life in ancient Egypt, Greece, and Rome.
- Tomorrow's test will be difficult because it **encompasses** all the material covered this semester.

<u>C</u> *Encompass* means   A. to suggest.   B. to omit.   C. to include.

3 entrepreneur
(ŏn′trə-prə-nûr′)
-*noun*

- Glenville has no shopping center, but the city is growing so quickly that smart **entrepreneurs** are sure to start up new businesses there soon.
- My ten-year-old neighbor is already an **entrepreneur**. He set up a lemonade stand last summer and sold homemade cookies at Halloween.

<u>A</u> *Entrepreneur* means   A. a business investor.   B. an overconfident person.   C. a conformist.

4 eradicate
(ĭ-răd′ĭ-kāt′)
-*verb*

- In recent years, smallpox has been **eradicated**—the first time in history that humans have been able to wipe out a disease.
- What makes so many people feel they must **eradicate** all signs of aging? Why should we have to get rid of our wrinkles and gray hair?

<u>C</u> *Eradicate* means   A. to reveal.   B. to regulate strictly.   C. to erase.

5 homogeneous
(hō′mō-jē′nē-əs)
-*adjective*

- The student body at the local college appears quite **homogeneous**, but there are significant social and economic differences among the students.
- "Homogenized" milk has been made **homogeneous**. This means that it's treated so it will be of uniform consistency, rather than having the cream rise to the top.

<u>B</u> *Homogeneous* means   A. strictly controlled.   B. the same throughout.   C. of high quality.

6 presumptuous
(prē-zŭmp′chōō-əs)
-*adjective*

- It was **presumptuous** of Eric to announce his engagement to Phyllis before she had actually agreed to marry him.
- If you ask personal questions at a job interview, you'll be considered **presumptuous**. So, for example, don't ask the interviewer, "What are they paying you?"

<u>A</u> *Presumptuous* means   A. too forward.   B. skilled.   C. cautious.

7 sordid
(sôr′dĭd)
-adjective

- Supermarket tabloids sell well because many people want to know the **sordid** details of celebrities' addictions and messy divorces.
- The reformed criminal now lectures at high schools on how to avoid the mistakes that led him into a **sordid** life as a drug dealer.

B *Sordid* means   A. proud.   B. ugly.   C. natural.

8 standardize
(stăn′dər-dīz′)
-verb

- When the company **standardized** its pay scale, the salary for each type of job became identical throughout all the departments.
- If Jamila begins selling her homemade soup, she'll have to **standardize** the ingredients. Now she just puts in whatever she has on hand, so the soup is never the same from one day to the next.

B *Standardize* means   A. to do away with.   B. to make the same.   C. to vary.

9 stint
(stĭnt)
-noun

- My **stint** serving hamburgers and fries at a fast-food restaurant convinced me that I needed to get a college degree.
- After traveling during her **stint** in the Navy, Alise wanted a job that would let her continue to see the world.

A *Stint* means   A. a length of time.   B. a risky undertaking.   C. future work.

10 stringent
(strĭn′jənt)
-adjective

- Ms. Jasper has the most **stringent** standards in the English department. Passing her course is difficult; getting an A is next to impossible.
- Elected officials should be held to a **stringent** code of ethics, requiring them to avoid even the appearance of wrongdoing.

C *Stringent* means   A. different.   B. flexible.   C. demanding.

Matching Words with Definitions

Following are definitions of the ten words. Clearly write or print each word next to its definition. The sentences above and on the previous page will help you decide on the meaning of each word.

1. _____entrepreneur_____ A person who organizes, manages, and takes the risk of a business undertaking

2. _____adept_____ Highly skilled; expert

3. _____stint_____ A specific period of work or service; amount of time spent

4. _____presumptuous_____ Too bold; overly confident

5. _____eradicate_____ To get rid of altogether; wipe out

6. _____stringent_____ Strictly controlled or enforced; strict; severe

7. _____standardize_____ To make consistent; cause to conform to a model

8. _____encompass_____ To include; contain

9. _____homogeneous_____ Made up of similar or identical parts; unvarying throughout

10. _____sordid_____ Indecent; morally low; corrupt

CAUTION: Do not go any further until you are sure the above answers are correct. Then you can use the definitions to help you in the following practices. Your goal is eventually to know the words well enough so that you don't need to check the definitions at all.

Sentence Check 1

Using the answer line provided, complete each item below with the correct word from the box. Use each word once.

| A. adept | B. encompass | C. entrepreneur | D. eradicate | E. homogeneous |
| F. presumptuous | G. sordid | H. standardize | I. stint | J. stringent |

presumptuous 1. It's ___ of Amy to assume she's got the job when others are still being interviewed.

adept 2. It takes years of study and practice to become ___ at acupuncture.

sordid 3. In the novel *Oliver Twist*, innocent young Oliver falls into the hands of a gang of pickpockets, who teach him their ___ trade.

stint 4. My grandfather held many jobs during his life. He even did a(n) ___ as a circus performer.

eradicate 5. Joyce and Steven's adopted son was abused in an earlier home. They're working hard to ___ the lingering effects on him of that experience.

homogeneous 6. The town is so close-knit and ___ that newcomers feel out of place. Many of the residents are even related to each other.

encompass 7. The articles in our small newspaper ___ local and statewide news, but not national or international events.

stringent 8. My sister applied to several colleges, some with very high admission standards for their students and others with less ___ requirements.

entrepreneur 9. Ramon has just opened an auto repair shop. Now that he's a(n) ___, he can join the National Association for the Self-Employed.

standardize 10. Should the high-school curriculum be ___(e)d throughout the state? Or should each school district be free to design its own courses?

NOTE: Now check your answers to these items by turning to page 178. Going over the answers carefully will help you prepare for the next two practices, for which answers are not given.

Sentence Check 2

Using the answer lines provided, complete each item below with **two** words from the box. Use each word once.

entrepreneur
adept
1–2. To succeed, ___s must be ___ at organization and management. In addition, they must be resilient° enough to deal with the ups and downs of running a business.

stint
stringent
3–4. During Nate's ___ as a teacher at a military academy, he felt that the ___ rules impeded° his easygoing, flexible approach.

eradicate
sordid
5–6. After serving a prison term for theft, Charlie is contrite°. He's decided to begin a new life as an honest citizen and ___ all traces of his ___ past.

presumptuous

encompass

7–8. I've been working at the daycare center only one week, so this suggestion may be ___, but I think the center's program should ___ activities geared to shy children as well as ones for gregarious° kids.

standardize

homogeneous

9–10. The instructors of the English as a Second Language class have finally ___(e)d their approach. At the first class, all students meet as a group and take a placement test. After that, they are divided into smaller, more ___ classes.

Final Check: *An Ohio Girl in New York*

Here is a final opportunity for you to strengthen your knowledge of the ten words. First read the following selection carefully. Then fill in each blank with a word from the box at the top of the previous page. (Context clues will help you figure out which word goes in which blank.) Use each word once.

Soon after Gina moved from her small Ohio town to New York City, she became so discouraged that she nearly returned home. It was easy to see why she was despondent°: New York had the glamour and excitement that she had expected, but not the high-paying jobs. However, Gina decided to stay in the big city and put in a(n) (1)_____ stint _____ as a waitress in a coffee shop while hoping for something better to turn up. She had been offered only one higher-paying job, calling senior citizens and trying to scare them into buying an expensive, unproven "anti-cancer pill," but she thought this kind of work was too (2)_____ sordid _____.

At least she enjoyed the coffee shop. For someone used to a small, (3)_____ homogeneous _____ town, the customers seemed to come in an enormous variety. Also, the low salary forced her to stick to a(n) (4)_____ stringent _____ budget. As a result of her precarious° financial situation, she was becoming (5)_____ adept _____ at making one dollar go as far as two did before.

One day, Gina met a customer who had recently opened a furniture rental store. This (6)_____ entrepreneur _____ mentioned to her that he was about to open a second store. Although she worried that he might think it (7)_____ presumptuous _____ of a waitress to offer a suggestion about the furniture business, Gina told him a thought she had about how he might (8)_____ standardize _____ his rental system. He could ask all his customers to fill out the same form. Then a single computer file could (9)_____ encompass _____ all the information. Customers would be signed up automatically for both stores at once. To Gina's relief, the customer didn't scoff° at her idea; in fact, he thanked her for the advice.

Sometime later, he stopped in at the coffee shop to say he needed a capable person to manage his new store. He offered Gina the job. Within a year, she was the manager of three furniture rental stores and earning an excellent salary. She was euphoric°, but her happiness would never fully (10)_____ eradicate _____ her memories of those difficult first months in New York.

Scores   Sentence Check 2 _____%   Final Check _____%

exhort	masochist
flamboyant	meticulous
foible	rancor
innocuous	recrimination
magnanimous	repugnant

Ten Words in Context

In the space provided, write the letter of the meaning closest to that of each **boldfaced** word. Use the context of the sentences to help you figure out each word's meaning.

1 exhort
(ĕg-zôrt′)
-verb

- The school counselor gave an impassioned speech to the parents, in which she **exhorted** them to make every effort to keep their children off drugs.
- On the eve of the invasion, the general **exhorted** the troops to fight bravely for their homeland.

C *Exhort* means
A. to accuse.   B. to praise.   C. to urge.

2 flamboyant
(flăm-boi′ənt)
-adjective

- Lily can't resist **flamboyant** clothes. She'd wear a hot-pink dress with gold satin trim to a funeral.
- The **flamboyant** pianist always wore sequined suits and glittering jewelry when he sat down at his silver piano.

A *Flamboyant* means
A. flashy.   B. self-centered.   C. concerned with details.

3 foible
(foi′bəl)
-noun

- Serious character flaws, such as abusiveness, are hard to overlook, but **foibles**—such as drinking soup through a straw—can often be easily tolerated.
- "I accept my husband's **foible** of leaving clothes lying around," Kia remarked, "because it lets me be messy without feeling guilty."

B *Foible* means
A. a serious problem.   B. a minor fault.   C. a complaint.

4 innocuous
(ĭn-nŏk′yoo-əs)
-adjective

- Although most children engage in **innocuous** pranks on Halloween, some get out of control and do serious damage.
- Experts at the Poison Information Center can tell you if a household substance is harmful or **innocuous**.

A *Innocuous* means
A. without bad effects.   B. expensive.   C. satisfying.

5 magnanimous
(măg-năn′ə-məs)
-adjective

- At age 5, Jonathan is already learning to be **magnanimous**. He hugs his baby sister, even when she hits him on the head with a wooden block.
- Last Thanksgiving, someone at work drew a funny picture of our boss as an enormous turkey. When the boss saw it, he was **magnanimous**—he laughed, said it was terrific, and even hung it up over his desk.

A *Magnanimous* means
A. forgiving.   B. consistent.   C. resentful.

6 masochist
(măs′ə-kĭst)
-noun

- Psychologists are trying to understand why **masochists** obtain satisfaction from suffering.
- "A **masochist's** idea of a good time," said the comedian, "is getting hit by a truck on the way home from having all his teeth pulled."

B *Masochist* means
A. someone filled with hatred.   B. someone who enjoys being hurt.   C. someone who enjoys hurting others.

7 meticulous
(mə-tĭk′yoo-ləs)
-*adjective*

- When you proofread your own writing, be **meticulous**—check every detail.
- Marcus is **meticulous** about his appearance. He never has a wrinkle in his clothing or a hair out of place.

A *Meticulous* means   A. very careful.   B. bold.   C. unconcerned.

8 rancor
(răn′kər)
-*noun*

- The **rancor** between my uncles has lasted for twenty years, ever since Uncle Dmitri married the woman to whom Uncle Sergei had proposed.
- When there is long-lasting **rancor** between divorced parents, their children may also start to share this bitterness.

B *Rancor* means   A. a minor fault.   B. deep hostility.   C. secrecy.

9 recrimination
(rĭ-krĭm′ə-nā′shən)
-*noun*

- The couple's session with the marriage counselor failed miserably; it began with the husband and wife hurling accusations at each other, and it never progressed beyond these **recriminations**.
- When Lainie's father and her teacher met to discuss Lainie's poor grades, they exchanged **recriminations**—each accused the other of not helping her do better.

C *Recrimination* means   A. an urgent plea.   B. a detailed suggestion.   C. an accusation in reply.

10 repugnant
(rĭ-pŭg′nənt)
-*adjective*

- My parents find some of my eating habits **repugnant**, but I see nothing offensive about mixing peas and ketchup into mashed potatoes.
- A snake is **repugnant** to many people—"Slimy!" they say, shivering with distaste. However, snakes are not at all slimy, and most are harmless.

A *Repugnant* means   A. disgusting.   B. amusing.   C. remarkable.

Matching Words with Definitions

Following are definitions of the ten words. Clearly write or print each word next to its definition. The sentences above and on the previous page will help you decide on the meaning of each word.

1. _____rancor_____   Intense hatred or ill will; long-lasting resentment

2. _____innocuous_____   Harmless; inoffensive

3. _____repugnant_____   Offensive; distasteful; repulsive

4. _____masochist_____   A person who gains satisfaction from suffering physical or psychological pain

5. _____flamboyant_____   Very showy; strikingly bold

6. _____foible_____   A minor weakness or character flaw; a minor fault in behavior

7. _____recrimination_____   An accusation made in response to an accuser; countercharge

8. _____exhort_____   To urge with argument or strong advice; plead earnestly

9. _____magnanimous_____   Noble in mind and spirit; especially generous in forgiving

10. _____meticulous_____   Extremely careful and exact; showing great attention to details

CAUTION: Do not go any further until you are sure the above answers are correct. Then you can use the definitions to help you in the following practices. Your goal is eventually to know the words well enough so that you don't need to check the definitions at all.

Sentence Check 1

Using the answer line provided, complete each item below with the correct word from the box. Use each word once.

| A. exhort | B. flamboyant | C. foible | D. innocuous | E. magnanimous |
| F. masochist | G. meticulous | H. rancor | I. recrimination | J. repugnant |

repugnant   1. Why is it that bats seem so ___? Do we think a flying mouselike creature is distasteful, or do we associate bats with vampires?

magnanimous   2. It was ___ of the Greens to forgive the driver who ran over their dog.

masochist   3. Battered women who stay with their abusive partners aren't necessarily ___s; they don't enjoy being hurt, but often they can't see any way to escape.

foible   4. Although nail-biting is only a ___, it can become maddening to a companion who observes it day after day.

exhort   5. Before the football game, the coach gave a fiery pep talk. He___(e)d the players to fight for the honor of the team and the school.

innocuous   6. To an allergic person, foods that are normally ___, such as milk or wheat, can cause discomfort and even serious illness.

rancor   7. The long-standing ___ between the two women finally came to an end when one of them fell and the other rushed over to help her.

recrimination   8. The angry neighbors traded ___s: "Your wild kids trampled all over my flower bed!" "Well, your crazy dog dug up my lawn!"

meticulous   9. Some jobs needn't be done in a(n) ___ way. For instance, why sweep every speck of dust off a floor that's only going to get dirty again in an hour?

flamboyant   10. On New Year's Day in Philadelphia, string bands called "Mummers" strut their stuff in ___ costumes designed to outshine all other bands in the parade.

NOTE: Now check your answers to these items by turning to page 178. Going over the answers carefully will help you prepare for the next two practices, for which answers are not given.

Sentence Check 2

Using the answer lines provided, complete each item below with **two** words from the box. Use each word once.

exhort
meticulous   1–2. My second-grade teacher had stringent° standards. For one thing, she ___(e)d us to be ___ about our handwriting. "Dot every *i*," she would say, "and cross every *t*."

rancor
magnanimous   3–4. In a small business, it's important never to instigate° quarrels or let ___ develop. People must learn to be ___ and forgive each other's errors.

masochist
repugnant   5–6. Many people find the thought of a ___ seeking out and enjoying suffering to be as ___ as the idea of causing someone else to suffer.

_____foible_____

_____innocuous_____

7–8. Walter is certainly odd. Still, most of his ___s—like wearing bedroom slippers to work and leaving bags of pretzels all over the office—are so ___ that nobody really minds them.

_____recrimination_____

_____flamboyant_____

9–10. When Martha put on a bright red beaded dress with huge rhinestone earrings, ___s flew back and forth between her and her sister. "You look preposterous° in that outfit," her sister said. "It's much too ___." Martha replied, "Well, *your* clothes are the most boring I've ever seen."

Final Check: *How Neat Is Neat Enough?*

Here is a final opportunity for you to strengthen your knowledge of the ten words. First read the following selection carefully. Then fill in each blank with a word from the box at the top of the previous page. (Context clues will help you figure out which word goes in which blank.) Use each word once.

Experts say that the most ordinary matters sometimes create the biggest problems in a marriage. If one spouse is a slob and the other is (1)_____meticulous_____, there is bound to be trouble.

At first, newlyweds tend to be (2)_____magnanimous_____, readily forgiving each other's (3)_____foible_____s. The wife says it's "sweet" that her husband made the bed while she was still in it and "cute" that he grabbed her plate to wash it when she picked up her sandwich to take a bite. "You're so helpful," she coos. And he manages a smile when she dumps her too-expensive, too-(4)_____flamboyant_____ gold sequined dress in the middle of the bedroom floor. "We've sure got a high-priced, flashy rug," he jokes.

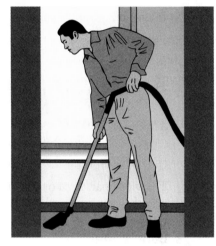

But the honeymoon ends, and the idiosyncrasies° that once seemed (5)_____innocuous_____ start to be seriously annoying. He begins to think, "Since my housekeeping is so impeccable°, why isn't she picking up my good habits? Why must I wade through dirty pantyhose to reach the closet? Why is there spaghetti sauce on the kitchen ceiling fan again?" He (6)_____exhort_____s her to have some self-respect and stop living like a pig.

And she begins to wonder about him: Why does he insist on dusting the tops of the door frames when no one can see them? So what if she squeezes the toothpaste from the middle of the tube—why should he find that harmless habit so (7)_____repugnant_____? Maybe he's a (8)_____masochist_____— why else would he be so happy down on his knees, scrubbing the bathroom floor with a toothbrush (one of the "old" ones that he replaced after using it for a week)?

Soon the accusations and (9)_____recrimination_____s start. She yells, "You're a zealot° for neatness—that's all you care about. You spend more time holding that vacuum cleaner than you spend holding me!" He responds, "If you weren't so sloppy, I'd hold you more often. As it is, I have to climb over a mountain of junk just to get near you!"

Eventually, as the two of them continue arguing with each other and berating° each other, their feelings of (10)_____rancor_____ become so strong that a breakup is imminent°. It won't be long before another relationship—so to speak—bites the dust.

Scores	Sentence Check 2 _____%	Final Check _____%

anima	miss, mit
arch, -archy	mort
ben-, bene-	poly-
-ee	tempo, tempor
-log, -logue	ten

Ten Word Parts in Context

Figure out the meanings of the following ten word parts by looking *closely* and *carefully* at the context in which they appear. Then, in the space provided, write the letter of the meaning closest to that of each word part.

1 anima

- During the worst part of her illness, Trina lay quietly in bed. We knew she was recovering when she sat up and began to talk in an **animated** way.
- A Japanese scientist recently invented a robot cat that sells for $1500. But why would someone want an **inanimate** pet instead of a living animal?

_C_ The word part *anima* means   A. good.   B. experience.   C. life.

2 arch, -archy

- Many fictional heroes have an **archenemy**. For instance, Sherlock Holmes's main opponent was the evil Dr. Moriarty.
- Among Amish people, the family is a **patriarchy**. The father rules the household, and the women and children are expected to obey.

_A_ The word part *arch* or *–archy* means   A. chief.   B. sender.   C. receiver.

3 ben-, bene-

- Southern California has a **benign** climate—sunny and warm.
- For Cheryl, day care has been **beneficial**. She's much less shy now.

_C_ The word part *ben-* or *bene-* means   A. experience.   B. deadly.   C. good.

4 -ee

- The mayor had to appoint a new chief of police. The first **appointee** became unavailable—he was serving a two-year sentence in prison.
- Today's **employees** expect to receive benefits as well as a salary.

_B_ The word part *-ee* means   A. a ruler.   B. someone who receives.   C. someone who sends.

5 -log, -logue

- It's almost impossible to have a **dialog** with Aaron because he does all the talking.
- The play opened with a **prologue**: before the action began, one of the characters came onstage and made a speech to the audience.

_A_ The word part *-log* or *-logue* means   A. speaking.   B. time.   C. send.

6 miss, mit

- The United Nations sends peacekeeping **missions** to trouble spots around the world, although not all of these efforts succeed.
- I use a cell phone every day, but to tell you the truth, I really have no idea how it **transmits** sound across a distance.

_A_ The word part *miss* or *mit* means   A. send.   B. well.   C. hold.

7 mort

- Ms. Patterson took her class to visit a **mortician**, who explained how he prepares a body for burial.
- Shakespeare's works are said to have achieved **immortality**: they will never die, since they will be read and performed forever.

A The word part *mort* means   A. death.   B. breath.   C. name.

8 poly-

- A **polytechnic** school is one which teaches many different sciences and industrial arts.
- **Polygamy** is a form of marriage in which a person can have a number of spouses at the same time.

C The word part *poly-* means   A. difficult.   B. time.   C. many.

9 tempo, tempor

- The chorus sang the difficult piece slowly at first. When they seemed sure of all the notes, the director speeded up the **tempo**.
- The trailer in the Langs' yard is there only **temporarily**, until the repairs to their house are finished and they can move back in.

B The word part *tempo* or *tempor* means   A. holding.   B. time.   C. number.

10 ten

- **Detention** is a common punishment in elementary and high school. Students who misbehave must stay in school for an hour or so after the other students go home.
- **Tenant** farmers hold the right to work someone else's land; they pay rent in cash or with a portion of the produce.

B The word part *ten* means   A. spirit.   B. keep.   C. divide.

Matching Word Parts with Definitions

Following are definitions of the ten word parts. Clearly write or print each word part next to its definition. The sentences above and on the previous page will help you decide on the meaning of each word part.

1. _____poly-_____ Many

2. ___tempo, tempor___ Time

3. _____ten_____ Hold; keep

4. _____mort_____ Death

5. ___-log, -logue___ A specific way of speaking or writing

6. ___arch, -archy___ Chief, ruler

7. _____anima_____ Life, breath; spirit

8. ___ben-, bene-___ Good, well

9. ___miss, mit___ Send

10. _____-ee_____ One who receives or experiences something; one who is in a certain condition

CAUTION: Do not go any further until you are sure the above answers are correct. Then you can use the definitions to help you in the following practices. Your goal is eventually to know the word parts well enough so that you don't need to check the definitions at all.

Sentence Check 1

Using the answer line provided, complete each *italicized* word below with the correct word part from the box. Use each word part once.

A. **anima**	B. **arch, -archy**	C. **ben-, bene-**	D. **-ee**	E. **-log, -logue**
F. **miss, mit**	G. **mort**	H. **poly-**	I. **tempo, tempor**	J. **ten**

__archangel__   1. A high-ranking angel is called a(n) (. . . *angel*) ___ .

__benefactor__   2. A(n) (. . . *factor*) ___ has been good enough to give the city blankets to pass out to the homeless.

__temporized__   3. When Ruben asked Luisa to marry him, she (. . . *ized*), saying, "I need some time to think it over."

__travelogues__
__(OR travelogs)__   4. I enjoy (*trave* . . . *s*) ___ on TV. It's interesting to hear people talk about their travels.

__tenets__   5. Certain (. . . *ets*) ___ , such as the belief in the sanctity of marriage, are held by many religions.

__dismissed__   6. When the bell rang and the teacher said "Class is (*dis* . . . *ed*) ___ ," that was enough to send the children hurtling into the hallway like popcorn exploding from a popper.

__postmortem__   7. There was suspicion that the evil dictator had been murdered, but a (*post* . . . *em*) ___ examination showed that he had died of natural causes.

__polygraph__   8. A(n) (. . . *graph*) ___ , or "lie detector," records several physical responses of the person hooked up to it, including heart rate, breathing rate, and blood pressure.

__animation__   9. Many cartoons today are excellent. The (. . . *tion*) ___ is so good that the characters seem to be alive—they move smoothly and naturally, like real people or animals.

__nominees__   10. "We are here to nominate the candidates for president of the Liars' Club," said the club's current president. "Remember," she said with a smile, "that the (*nomin* . . . *s*) ___ should be exceptionally honest."

NOTE: Now check your answers to these items by turning to page 178. Going over the answers carefully will help you prepare for the next two practices, for which answers are not given.

Sentence Check 2

Using the answer line provided, complete each *italicized* word in the sentences below with the correct word part from the box. Use each word part once.

__catalog__
__emits__   1–2. The (*cata* . . .) ___ of unusual gifts includes a plastic skunk named "Rosebud" which (*e* . . . *s*) ___ a rose-scented air freshener.

__benevolent__
__archbishop__   3–4. Our parish priest was especially (. . . *volent*) ___ and wise. I wasn't surprised to hear that he eventually became a(n) (. . . *bishop*) ___ , with a large number of churches in his jurisdiction°.

_____contents_____
_____temporarily_____

5–6. The owner of the safe-deposit box had to relinquish° it to the police. The (*con . . . ts*) ___ are now being held (*. . . arily*) ___ by the district attorney, until the trial.

_____Polynesia_____
_____refugees_____

7–8. Our visitor from (*. . . nesia*) ___, a country of many islands, told us about the plight° of (*refug . . . s*) ___ who had to flee from one island after it was struck by a hurricane.

_____mortal_____
_____animate_____

9–10. Mary Shelley's classic novel *Frankenstein* tells the story of a doctor who had the presumptuous° belief that a mere (*. . . al*) ___ could achieve godlike power and (*. . . te*) ___ a lifeless body.

Final Check: *A Cult Community*

Here is a final opportunity for you to strengthen your knowledge of the ten word parts. First read the following selection carefully. Then complete each *italicized* word in the parentheses below with a word part from the box at the top of the previous page. (Context clues will help you figure out which word part goes in which blank.) Use each word part once.

My friend Lucy recently visited her brother Ben in British Columbia. She was shocked to discover that Ben was living in a cult—a community of about forty followers, headed by a (*patri . . .*) (1)_____patriarch_____ whom they all called Uncle. Uncle was a (*. . . ign*) (2)_____benign_____ leader as long as his authority wasn't questioned, but he wouldn't tolerate troublemakers or dissidents°. Uncle's followers were expected to regard him as infallible° and to uphold the stringent° (*. . . ets*) (3)_____tenets_____ of his "religion." These strict rules included sticking to a monogamous lifestyle and living in an austere° manner, without any luxuries. Uncle himself, however, was a(n) (*. . . gamist*) (4)_____polygamist_____ who chose the prettiest cult members as his wives, and he drove around in an ostentatious° car, a shiny gold Rolls-Royce. Several times each day, all the cult members would be gathered to hear Uncle's verbose° (*mono . . . s*) (5)_____monologues_____—long speeches in which he exhorted° them to think of eternal life, not of their brief, (*. . . ary*) (6)_____temporary_____ existence on Earth. Many of them believed Uncle to be (*im . . . al*) (7)_____immortal_____. Others admitted that he might indeed die someday, but they fully expected that his body would be (*re . . . ted*) (8)_____reanimated_____ very soon thereafter.

Lucy's brother was a particularly strong (*devot . . .*) (9)_____devotee_____ of the cult; he believed that God had sent him on a (*. . . ion*) (10)_____mission_____ to follow Uncle. To Lucy, however, it seemed that Ben had been mesmerized° by an egocentric° charlatan.° She wished she knew how to break the spell that this dishonest leader had cast on her brother.

Scores   Sentence Check 2 _____%   Final Check _____%

UNIT THREE: Review

The box at the right lists twenty-five words from Unit Three. Using the clues at the bottom of the page, fill in these words to complete the puzzle that follows.

1 ESOTERIC
3 METICULOUS
4 ADEPT
5 CONTRITE
10 NOTORIOUS
11 GROTESQUE
12 SUPERFICIALLY
19 SORDID
20 IMMINENT
21 AUSTERE
22 VERBOSE
1 EXHORT
2 ERADICATE
3 MASOCHIST
6 TRAVESTY
7 FOIBLE
8 ANTIPATHY
9 GERMANE
12 STINT
13 PRECARIOUS
14 RANCOR
15 IMPEDE
16 INCLUSIV
17 LUCID
18 STRINGENT

adept
antipathy
austere
contrite
eradicate
esoteric
exhort
foible
germane
grotesque
imminent
impede
inclusive
lucid
masochist
meticulous
notorious
precarious
rancor
sordid
stint
stringent
superficially
travesty
verbose

ACROSS

1. Beyond the understanding of most people
3. Extremely careful and exact; showing great attention to details
4. Highly skilled; expert
5. Truly sorry for having done wrong; repentant
10. Known widely but unfavorably
11. Distorted or strikingly inconsistent in shape, appearance, or manner
12. Not thoroughly
19. Indecent; morally low
20. About to happen
21. Without decoration or luxury; severely simple
22. Using too many words

DOWN

1. To urge with argument or strong advice; plead earnestly
2. To get rid of; wipe out
3. A person who enjoys suffering or physical pain
6. A crude, exaggerated, or ridiculous representation
7. A minor weakness or character flaw
8. A strong dislike or distaste
9. Having to do with the issue at hand; relevant
12. A specific period of work or service
13. Dangerous; risky
14. Intense hatred or ill will
15. To delay or slow up; get in the way of
16. Including much or everything
17. Clearly expressed
18. Strictly controlled or enforced; strict; severe

PART A

Choose the word that best completes each item and write it in the space provided.

___sordid___ 1. Working-class housing in nineteenth-century England was ___ by today's standards: crowded, dark, badly ventilated, and unsanitary.

    A. meticulous   B. distraught   C. sordid   D. innocuous

___standardized___ 2. Even when textbooks are ___ throughout a school system, methods of teaching may vary greatly.

    A. standardized   B. mesmerized   C. contrite   D. symmetrical

___precarious___ 3. The existence of nuclear weapons puts everyone in a(n) ___ situation.

    A. austere   B. precarious   C. magnanimous   D. flamboyant

___jurisdiction___ 4. As long as the thief was in Europe, American courts had no ___ over him.

    A. metamorphosis   B. connoisseur   C. jurisdiction   D. travesty

___connoisseur___ 5. Having lived in Italy and studied cooking there, the newspaper's food critic is a ___ of Italian cuisine.

    A. masochist   B. rancor   C. plight   D. connoisseur

___notorious___ 6. If you're planning to visit New York City, don't drive. New York is ___ for its traffic jams and expensive parking fees—as much as $50 a day—and if your car is towed, you'll owe $300.

    A. stringent   B. symmetrical   C. notorious   D. magnanimous

___travesty___ 7. Some people feel that a circus act in which costumed elephants dance or stand on their heads is a ___ of these intelligent animals' true nature.

    A. foible   B. recrimination   C. conspiracy   D. travesty

___stint___ 8. My ___ as a worker in the hotel laundry lasted only a day. It turned out that I was allergic to the soap.

    A. facsimile   B. idiosyncrasy   C. foible   D. stint

___grotesque___ 9. The Englishman John Merrick had an illness that gave him a(n) ___ appearance, which is why he was called "The Elephant Man." Despite people's reactions to his misshapen head and body, Merrick remained affectionate and gentle.

    A. germane   B. imminent   C. contrite   D. grotesque

___idiosyncrasy___ 10. A founder of the U.S. Steel Company was wealthy enough to have an expensive ___. It was his habit to bet a thousand dollars on which of two raindrops falling down a windowpane would reach the bottom first.

    A. masochist   B. recrimination   C. facsimile   D. idiosyncrasy

(Continues on next page)

PART B

On the answer line, write the letter of the choice that best completes each item.

  B   11. Since the President's speech was **imminent**, the reporters
- A. left to write their stories.
- B. got ready to take notes on it.
- C. planned to come back in an hour.
- D. had difficulty understanding it.

  A   12. The **austere** office
- A. had bare walls, a small desk, and one chair.
- B. was filled with desks and file cabinets.
- C. contained fake flowers and cheap posters.
- D. had fine art, live plants, and plush carpets.

  D   13. Rita wears **flamboyant** hairstyles. Today, her hair is
- A. chin-length.
- B. in a ponytail.
- C. easily cared for.
- D. in green braids.

  D   14. When Annabelle broke off their engagement, Arthur showed he was **magnanimous** by saying,
- A. "How weird. I was just about to dump *you*."
- B. "You don't deserve me, and that's that."
- C. "I'm the unhappiest man in the world."
- D. "*Please* keep the three-carat diamond ring."

  D   15. When told he needed to have an operation, the **masochist**
- A. panicked, saying, "I just can't face that."
- B. wanted a second opinion.
- C. assumed that he would die.
- D. secretly hoped it would hurt quite a lot.

  A   16. "Let me tell you of my **plight**," the stranger said. "You see,
- A. I've left my wallet in a taxi and I have no money to get home."
- B. I was born in Kansas and my parents were farmers."
- C. I collect rare stamps and coins."
- D. I'd like to offer you a tremendous opportunity to make money."

  C   17. It was **presumptuous** of my brother to
- A. volunteer his free time to work at a homeless shelter.
- B. refuse to lend money to his spendthrift pal Leon.
- C. call elderly, dignified Mr. Jackson "Larry" as soon as he met him.
- D. start giggling in the middle of a quiet church service.

  C   18. The police officer was **superficially** wounded, so the doctor
- A. rushed him to the hospital for immediate surgery.
- B. suggested that he call his family and clergyperson.
- C. put on a bandage and told him he could return to work.
- D. asked to consult with a specialist.

  B   19. I hadn't realized how much **antipathy** Jack felt for Tara until I saw him
- A. staring at her like a lovesick puppy.
- B. stick out his tongue at her as she turned away from him.
- C. secretly send her small amounts of cash just to help her make ends meet.
- D. cover up for some mistakes she made at work.

  A   20. "You cheated!" one child yelled. The other child answered with this **recrimination**:
- A. "Well, you're the biggest, most rotten cheater of them all."
- B. "Let's start the game over again, and this time I'll try to do better."
- C. "No, I didn't."
- D. "I'm going home."

Score	(Number correct) _____	x	5 =	_____%

Enter your scores above and in the **Vocabulary Performance Chart** on the inside back cover of the book.

PART A

Complete each item with a word from the box. Use each word once.

A. **advocate**	B. **conspiracy**	C. **contrite**	D. **emancipate**	E. **eradicate**
F. **exhort**	G. **facsimile**	H. **foible**	I. **inclusive**	J. **lucid**
K. **metamorphosis**	L. **preposterous**	M. **repugnant**		

repugnant   1. The furry white and green mold growing on the old tomato sauce was a(n) ___ sight.

lucid   2. Correct punctuation makes prose more ___.

foible   3. One of my ___s is biting into many chocolates in a box until I find one I like.

conspiracy   4. The dictator arrested everyone involved in the ___ to overthrow him, including his wife.

facsimile   5. A(n) ___ of a transcript isn't official unless it has been stamped with the seal of the school registrar.

contrite   6. The boys were ___ when they realized that their teasing had made Mary afraid to go to school the next day.

eradicate   7. If the common cold were ever ___(e)d, it would be economically unhealthy for the makers of cold remedies.

exhort   8. The TV preacher ___(e)d viewers to support his ministry with whatever funds they could manage to send.

inclusive   9. "It's an all-___ tour," the travel agent said. "Hotel, meals, flights both ways—everything is covered in one package."

advocate   10. Environmentalists ___ stricter controls on American industry, which releases billions of pounds of pollution into the air each year.

metamorphosis   11. After Cristina learned to read at age 30, she underwent a(n) ___. She changed from being shy to being confident, got an interesting new job, and started taking college classes at night.

emancipate   12. When I told my son to mow the lawn after he'd cleaned his room, he groaned and said, "I thought Lincoln ___(e)d all the slaves, but it looks like he forgot one."

preposterous   13. The man made the ___ claim that he had been taken aboard a Martian spaceship by someone who looked like Woody Allen, except that his skin was green.

(Continues on next page)

PART B

Write **C** if the italicized word is used **correctly**. Write **I** if the word is used **incorrectly**.

___I___ 14. I was *distraught* when I got the raise I had asked for.

___C___ 15. Only female black widow spiders are dangerous to humans. The bite of a male is *innocuous*.

___I___ 16. Ricardo writes thoughtful essays and then spoils them by handing in a *meticulous* final draft filled with spelling and typing errors.

___I___ 17. Marsha, as *verbose* as always, signed her letter only "Best," instead of "Best wishes."

___C___ 18. Rose's "How are you?" always seems *perfunctory*, just a matter of routine courtesy, not genuine interest.

___I___ 19. As kids, my brother and I loved staying with our grandparents because of their *stringent* rules; they let us stay up as late as we liked and eat candy for breakfast.

PART C

On the answer line, write the letter of the word that is the **synonym** of the boldfaced word.

Example: ___C___ antipathy   A. illness   B. admiration   C. hatred

___C___ 20. **rancor**   A. noise   B. good will   C. bitterness

___A___ 21. **encompass**   A. include   B. turn   C. omit

___C___ 22. **provocative**   A. boring   B. foreign   C. fascinating

PART D

On the answer line, write the letter of the word that is the **antonym** of the boldfaced word.

Example: ___B___ antipathy   A. illness   B. admiration   C. hatred

___B___ 23. **impede**   A. discover   B. aid   C. block

___A___ 24. **germane**   A. unrelated   B. relevant   C. healthy

___A___ 25. **adept**   A. clumsy   B. experienced   C. skilled

Score   (Number correct) _____ x 4 = _____%

Enter your scores above and in the **Vocabulary Performance Chart** on the inside back cover of the book.

Each item below starts with a pair of words in CAPITAL LETTERS. For each item, figure out the relationship between these two words. Then decide which of the choices (A, B, C, or D) expresses a similar relationship. Write the letter of your choice on the answer line.

D 1. ADVOCATE : OPPOSE ::
  A. rush : hurry   C. debate : win
  B. predict : know   D. contradict : agree with

C 2. ANTIPATHY : ENEMIES ::
  A. romance : siblings   C. affection : friends
  B. love : hate   D. intimacy : strangers

D 3. EMANCIPATE : ENSLAVE ::
  A. say : speak   C. convict : jurors
  B. elect : vote   D. arrest : release

B 4. IMMINENT : THE YEAR 4000 ::
  A. high : Mount Everest C. dry : Sahara Desert
  B. hot : North Pole   D. wet : Pacific Ocean

B 5. AUSTERE : PLAIN ::
  A. remote : control   C. strict : easygoing
  B. nearby : close   D. selfish : tantrum

D 6. ESOTERIC : BRAIN SURGERY ::
  A. logical : infancy   C. noisy : sleeping
  B. daring : jogging   D. challenging : mountain climbing

B 7. FACSIMILE : ORIGINAL ::
  A. parent : adult   C. brother : man
  B. reproduction : painting D. piano : pianist

A 8. MESMERIZE : HYPNOTIST ::
  A. operate : surgeon   C. disappear : announcer
  B. listen : lecturer   D. repair : undertaker

C 9. CONNOISSEUR : TASTE ::
  A. computer programmer : height C. comedian : wit
  B. proofreader : courage   D. acrobat : clumsiness

B 10. CONSPIRACY : PLOTTERS ::
  A. football field : athletes C. railroad : conductors
  B. blueprint : architects   D. television : viewers

(Continues on next page)

_C_   11. SUPERFICIALLY : UNDERSTAND ::
     A. thoroughly : examine   C. briefly : visit
     B. slowly : read   D. race : run

_D_   12. SYMMETRICAL : SQUARE ::
     A. boxy : circle   C. triangular : hoop
     B. circular : rectangle   D. egg-shaped : oval

_C_   13. ADEPT : PICKPOCKET ::
     A. thin : chess player   C. graceful : dancer
     B. scholarly : shortstop   D. cheerful : worrier

_D_   14. ENCOMPASS : EXCLUDE ::
     A. explain : clarify   C. erase : remove
     B. insert : write   D. omit : include

_B_   15. ENTREPRENEUR : BUSINESS ::
     A. dentist : patient   C. cook : fry
     B. producer : movie   D. company : employee

_C_   16. HOMOGENEOUS : MILK ::
     A. juicy : cornflakes   C. grainy : sugar
     B. fattening : celery   D. greasy : water

_A_   17. FLAMBOYANT : GRAY SUIT ::
     A. economical : ten-course banquet   C. luxurious : palace
     B. generous : thirty-percent tip   D. competitive : Olympics

_B_   18. FOIBLE : NAIL-BITING ::
     A. weakness : self-control   C. strength : compulsive gambling
     B. phobia : fear of heights   D. skill : blue eyes

_D_   19. MAGNANIMOUS : GENEROUS ::
     A. angelic : heaven   C. delicate : flower
     B. softhearted : brutal   D. affectionate : loving

_C_   20. REPUGNANT : COCKROACHES ::
     A. cheerful : ants   C. musical : songbirds
     B. sturdy : butterflies   D. ruthless : doves

Score   (Number correct) _____ x 5 = _____ %

PART A

Listed in the left-hand column below are ten common word parts, followed by words in which the parts are used. In each blank, write in the letter of the correct definition on the right.

Word Parts	Examples	Definitions
I 1. **anima**	animated, inanimate	A. Hold; keep
G 2. **arch, -archy**	archenemy, patriarchy	B. Send
F 3. **ben-, bene-**	benign, beneficial	C. A specific way of speaking or writing
E 4. **-ee**	appointee, employee	D. Many
C 5. **-log, -logue**	dialog, prologue	E. One who receives or experiences something; one who is in a certain condition
B 6. **miss, mit**	mission, transmit	F. Good, well
J 7. **mort**	mortician, immortality	G. Chief, ruler
D 8. **poly-**	polytechnic, polygamy	H. Time
H 9. **tempo, tempor**	tempo, temporarily	I. Life, breath; spirit
A 10. **ten**	detention, tenant	J. Death

PART B

Using the answer line provided, complete each *italicized* word in the sentences below with the correct word part from the box. Not every word part will be used.

A. **anima**	B. **arch**	C. **bene-**	D. **-ee**	E. **-logue**
F. **miss**	G. **mort**	H. **poly-**	I. **tempor**	J. **ten**

_____ monarch _____   11. One (*mon . . .*) ___ in Persia was king for seventy years—his entire life.

_____ benediction _____   12. My brother and I always loved the minister's (. . . *diction*) ___ because that final blessing meant the service was over.

_____ contemporary _____   13. My sister-in-law likes early American furniture, but I prefer (*con . . . ary*) ___ styles, designs that reflect today's times.

_____ epilogue _____   14. Shakespeare sometimes wrote an (*epi . . .*) ___ to a play, a final speech spoken by a character directly to the audience.

_____ inanimate _____   15. Stick insects are so named because when they don't move, they resemble (*in . . . te*) ___ twigs more than living insects.

(Continues on next page)

PART C

Use your knowledge of word parts to determine the meaning of the **boldfaced** words. On the answer line, write the letter of each meaning.

___B___ 16. Instead of using the perfectly good words *no* and *yes*, Evan insists on using the **polysyllabic** words *negative* and *affirmative*.

     A. having long syllables   B. having many syllables   C. hard to pronounce

___C___ 17. My brother has a **retentive** memory.

     A. tending to forget   B. highly selective   C. tending to hold

___C___ 18. Giving the **emissary** a hollow nickel containing a microchip full of key information, the spy told him to bring the nickel to army headquarters.

     A. a king   B. a recipient   C. a messenger sent on an errand

___A___ 19. My mother and I donated blood today. The **donee** is a neighbor.

     A. a person receiving blood   B. a doctor   C. a chief of a blood bank

___B___ 20. After recovering from breaking many bones while going over Niagara Falls in a barrel, Bobby Leech was **mortally** injured in 1911 when he slipped on a banana peel.

     A. painfully   B. fatally   C. strangely

Score   (Number correct) _____ x 5 = _____%

Enter your scores above and in the **Vocabulary Performance Chart** on the inside back cover of the book.

Unit Four

Chapter 19

chide	dilapidated
coalition	integral
commensurate	noxious
connotation	scenario
diabolic	yen

Chapter 20

atrophy	mitigate
deplore	objective
deprivation	panacea
exacerbate	unprecedented
imperative	utilitarian

Chapter 21

decorum	facilitate
espouse	orthodox
exhilaration	rejuvenate
exorbitant	synchronize
extricate	tenuous

Chapter 22

assimilate	indolent
belligerent	inherent
demeanor	nonchalant
denunciation	unassuming
dissipate	unilateral

Chapter 23

analogy	placebo
annihilate	proficient
criterion	staunch
emanate	subversive
holistic	vindicate

Chapter 24

-cian, -ian	oct-, octo-
dec-	-ous
duc, duct	phil, -phile
-en	sur
homo-	vol

chide	dilapidated
coalition	integral
commensurate	noxious
connotation	scenario
diabolic	yen

Ten Words in Context

In the space provided, write the letter of the meaning closest to that of each **boldfaced** word. Use the context of the sentences to help you figure out each word's meaning.

1 chide
(chīd)
-*verb*

● My parents **chided** me for getting sunburned, but my blistered skin hurt a lot more than their scolding.

● Elise was right to **chide** me when I lazily threw the newspapers into the trash instead of stacking and tying them for recycling.

B *Chide* means   A. to command.   B. to criticize.   C. to be cruel to.

2 coalition
(kō′ə-lĭsh′ən)
-*noun*

● Four colleges formed a **coalition** to operate a shared Center of Higher Education.

● A **coalition** of one sheriff, two horse thieves, three stagecoach robbers, and a couple of crooked gamblers once made up the government of Virginia City.

C *Coalition* means   A. one part of a whole.   B. a neighborhood.   C. a partnership.

3 commensurate
(kə-mĕn′sər-ĭt)
-*adjective*

● Most students who work hard will eventually see results **commensurate** with their efforts.

● The expression "make the punishment fit the crime" means that a penalty should be **commensurate** with the degree of wrongdoing.

C *Commensurate with* means   A. essential to.   B. delayed by.   C. equal to.

4 connotation
(kŏn′ə-tā′shən)
-*noun*

● For many of us, the word *sea* has a **connotation** of salty air and vast openness.

● *Sayonara*, the Japanese word for "goodbye," actually means "if it must be so" and thus has **connotations** of sadness at parting.

A *Connotation* means   A. a suggested meaning.   B. a handicap.   C. a warning.

5 diabolic
(dī′ə-bŏl′ĭk)
-*adjective*

● In the musical *Sweeney Todd: The Demon Barber of Fleet Street*, the barber is indeed **diabolic**: he kills his clients by cutting their throats so that his friend Mrs. Lovett can make the victims into meat pies.

● The horror story featured open graves, walking corpses, and a **diabolic** villain who turned an entire townful of people into zombies.

C *Diabolic* means   A. lazy.   B. frightened.   C. devilish.

6 dilapidated
(də-lăp′ə-dāt′ĭd)
-*adjective*

● The **dilapidated** house must have once been handsome. Some of its broken windows are stained glass, and the loose door hinges are fine metalwork.

● His teddy bear is **dilapidated**, with its ears hanging by threads and the stuffing coming out, but the little boy won't let go of it long enough for anyone to repair it.

C *Dilapidated* means   A. out of proportion.   B. strongly desired.   C. run-down.

7 integral
(ĭn′tə-grəl)
-adjective

● Arguing seems to be an **integral** part of Laura and Nate's relationship. If they weren't fighting, they'd have nothing to say to each other.

● Voting is **integral** to democracy. Without free elections, a democratic system cannot continue to exist.

_A_ *Integral* means   A. essential.   B. very small.   C. predicted.

8 noxious
(nŏk′shəs)
-adjective

● When you are cleaning, never mix ammonia and bleach. The **noxious** gas they produce could send you to the hospital.

● The entire office building had to be evacuated when **noxious** fumes started coming out of the air vents and dozens of workers got sick.

_B_ *Noxious* means   A. potential.   B. unhealthy.   C. impossible.

9 scenario
(sĭ-nâr′ē-ō)
-noun

● "I've worked out an overall **scenario** for the movie," the screenwriter said, "but I haven't gone beyond the basic plot."

● To help governments and industries plan for the future, experts sometimes develop **scenarios** describing what might happen in the next year or decade.

_A_ *Scenario* means   A. an outline of possible events.   B. a budget.   C. an actual occurrence.

10 yen
(yĕn)
-noun

● Whenever I have a **yen** for something sweet, I try to eat fruit instead of cookies or candy.

● My **yen** for garlic bagel chips doesn't go away even after I've eaten a whole bagful.

_A_ *Yen* means   A. a longing.   B. a feeling of disapproval.   C. a memory.

Matching Words with Definitions

Following are definitions of the ten words. Clearly write or print each word next to its definition. The sentences above and on the previous page will help you decide on the meaning of each word.

1. _noxious_ Harmful to life or health; poisonous

2. _scenario_ A sequence of events that is imagined, assumed, or suggested

3. _diabolic_ Very cruel; wicked; demonic

4. _chide_ To scold mildly or express disapproval

5. _yen_ A strong desire; craving

6. _integral_ Necessary to the whole; belonging to the whole

7. _coalition_ A union of individuals, groups, or nations for some specific purpose

8. _commensurate_ Corresponding in degree, number, or size; in proportion

9. _connotation_ A secondary meaning suggested by a word, in addition to the word's dictionary definition

10. _dilapidated_ Fallen into a state in which repairs are badly needed; broken down

CAUTION: Do not go any further until you are sure the above answers are correct. Then you can use the definitions to help you in the following practices. Your goal is eventually to know the words well enough so that you don't need to check the definitions at all.

Sentence Check 1

Using the answer line provided, complete each item below with the correct word from the box. Use each word once.

A. **chide**	B. **coalition**	C. **commensurate**	D. **connotation**	E. **diabolic**
F. **dilapidated**	G. **integral**	H. **noxious**	I. **scenario**	J. **yen**

chide   1. The doctor ___(e)d Rick for not following her advice about switching to a low-fat diet.

diabolic   2. One Chinese emperor was so quick to have people executed that his officials always said their last goodbyes when they were summoned to the presence of their ___ ruler.

integral   3. We may argue about whether character or plot is more important, but they are both ___ to any novel.

coalition   4. The New York telephone directory lists hundreds of different ___s, including action groups for "Korean-American Voters," "Fairness to Africa," and "A Smoke-Free City."

yen   5. Often, to satisfy a ___, I eat something sweet, only to find that the sweetness has produced an equally strong craving for something salty.

commensurate   6. "I wish I could give you a grade ___ with the excellence of your paper," the teacher said. "Unfortunately, there is no such grade as 'A plus-plus.'"

connotation   7. Dictionaries usually don't give the ___s of words. These associated meanings become familiar to us only through experience.

dilapidated   8. My parents always know when my friend Theo has been here because his ___ old car, which has a leaky radiator, leaves a puddle of water in the driveway.

noxious   9. Cigarettes aren't bad only for smokers. Secondhand smoke is also ___ and can be harmful to everyone nearby.

scenario   10. I had thought up several ___s of how my widowed mother might marry again, but I never would have predicted what actually happened: she married my widowed father-in-law.

NOTE: Now check your answers to these items by turning to page 178. Going over the answers carefully will help you prepare for the next two practices, for which answers are not given.

Sentence Check 2

Using the answer lines provided, complete each item below with **two** words from the box. Use each word once.

chide
Coalition   1–2. When red M&M's were discontinued, angry consumers ___(e)d the company and formed a "___ for the Restoration and Preservation of Red M&M's." The company hastily reinstated° the red pieces.

noxious
commensurate   3–4. The developers who endangered the local water supply by dumping ___ wastes in the landfill did not get a punishment that was ___ with their reprehensible° act: they had to pay only a small fine.

<u>_____dilapidated_____</u>
<u>_____diabolic_____</u>

5–6. A dark, ___ old house in our neighborhood scares local children, who feel that the quiet, unfriendly owner is some sort of ___ villain.

<u>_____scenario_____</u>
<u>_____integral_____</u>

7–8. The TV writer was distraught°: "The producer told me to shorten the script by cutting the deathbed scene out of my ___. But how can I? It's a(n)___ part of the story."

<u>_____yen_____</u>
<u>_____connotation_____</u>

9–10. While the word "___" can refer to a strong desire for anything, to many people it has the specific ___ of a sharp longing for a particular food.

Final Check: *Halloween Troubles*

Here is a final opportunity for you to strengthen your knowledge of the ten words. First read the following selection carefully. Then fill in each blank with a word from the box at the top of the previous page. (Context clues will help you figure out which word goes in which blank.) Use each word once.

Discomfort was such a(n) (1)_____integral_____ part of my childhood Halloweens that I wouldn't have recognized the holiday without it. In retrospect°, I think I must have been a masochist°. As a Dutch girl, I limped from door to door in crippling wooden shoes. As a vampire with sharp fangs, I cut my lower lip every time I said "Trick or treat." Even today the word *Halloween* carries for me (2)_____connotation_____s of physical misery.

My (3)_____scenario_____ for the perfect Halloween encompassed° not only frightening others, but also frightening myself. So I was willing to approach even the most scary-looking houses, ones sure to be haunted or to belong to (4)_____diabolic_____ witches waiting to boil children for dinner. Generally, such houses were (5)_____dilapidated_____,

with cracked windows, creaking steps, and loose shutters banging in the wind. Even scarier than those places, however, were the (6)_____coalition_____s of high-school students. At any moment, these gangs might corner me and, without wasting words, make the terse° demand, "Your candy or your life." I might die if I refused to relinquish° my Baby Ruths, Hershey's Kisses, and Three Musketeers.

My candy haul was always disappointing, never (7)_____commensurate_____ with what I had suffered on my rounds. In addition, as soon as I returned home, my parents would order me to throw out all unwrapped candy, since it might contain some (8)_____noxious_____ substance, even poison. By then, of course, I had built up a powerful and indiscriminate° (9)_____yen_____ for candy—any candy at all. So I would stuff myself with the loot that remained—and then be (10) _____chide_____(e)d for getting sick.

Scores	Sentence Check 2 _____%	Final Check _____%

Enter your scores above and in the **Vocabulary Performance Chart** on the inside back cover of the book.

atrophy	mitigate
deplore	objective
deprivation	panacea
exacerbate	unprecedented
imperative	utilitarian

Ten Words in Context

In the space provided, write the letter of the meaning closest to that of each **boldfaced** word. Use the context of the sentences to help you figure out each word's meaning.

1 atrophy
(ă′trə-fē)
-verb

- Since unused muscles **atrophy**, an arm or a leg that remains in a cast for some time becomes thinner.
- "If you watch any more of those mindless television programs," my father said, "your brain will **atrophy**."

__B__ *Atrophy* means   A. to grow.   B. to waste away.   C. to cause pain.

2 deplore
(dĭ-plôr′)
-verb

- Bernie **deplored** his coworkers' habit of taking home paper clips, Scotch tape, pens, and stationery from the office, a practice he felt was dishonest.
- Many people **deplore** some of the content on the Internet but feel they must tolerate it, because they disapprove just as strongly of censorship.

__A__ *Deplore* means   A. to condemn.   B. to ignore.   C. to make worse.

3 deprivation
(dĕp′rə-vā′shən)
-noun

- Children who spend their early years in institutions where they receive no love may suffer throughout life from the effects of this **deprivation**.
- Weight-loss programs typically claim that their members experience no sense of **deprivation**. "You'll never be hungry!" they promise.

__A__ *Deprivation* means   A. a deficiency.   B. a feeling of disapproval.   C. a strong desire.

4 exacerbate
(ĕg-zăs′ər-bāt′)
-verb

- Scratching a mosquito bite only makes it worse: the scraping **exacerbates** the itching and may even cause an infection.
- Instead of soothing the baby, the sound of the music box seemed only to **exacerbate** his crying.

__C__ *Exacerbate* means   A. to find the cause of.   B. to relieve.   C. to make worse.

5 imperative
(ĭm-pĕr′ə-tĭv)
-adjective

- It is **imperative** that I renew my driver's license today—it expires at midnight.
- "It is **imperative** for this letter to reach Mr. Rivera tomorrow," the boss said, "so please send it by Express Mail."

__C__ *Imperative* means   A. impossible.   B. difficult.   C. essential.

6 mitigate
(mĭt′ə-gāt′)
-verb

- The disabilities resulting from Mr. Dobbs's stroke were **mitigated** by physical therapy, but he still has difficulty using his right arm.
- Time usually **mitigates** the pain of a lost love. When Richard's girlfriend broke their engagement, he was miserable, but now the hurt is much less.

__A__ *Mitigate* means   A. to relieve.   B. to worsen.   C. to reveal.

7 objective
(əb-jĕk′tĭv)
-*adjective*

● Scientists must strive to be totally **objective** in their observations and experiments, putting aside their personal wishes and expectations.

● All too often, we let our own prejudices prevent us from being **objective** in judging others.

B   *Objective* means   A. personal.   B. fair.   C. persuasive.

8 panacea
(păn′ə-sē′ə)
-*noun*

● My aunt considers vitamins a **panacea**. She believes that they can cure everything from chapped lips to heart disease.

● Ravi thinks his troubles would be over if he just had plenty of money. But money isn't a **panacea**; it wouldn't solve all his problems.

C   *Panacea* means   A. a belief.   B. a basic necessity.   C. a complete solution.

9 unprecedented
(ŭn-prĕs′ĭ-dĕn′tĭd)
-*adjective*

● When Hillary Clinton and Barack Obama ran against each other for the 2008 Democratic nomination for president of the United States, the situation was **unprecedented**. All the previous major-party nominees for president had been white men.

● The spring concert was "standing room only." This was **unprecedented**, the first time in our school's history that the concert had been sold out.

A   *Unprecedented* means   A. unheard-of.   B. unprejudiced.   C. controversial.

10 utilitarian
(yōō-tĭl′ə-târ′ē-ən)
-*adjective*

● One difference between "arts" and "crafts" is that crafts tend to be more **utilitarian**. They are generally created to serve a specific purpose.

● I prefer **utilitarian** gifts, such as pots and pans, to gifts that are meant to be just ornamental or beautiful.

B   *Utilitarian* means   A. unique.   B. practical.   C. inexpensive.

Matching Words with Definitions

Following are definitions of the ten words. Clearly write or print each word next to its definition. The sentences above and on the previous page will help you decide on the meaning of each word.

1. _____exacerbate_____   To aggravate (a situation or condition); make more severe

2. _____mitigate_____   To make less severe or less intense; relieve

3. _____unprecedented_____   Being the first instance of something; never having occurred before

4. _____panacea_____   Something supposed to cure all diseases, evils, or difficulties; cure-all

5. _____atrophy_____   To wear down, lose strength, or become weak, as from disuse, disease, or injury (said of a body part); to wither away

6. _____deprivation_____   Lack or shortage of one or more basic necessities

7. _____imperative_____   Necessary; urgent

8. _____objective_____   Not influenced by emotion or personal prejudice; based only on what can be observed

9. _____utilitarian_____   Made or intended for practical use; stressing usefulness over beauty or other considerations

10. _____deplore_____   To feel or express disapproval of

CAUTION: Do not go any further until you are sure the above answers are correct. Then you can use the definitions to help you in the following practices. Your goal is eventually to know the words well enough so that you don't need to check the definitions at all.

Sentence Check 1

Using the answer line provided, complete each item below with the correct word from the box. Use each word once.

A. atrophy	B. deplore	C. deprivation	D. exacerbate	E. imperative
F. mitigate	G. objective	H. panacea	I. unprecedented	J. utilitarian

deprivation   1. When families go camping and decide to spend a whole weekend without video games and TV, some kids think they are experiencing a great ___.

mitigate   2. The last time I had a migraine headache, I tried draping a cold, wet cloth over my eyes to ___ the pain and nausea, but my symptoms only got worse.

exacerbate   3. First-aid instructions usually advise against moving an accident victim, because movement can ___ an injury.

unprecedented   4. The election of Barack Obama to the presidency was ___ in American history—he was the first African American president.

deplore   5. No one could ___ drinking and driving more than Lin; her son was killed by a drunk driver.

utilitarian   6. Although an Academy Award is not meant to be ___, one winner uses his as a paperweight.

objective   7. If you find it difficult to be ___ about your own writing, try asking a classmate to read it and give you an unbiased opinion.

panacea   8. Our city has many different crime-related problems, but the mayor has only one solution to offer: more police officers on the streets. She believes an enlarged police force is a ___.

imperative   9. When told that Ms. Thomas was in conference and could not be disturbed, the caller said urgently, "It's ___ that I speak to her. Her house is on fire."

atrophy   10. In Burma, some women lengthen their necks by stretching them with copper coils. This practice damages the muscles, causing them to ___: they become thin and weak.

NOTE: Now check your answers to these items by turning to page 178. Going over the answers carefully will help you prepare for the next two practices, for which answers are not given.

Sentence Check 2

Using the answer lines provided, complete each item below with **two** words from the box. Use each word once.

mitigate
deprivation   1–2. "Hands Across America" was a fund-raising effort to help ___ hunger in regions where ___ was widespread.

deplore
unprecedented   3–4. Many people are so opposed to change that they ___ as potentially harmful just about anything that is new and ___.

_____ exacerbate _____   5–6. It's hard to know what treatment is optimum° for a sprained ankle. Walking
_____ atrophy _____   on the ankle can ___ the injury, but if you don't walk on it for a long time,
                                        the muscles will start to ___.

_____ objective _____   7–8. If you want to be ___, it is ___ that you put aside your emotions and
_____ imperative _____   prejudices.

_____ utilitarian _____   9–10. In deciding which over-the-counter medicine to take, it's important to use
_____ panacea _____   a(n) ___ approach. Choose a drug for the specific purpose it serves, and don't
                                        rely on any one drug as a ___.

Final Check: *Thomas Dooley*

Here is a final opportunity for you to strengthen your knowledge of the ten words. First read the following selection carefully. Then fill in each blank with a word from the box at the top of the previous page. (Context clues will help you figure out which word goes in which blank.) Use each word once.

In the 1950s, a young American doctor named Thomas Dooley arrived in Laos, in southeast Asia. He was shocked by the ubiquitous° sickness and poverty he found there. The people lived without plumbing or electricity, and they had no knowledge of health care or even of basic hygiene. For example, one boy with an infected leg had been told not to walk at all, which caused both of his legs to (1)_____ atrophy _____. The people's lack of knowledge was (2)_____ exacerbate _____(e)d by superstitions and by a reliance on well-meaning traditional healers, who sometimes inadvertently° gave useless or harmful advice. They might, for example, advocate° pig grease for a burn or treat a fracture by chanting. Dooley

(3)_____ deplore _____(e)d the terrible (4)_____ deprivation _____ he saw. He felt that it was (5)_____ imperative _____ to help these communities learn about modern medicine—to help them apply (6)_____ objective _____ scientific knowledge—and equally essential for them to relinquish° their harmful superstitions. Dooley did not believe that modern medicine would be a (7)_____ panacea _____ for every problem in Laos, nor did he expect to eradicate° all disease there, but he firmly believed that he could at least (8)_____ mitigate _____ the people's suffering.

Dooley's (9)_____ utilitarian _____ approach to health care, based specifically on practical instruction, was (10)_____ unprecedented _____: no one before him had tried to teach the communities how to care for themselves. Dooley believed that teaching was an integral° part of medical care, that it was useless to treat symptoms and allow the causes to continue. So, subsidized° by local governments, he set up hospitals and taught the rudimentary° principles of hygiene, nursing, and medical treatment.

Tom Dooley died at a tragically young age, but his work and the tenets° that guided it benefited countless people.

Scores   Sentence Check 2 _____%   Final Check _____%

Enter your scores above and in the **Vocabulary Performance Chart** on the inside back cover of the book.

CHAPTER 21

decorum	facilitate
espouse	orthodox
exhilaration	rejuvenate
exorbitant	synchronize
extricate	tenuous

Ten Words in Context

In the space provided, write the letter of the meaning closest to that of each **boldfaced** word. Use the context of the sentences to help you figure out each word's meaning.

1 decorum
(dĭ-kô′rəm)
-noun

- **Decorum** demands that you send a thank-you note for all birthday gifts, even those you don't like or will never use.
- In her newspaper columns, Miss Manners gives advice on **decorum** in all kinds of situations. For example, she says that at a dinner party, you must be polite even if you find a bug crawling in your salad.

_C_ *Decorum* means   A. a difficult situation.   B. beauty.   C. proper conduct.

2 espouse
(ĕ-spouz′)
-verb

- Some politicians **espouse** whatever ideas they think will win them votes.
- People who **espouse** animals' rights often find themselves in conflict with scientists who argue for the use of animals in medical experiments.

_A_ *Espouse* means   A. to speak for.   B. to argue against.   C. to study.

3 exhilaration
(ĕg-zĭl′ə-rā′shən)
-noun

- After the last exam of the year, Olivia and I were so filled with **exhilaration** that we skipped all the way to the car.
- A marching band gives most people a feeling of **exhilaration**. The lively music makes them feel excited.

_B_ *Exhilaration* means   A. appropriateness.   B. happiness.   C. commitment.

4 exorbitant
(ĕg-zôr′bĭ-tənt)
-adjective

- Even if I were rich, I wouldn't pay three hundred dollars for those shoes. That's an **exorbitant** price.
- The armed forces often spend **exorbitant** amounts on minor items, including an eight-hundred-dollar ashtray and a toilet seat that cost thousands of dollars.

_C_ *Exorbitant* means   A. estimated.   B. inconvenient.   C. extremely high.

5 extricate
(ĕks′trĭ-kāt′)
-verb

- The fly struggled and struggled but was unable to **extricate** itself from the spider's web.
- The young couple ran up so many debts that they finally needed a counselor to help them **extricate** themselves from their financial mess.

_A_ *Extricate* means   A. to untangle.   B. to distinguish.   C. to excuse.

6 facilitate
(fə-sĭl′ə-tāt′)
-verb

- Automatic doors in supermarkets **facilitate** the entry and exit of customers with bags or shopping carts.
- For those with poor eyesight, large print **facilitates** reading.

_C_ *Facilitate* means   A. to decrease.   B. to cause.   C. to make possible.

118

7 orthodox
(ôr′thə-dŏks′)
-adjective

- When Father McKenzie brought drums and electric guitars into church, he shocked the more **orthodox** members of his congregation.
- The **orthodox** footwear for a sprint or distance race is some kind of running shoes, but a champion Ethiopian runner competed in the Olympics barefoot.

_B_ *Orthodox* means   A. revolutionary.   B. traditional.   C. important.

8 rejuvenate
(rĭ-jōō′və-nāt′)
-verb

- The Fountain of Youth was a legendary spring whose water could **rejuvenate** people.
- The grass had become brown and matted, but a warm spring rain **rejuvenated** it, perking it up and turning it green again.

_C_ *Rejuvenate* means   A. to set free.   B. to excite.   C. to give new life to.

9 synchronize
(sĭng′krə-nīz′)
-verb

- The secret agents **synchronized** their watches so that they could cross the border at exactly the same minute.
- We need to **synchronize** the clocks in our house: the kitchen clock is ten minutes slower than the alarm clock in the bedroom.

_A_ *Synchronize* means   A. to coordinate.   B. to repair.   C. to find.

10 tenuous
(tĕn′yōō-əs)
-adjective

- It doesn't take much to destroy an already **tenuous** relationship. Something as slight as forgetting to telephone can cause an unstable relationship to collapse.
- Del was opposed to the Equal Rights Amendment, but his position seemed **tenuous**. He couldn't support it with any facts, and his logic was weak.

_A_ *Tenuous* means   A. shaky.   B. easy.   C. established.

Matching Words with Definitions

Following are definitions of the ten words. Clearly write or print each word next to its definition. The sentences above and on the previous page will help you decide on the meaning of each word.

1. ____exhilaration____ Cheerfulness; high spirits

2. ____extricate____ To free from a tangled situation or a difficulty

3. ____tenuous____ Having little substance or basis; weak; poorly supported

4. ____decorum____ Correctness in behavior and manners; standards or conventions of socially acceptable behavior

5. ____rejuvenate____ To make (someone) feel or seem young again; to make (something) seem fresh or new again

6. ____espouse____ To support, argue for, or adopt (an idea or cause)

7. ____synchronize____ To cause to occur at exactly the same time; to cause (clocks and watches) to agree in time

8. ____facilitate____ To make easier to do or to get

9. ____orthodox____ Following established, traditional rules or beliefs, especially in religion; following what is customary or commonly accepted

10. ____exorbitant____ Excessive, especially in amount, cost, or price; beyond what is reasonable or appropriate

CAUTION: Do not go any further until you are sure the above answers are correct. Then you can use the definitions to help you in the following practices. Your goal is eventually to know the words well enough so that you don't need to check the definitions at all.

Sentence Check 1

Using the answer line provided, complete each item below with the correct word from the box. Use each word once.

A. **decorum**	B. **espouse**	C. **exhilaration**	D. **exorbitant**	E. **extricate**
F. **facilitate**	G. **orthodox**	H. **rejuvenate**	I. **synchronize**	J. **tenuous**

_____decorum_____ 1. Ignoring all standards of cafeteria ___, students sat on the tables and threw french fries at each other.

_____tenuous_____ 2. Some premature babies are so tiny and weak that their hold on life is very ___.

_____rejuvenate_____ 3. The ads for the anti-wrinkle cream claim that it will ___ aging skin.

_____exorbitant_____ 4. The new restaurant went out of business because of its ___ prices.

_____exhilaration_____ 5. The children's ___ at the amusement park was contagious—their parents soon felt excited too.

_____facilitate_____ 6. If you're giving a dinner party, preparing some food platters ahead of time will ___ your work when the guests arrive.

_____extricate_____ 7. At age two, Carlos got his head stuck between the bars of an iron railing. His parents had to call the fire department to come and ___ him.

_____espouse_____ 8. During the 1960s and 1970s, there were bitter clashes between those who ___(e)d the United States' involvement in Vietnam and those who were opposed to it.

_____synchronize_____ 9. New members of the water ballet club have trouble coordinating their swimming, but with practice, the group is able to ___ its movements.

_____orthodox_____ 10. "The ___ treatment in this kind of case," the doctor said, "is surgery followed by chemotherapy. But some specialists are exploring the possibility of using surgery alone."

NOTE: Now check your answers to these items by turning to page 179. Going over the answers carefully will help you prepare for the next two practices, for which answers are not given.

Sentence Check 2

Using the answer lines provided, complete each item below with **two** words from the box. Use each word once.

_____exhilaration_____
_____synchronize_____ 1–2. It filled the audience with ___ to see the dexterous° dancers in the chorus line ___ their turns and kicks so perfectly.

_____orthodox_____
_____tenuous_____ 3–4. In any religion, ___ practices are slow to change. New ones are always in a(n) ___ position at first and require time to become widely accepted.

_____exorbitant_____
_____rejuvenate_____ 5–6. Although the price may seem ___, an expensive vacation may be worth the money, as it can often ___ one's mind and body.

_____decorum_____

_____extricate_____

7–8. Foreign Service officers must observe strict rules of conduct. If their behavior violates ___, their government may have to ___ itself from a diplomatic mess.

_____espouse_____

_____facilitate_____

9–10. My grandmother ___(e)d garlic as a treatment for chest colds, in the belief that it ___(e)d breathing. Sometimes she made us eat it, and sometimes she rubbed it on our chests. As a result, we were often ostracized° by our friends, who found the smell of garlic repugnant°.

Final Check: *Twelve Grown Men in a Bug*

Here is a final opportunity for you to strengthen your knowledge of the ten words. First read the following selection carefully. Then fill in each blank with a word from the box at the top of the previous page. (Context clues will help you figure out which word goes in which blank.) Use each word once.

My college reunions are very traditional occasions, but there is usually very little that's (1)_____orthodox_____ about my husband's.

Take, for example, one of the final events of his reunion last year. It all began when a big, bearded man stood up to address the raucous° crowd. Over the noise, the man yelled, "You are about to see an amazing sight. The twelve large, robust° hunks of manhood you see up here, none with a waistline smaller than forty-two inches, are about to squeeze into this Volkswagen Beetle. We're not here to (2)_____espouse_____ the use of economy cars, and we're not masochists° trying to torture ourselves. It's just that we all fit into the Beetle twenty years ago, and we aim to do it again today. Unless we occasionally (3)_____rejuvenate_____ ourselves by letting go of our serious side and doing something inane°, how can we stay young?

"Now, I know that some of you have (4)_____exorbitant_____ bets in the amount of two whole bucks riding on this," he joked. "We won't fail those who believe in us. And those of you who consider our claim (5)_____tenuous_____, just watch."

Then the big, bearded man turned to the eleven others. "Okay, you heroes," he exhorted° them, "this is no time for (6)_____decorum_____. Forget your manners, and do anything you can to (7)_____facilitate_____ this mighty task. Now, let's (8)_____synchronize_____ our start—all together: ready, set, go!"

Shoving, yelling, and cursing, the twelve men tried to squeeze into the car. "If they do get in," I said to my husband, "how will they ever (9)_____extricate_____ themselves?"

Moments later, however, everyone was cheering vociferously°. All twelve men were inside the car. After a few seconds, they exploded out of it, wild with (10)_____exhilaration_____. Sweaty but triumphant, they jumped up and down and hugged one another.

Scores   Sentence Check 2 _____%   Final Check _____%

Enter your scores above and in the **Vocabulary Performance Chart** on the inside back cover of the book.

assimilate	indolent
belligerent	inherent
demeanor	nonchalant
denunciation	unassuming
dissipate	unilateral

Ten Words in Context

In the space provided, write the letter of the meaning closest to that of each **boldfaced** word. Use the context of the sentences to help you figure out each word's meaning.

1 assimilate
(ə-sĭm′ə-lāt′)
-verb

- To **assimilate** into the culture of a new country, it's essential to learn the language.
- The United States has often been called a "melting pot"—meaning that people of many cultures have **assimilated**, or blended together, within it.

A   *Assimilate* means   A. to be absorbed.   B. to spread thin.   C. to remain.

2 belligerent
(bə-lĭj′ə-rənt)
-adjective

- When anyone contradicts Bruce, he becomes **belligerent**. He has often started fights with people who disagreed with him.
- Angie was suspended for her **belligerent** behavior during an argument with one of her teachers. She actually shook her fist at him and threatened to hit him.

B   *Belligerent* means   A. overly casual.   B. quarrelsome.   C. confused.

3 demeanor
(dĭ-mēn′ər)
-noun

- Troy's **demeanor** was quiet and controlled, but inside he was boiling with anger.
- Proper **demeanor** during a funeral or lecture is obviously quite different from acceptable conduct at a ball game or rock concert.

A   *Demeanor* means   A. behavior.   B. feelings.   C. expectation.

4 denunciation
(dĭ-nŭn′sē-ā′shən)
-noun

- In an unusual **denunciation** of parents, the community leader said, "Parents have not been taking enough responsibility for their children."
- The mayor's public **denunciation** of the police chief angered many officers; local citizens, however, applauded the mayor's public statement of disapproval.

C   *Denunciation* means   A. appreciation.   B. ignoring.   C. criticism.

5 dissipate
(dĭs′ə-pāt′)
-verb

- After twenty minutes of meditation, I find that the stresses of my day have **dissipated**, and I'm relaxed enough to enjoy the evening.
- Teddy hates catching a cold. When anyone is sneezing and coughing in his presence, he opens a window and fans the air to **dissipate** the cold germs.

B   *Dissipate* means   A. to blend.   B. to scatter.   C. to assemble.

6 indolent
(ĭn′də-lənt)
-adjective

- My **indolent** sister says that the most work she ever wants to do is clicking the remote control to switch TV channels.
- My uncle has been fired from three jobs for being **indolent**. He shows up on time, but he does very little work and leaves early.

C   *Indolent* means   A. destructive.   B. shy.   C. unwilling to work.

7 inherent
(ĭn-hîr′ənt)
-*adjective*

- An **inherent** danger of life in San Francisco is the possibility of earthquakes.
- Marco believes that kindness is **inherent** in human nature, but I think people are born selfish. Maybe we're both right.

C *Inherent* means   A. shrinking.   B. humble.   C. natural.

8 nonchalant
(nŏn′shə-lŏnt′)
-*adjective*

- Because the automobile is so commonplace today, many people have become **nonchalant** about traveling by car. In the early twentieth century, however, people saw driving as an exciting and risky adventure.
- My friend was very **nonchalant** about giving her oral report in class, but I was a nervous wreck about giving mine.

A *Nonchalant* means   A. relaxed.   B. anxious.   C. angry.

9 unassuming
(ŭn′ə-sōō′mĭng)
-*adjective*

- In the business world, you shouldn't be too **unassuming**. If you're overly modest about your skills and achievements, for example, you might not get a promotion you deserve.
- As **unassuming** as ever, Alice accepted the award in a quiet, modest way.

C *Unassuming* means   A. argumentative.   B. lazy.   C. humble.

10 unilateral
(yōōn′ə-lăt′ər-əl)
-*adjective*

- Many people believe in **unilateral** disarmament; that is, they think their own nation should give up all weapons of war even if no other country will do so.
- Tanya's **unilateral** decisions are hurting her marriage. For instance, she recently bought nonrefundable tickets to Florida without consulting her husband.

B *Unilateral* means   A. gradual.   B. one-sided.   C. group.

Matching Words with Definitions

Following are definitions of the ten words. Clearly write or print each word next to its definition. The sentences above and on the previous page will help you decide on the meaning of each word.

1. _____demeanor_____   Conduct; outward behavior; manner

2. _____indolent_____   Lazy; avoiding or disliking work

3. _____unassuming_____   Modest; not boastful or arrogant

4. _____dissipate_____   To thin out or scatter and gradually vanish; drive away

5. _____nonchalant_____   Calm, carefree, and casually unconcerned

6. _____assimilate_____   To become more similar to a larger whole; especially, to blend into or adjust to a main culture

7. _____unilateral_____   Involving or done by only one side

8. _____inherent_____   Existing as a natural or essential quality of a person or thing; built-in

9. _____belligerent_____   Quick or eager to argue or fight; hostile; aggressive

10. _____denunciation_____   A strong expression of disapproval; an act of condemning, especially publicly

CAUTION: Do not go any further until you are sure the above answers are correct. Then you can use the definitions to help you in the following practices. Your goal is eventually to know the words well enough so that you don't need to check the definitions at all.

Sentence Check 1

Using the answer line provided, complete each item below with the correct word from the box. Use each word once.

| A. **assimilate** | B. **belligerent** | C. **demeanor** | D. **denunciation** | E. **dissipate** |
| F. **indolent** | G. **inherent** | H. **nonchalant** | I. **unassuming** | J. **unilateral** |

_____inherent_____ 1. The eye is not necessarily a(n) ___ part of the reading process. Blind people can read Braille—a system of raised dots—with their fingertips.

_____dissipate_____ 2. Anger builds up if you hold it in. But expressing anger can help it to ___, leaving you much calmer.

_____belligerent_____ 3. Jerry is a(n) ___ child who frequently pushes and hits other children.

_____denunciation_____ 4. In a ___ of the union, the company president said that its members were "selfish and narrow-minded."

_____nonchalant_____ 5. It's amazing how ___ kids can be about computers; they'll work at the keyboard as casually as if it were a coloring book.

_____indolent_____ 6. Because that boss herself is a workaholic, she thinks that anyone who works less than ten hours a day is ___.

_____demeanor_____ 7. Airport security guards are trained to observe people's ___ so that they can notice and respond to any suspicious behavior.

_____unassuming_____ 8. Even though Marta was the star of the team, she was always ___ and quick to give credit to the whole team for its successes.

_____assimilate_____ 9. Many Americans who live and work abroad make no attempt to ___ to foreign countries; they continue to eat only American food, speak only English, and see things only from an American perspective.

_____unilateral_____ 10. Governments are usually reluctant to take ___ action in international disputes. They want other countries to join them in their efforts.

NOTE: Now check your answers to these items by turning to page 179. Going over the answers carefully will help you prepare for the next two practices, for which answers are not given.

Sentence Check 2

Using the answer lines provided, complete each item below with **two** words from the box. Use each word once.

_____demeanor_____
_____belligerent_____
1–2. Estéban's ___ is consistently gentle and peaceful. By contrast, his brother Luis usually behaves in a rough and ___ way.

_____unilateral_____
_____dissipate_____
3–4. Tension was building between two gangs in the park when suddenly the leader of one gang made a brave ___ gesture: he held out his hand to the other leader. As they shook hands, the strain between the groups began to ___, and a fight was avoided.

_____inherent_____

_____nonchalant_____

5–6. Usha's calm, casual style seems to be a(n) ___ part of her personality. She remains ___ in tense situations that would make most people distraught°.

_____denunciation_____

_____indolent_____

7–8. My mother, a zealot° for exercise, is loud in her ___ of my ___ ways. "*Must* you be so sedentary°?" she says. "Don't just sit around all the time like a lump of mashed potatoes!"

_____unassuming_____

_____assimilate_____

9–10. Because Wes is so quiet and ___, he found it difficult to ___ into a company in which people were very aggressive and competitive.

Final Check: *Adjusting to a Group Home*

Here is a final opportunity for you to strengthen your knowledge of the ten words. First read the following selection carefully. Then fill in each blank with a word from the box at the top of the previous page. (Context clues will help you figure out which word goes in which blank.) Use each word once.

As Ken went up the path to the children's home, he dragged his feet, clenched his fists, and made faces. His whole (1)_____demeanor_____ announced, "You can make me come here, but you can't make me like it." Ken was 11, and he had been relegated° to a group home by the court because there seemed to be no other recourse°—his mother was an alcoholic and his father had abandoned him.

Ken reacted with rancor°. His attitude toward the other children was (2)_____belligerent_____; he started fights over the smallest matters. His antipathy° toward the home was equally obvious. When he was asked, "How are you getting on?" he would respond with a terse° (3)_____denunciation_____: "This place stinks." And his attitude toward his schoolwork and his assigned chores was (4)_____nonchalant_____; he was so casual about his responsibilities that he was often scolded for being (5)_____indolent_____.

One day, though, something happened that bolstered° Ken's spirits. A small, quiet boy was being teased by some older kids, while others stood by watching, doing nothing to help. Risking a(n) (6)_____unilateral_____ action, Ken stood up for the child. When the younger boy thanked him, Ken was (7)_____unassuming_____, saying, "It's okay. It was nothing." After that incident, Ken started to (8)_____assimilate_____ more and more into the life of the home. As his anger (9)_____dissipate_____(e)d, his (10)_____inherent_____ friendliness began to appear, and he became more gregarious°.

Naturally, Ken did not go through a complete metamorphosis°. He still fought now and then. But he had changed enough to become a happy and popular member of the group home.

| Scores | Sentence Check 2 _____% | Final Check _____% |

analogy	placebo
annihilate	proficient
criterion	staunch
emanate	subversive
holistic	vindicate

Ten Words in Context

In the space provided, write the letter of the meaning closest to that of each **boldfaced** word. Use the context of the sentences to help you figure out each word's meaning.

1 analogy
(ə-năl′ə-jē)
-noun

- To help students understand vision, teachers often draw an **analogy** between the eye and a camera.
- The commencement address, titled "You Are the Captain of Your Ship," used the **analogy** of life as an ocean-going vessel that the captain must steer between rocks.

B *Analogy* means   A. a picture.   B. a comparison.   C. a standard.

2 annihilate
(ə-nī′ə-lāt′)
-verb

- The movie was about a plot to **annihilate** entire cities by poisoning their water supply.
- "Universal Destroyer" is a warlike video game in which the aim is to **annihilate** the opponents.

C *Annihilate* means   A. to escape from.   B. to seize.   C. to wipe out.

3 criterion
(krī-tēr′ē-ən)
-noun

- One **criterion** by which writing teachers judge a paper is clear organization.
- Some advertisers aren't concerned about telling the truth. Their only **criterion** for a good commercial is selling the product.

A *Criterion* means   A. a standard.   B. a beginning.   C. an answer.

4 emanate
(ĕm′ə-nāt′)
-verb

- As the cinnamon bread baked, a wonderful smell **emanated** from the kitchen.
- The screeching and scraping **emanating** from Keisha's bedroom tell me that she is practicing her violin.

B *Emanate* means   A. to disappear.   B. to come out.   C. to expand.

5 holistic
(hō-lĭs′tĭk)
-adjective

- A good drug center takes a **holistic** approach to treatment, seeing each client not just as "an addict" but as a whole person. Along with medical aid, it provides emotional support, individual and family counseling, and follow-up services.
- Eastern cultures tend to take a more **holistic** view of learning than Western societies, focusing on the whole rather than analyzing parts.

B *Holistic* means   A. easygoing.   B. concerned with the whole.   C. nonfinancial.

6 placebo
(plə-sē′bō)
-noun

- When the little boy had a headache and there was no aspirin in the house, his mother gave him a **placebo**: a small candy that she told him was a "pain pill." It seemed to work—his headache went away.
- The doctor lost his license when it was found that the pills for depression he had been giving to many of his patients were actually a **placebo**—just sugar pills.

A *Placebo* means   A. a fake medicine.   B. an over-the-counter pill.   C. an expensive cure.

7 proficient
(prə-fĭsh′ənt)
-adjective

- It's not all that hard to become **proficient** on a computer. Be patient, and you'll develop the necessary skill.
- Wayne is a **proficient** woodworker. He is able to make professional-quality desks, bookshelves, and cabinets.

A *Proficient* means   A. expert.   B. hard-working.   C. enthusiastic.

8 staunch
(stônch)
-adjective

- Although the mayor had been accused of taking bribes, he still had some **staunch** supporters.
- The newspaper's astrological predictions are often way off the mark, yet Teresa remains a **staunch** believer in astrology and checks her horoscope every day.

C *Staunch* means   A. busy.   B. unsteady.   C. faithful.

9 subversive
(səb-vûr′sĭv)
-adjective

- To some Americans, criticizing the President is a **subversive** act, aimed at undermining his power. To others, it is simply an example of freedom of speech.
- The so-called "consulting company" was a cover for **subversive** activities; it was actually a ring of antigovernment agents.

B *Subversive* means   A. having faith.   B. intended to destroy.   C. blameless.

10 vindicate
(vĭn′də-kāt′)
-verb

- When Kai was accused of cheating on a geometry test, he **vindicated** himself by reciting several theorems from memory, proving that he knew the material.
- In our society, people falsely accused of crimes often must spend a great deal of money on legal fees in order to **vindicate** themselves.

A *Vindicate* means   A. to prove innocent.   B. to make a commitment.   C. to weaken.

Matching Words with Definitions

Following are definitions of the ten words. Clearly write or print each word next to its definition. The sentences above and on the previous page will help you decide on the meaning of each word.

1. _____vindicate_____   To clear from blame or suspicion; justify or prove right

2. _____placebo_____   A substance which contains no medicine, but which the receiver believes is a medicine

3. _____emanate_____   To flow or come out from a source; come forth

4. _____analogy_____   A comparison between two things in order to clarify or dramatize a point

5. _____annihilate_____   To destroy completely; reduce to nothingness

6. _____criterion_____   A standard by which something is or can be judged

7. _____subversive_____   Acting or intending to undermine or overthrow something established

8. _____staunch_____   Firm; loyal; strong in support

9. _____holistic_____   Emphasizing the whole and the interdependence of its parts, rather than the parts separately

10. _____proficient_____   Skilled; highly competent

CAUTION: Do not go any further until you are sure the above answers are correct. Then you can use the definitions to help you in the following practices. Your goal is eventually to know the words well enough so that you don't need to check the definitions at all.

Sentence Check 1

Using the answer line provided, complete each item below with the correct word from the box. Use each word once.

| A. analogy | B. annihilate | C. criterion | D. emanate | E. holistic |
| F. placebo | G. proficient | H. staunch | I. subversive | J. vindicate |

subversive   1. During the Vietnam War, some protesters poured blood over draft records. Supporters of the war considered this a ___ act.

annihilate   2. Passenger pigeons no longer exist. They were ___(e)d by hunters.

staunch   3. I'm a ___ fan of Alicia Keys. I have all her recordings.

criterion   4. One ___ used to judge the children's artwork was their use of vivid colors.

proficient   5. Although I'm quite a good cook, I'm not very ___ at baking. My pies tend to be runny, and my bread won't rise.

holistic   6. A ___ view of business would take into account not just profits but also such things as the work environment and employees' job satisfaction.

emanate   7. As the garbage-collectors' strike went into its third week, a dreadful odor began to ___ from all the garbage bags piled up in the city streets.

analogy   8. Explaining the importance of using a search engine to find information on the Internet, the instructor used a(n) ___. "The Internet is a huge ocean. The search engine is a guide showing you the best places to fish."

vindicate   9. Accused of shoplifting, the customer insisted that she had already paid for the items. She was ___(e)d when she pulled the receipt out of her purse.

placebo   10. To test a new painkiller, researchers gave it to one group of volunteers, while a second group got a(n) ___, identical in appearance to the new medicine but with no built-in power to relieve pain.

NOTE: Now check your answers to these items by turning to page 179. Going over the answers carefully will help you prepare for the next two practices, for which answers are not given.

Sentence Check 2

Using the answer lines provided, complete each item below with **two** words from the box. Use each word once.

emanate
annihilate   1–2. From the nasty smell that ___(e)d from the kitchen, I guessed that Mom was using a new kind of bug spray to try to ___ the ants there.

criterion
proficient   3–4. "One ___ by which I'll judge your papers," the teacher said, "is whether you are ___ at connecting your ideas into a cohesive° whole."

vindicate
subversive   5–6. The agent was accused of selling government secrets, but he was able to ___ himself by proving that it was his boss who was the ___ one.

_____ holistic _____

_____ analogy _____

7–8. To explain why she supported ___ medicine, the doctor used a(n) ___. She said that taking a narrow view of a health problem is like treating a dying tree's leaves but ignoring its roots, where the real problem lies.

_____ staunch _____

_____ placebo _____

9–10. Anton is a ___ believer in the power of a(n) ___. When his small daughter started having nightmares about monsters, he sprayed the room with water and told her it was "anti-monster medicine."

Final Check: *A Different Kind of Doctor*

Here is a final opportunity for you to strengthen your knowledge of the ten words. First read the following selection carefully. Then fill in each blank with a word from the box at the top of the previous page. (Context clues will help you figure out which word goes in which blank.) Use each word once.

Dr. Wilson considers (1)_____ holistic _____ medicine the optimum° approach to health care. He believes that to facilitate° healing and well-being, it is imperative° to consider a patient's entire lifestyle, not just specific aches and pains. To explain to patients how to keep well, he uses the (2)_____ analogy _____ of a garden. "If a garden gets too much or too little rain, sun, or fertilizer, it won't do well," he says. "But a proper balance keeps the garden healthy. In the same way, the body needs proper amounts of good food, exercise, work, and relaxation."

Dr. Wilson often treats patients without giving them drugs. Many of his patients have begun to feel healthier since they started taking his advice. They've adopted such new habits as eating more vegetables and taking a brisk walk every day. As a result, a new liveliness and an increased sense of pleasure and exhilaration° seem to (3)_____ emanate _____ from them; many say they feel rejuvenated°.

Despite Dr. Wilson's successes, many orthodox° physicians do not sanction° his methods, and some even deplore° them. They see him as dangerously (4)_____ subversive _____, a threat to the medical establishment; and they scoff° at his drug-free "prescriptions," calling them powerless (5)_____ placebo _____s. They fear he wants to (6)_____ annihilate _____ medical progress.

Dr. Wilson, however, has no wish to destroy medical progress. To the contrary, he believes that his methods actually *are* progressive and that they are (7)_____ vindicate _____(e)d by the improved health of his patients. There are other doctors worldwide who agree and who believe he is so (8)_____ proficient _____ at medicine that they often invite him to speak at professional conferences.

Dr. Wilson's patients also believe he is highly skilled, and they are the ones who are his most (9)_____ staunch _____ supporters. They judge him by a different (10)_____ criterion _____ from those who think medical progress lies only in finding new ways to treat disease. They judge him by the extent to which he helps his patients stay well.

Scores	Sentence Check 2 _____%	Final Check _____%

Enter your scores above and in the **Vocabulary Performance Chart** on the inside back cover of the book.

-cian, -ian	oct-, octo-
dec-	-ous
duc, duct	phil, -phile
-en	sur-
homo-	vol

Ten Word Parts in Context

Figure out the meanings of the following ten word parts by looking *closely* and *carefully* at the context in which they appear. Then, in the space provided, write the letter of the meaning closest to that of each word part.

1 -cian, -ian

- A **politician** must be a specialist both in getting elected and in governing.
- To become a **librarian**, Lian had to complete the course work in library science and also be an intern in a library during the summer.

_B_ The word part *-cian* or *-ian* means

A. a similarity.   B. a person with expertise.   C. made of.

2 dec-

- Another name for the Ten Commandments is the **Decalogue**.
- Around 800 A.D., the Hindus invented the modern **decimal** system, a number system based on 10.

_C_ The word part *dec-* means

A. eight.   B. having a certain knowledge.   C. ten.

3 duc, duct

- The **ducal** palace was the residence of the duke—the leader of his subjects.
- When my father listens to classical music on the radio, he often swings his arms as if he's **conducting** the orchestra.

_A_ The word part *duc* or *duct* means

A. to lead.   B. to be marked by.   C. to be above.

4 -en

- Chen can't wear a **woolen** sweater over bare skin. The scratchy wool drives him crazy.
- When the archaeologists opened the tomb of the ancient Egyptian king, they found dozens of **golden** bowls, necklaces, and bracelets.

_C_ The word part *-en* means

A. same as.   B. attracted to.   C. made of.

5 homo-

- The people working at the store are a fairly **homogeneous**° group. They're all in their early 20s, they've all had a year or two of college, and they're all single.
- Nowadays many **homosexuals** are more open about their lifestyles. They don't mind if people know they prefer same-sex relationships.

_B_ The word part *homo-* means

A. different.   B. alike.   C. loving.

6 oct-, octo-

- An **octagon** is a geometrical figure with eight sides and eight angles.
- An **octopus** has eight arms; that may seem like a lot, but a squid has ten.

_A_ The word part *oct-* or *octo-* means

A. eight.   B. ten.   C. above.

7 -ous

- Marla dreams of having great fame, but she has no idea what she wants to be **famous** for.
- Tomas is very **serious** lately. He seems to be full of deep thoughts.

A   The word part *-ous* means   A. characterized by.   B. loving.   C. beyond.

8 phil, -phile

- **Philadelphia** is often called the "city of brotherly love."
- Martin is a complete **Anglophile**. He adores English accents, clothes, music, manners, and cars, saying they're superior to anything on this side of the ocean.

B   The word part *phil* or *-phile* means   A. above.   B. love.   C. before.

9 sur-

- Siri polished the **surface** of the table until it shone like glass.
- Once our chickens started laying eggs, we had such a **surplus** that we were giving away dozens of extra eggs to our neighbors.

C   The word part *sur-* means   A. choose.   B. support.   C. over.

10 vol

- Many retirees offer their talents as **volunteers** in their communities, nationwide, and even throughout the world.
- According to the defense attorney, the defendant's confession was made under force, but the police and the prosecutor said that it had been **voluntary**.

A   The word part *vol* means   A. by choice.   B. without payment.   C. with skill.

Matching Word Parts with Definitions

Following are definitions of the ten word parts. Clearly write or print each word part next to its definition. The sentences above and on the previous page will help you decide on the meaning of each word part.

1. _____dec-_____ Ten

2. _____-ous_____ Having; full of; characterized by

3. _____sur-_____ Over; above; additional

4. _____duc, duct_____ To lead; guide; draw off

5. _____phil, -phile_____ Loving; lover; friend

6. _____-en_____ Made of

7. _____oct-, octo-_____ Eight

8. _____vol_____ To will; choose

9. _____-cian, -ian_____ A person with a certain ability or a certain kind of knowledge

10. _____homo-_____ Same; similar

CAUTION: Do not go any further until you are sure the above answers are correct. Then you can use the definitions to help you in the following practices. Your goal is eventually to know the word parts well enough so that you don't need to check the definitions at all.

Sentence Check 1

Using the answer line provided, complete each *italicized* word below with the correct word part from the box. Use each word part once.

A. -cian, -ian	B. dec-	C. duc, duct	D. -en	E. homo-
F. oct-, octo-	G. -ous	H. phil, -phile	I. sur-	J. vol

_____volition_____   1. Doing something on one's own (. . . *ition*) ___ means doing it by choice, of one's own free will.

_____wooden_____   2. Ralph sprayed a protective coating over the (*wood* . . .) ___ fence so that it wouldn't be eaten by termites.

_____physician_____   3. If Ana's pain isn't better by tomorrow, she really should see a (*physic* . . .) ___.

_____decathlon_____   4. The (. . . *athlon*) is an athletic competition made up of ten events.

_____octuplets_____   5. In 2009, a California woman became instantly famous when she gave birth to (. . . *uplets*) ___—six boys and two girls.

_____homophone_____   6. A(n) (. . . *phone*) ___ is a word that's pronounced the same as another word. Examples are the words *hear* and *here*.

_____aqueduct_____   7. An (*aque* . . .) ___ is a channel for bringing water from one place to another. The water is usually drawn along by gravity.

_____philanthropist_____   8. The wealthy woman was a true (. . . *anthropist*) ___; out of love for her fellow humans, she made generous donations to many causes.

_____surpass_____   9. If the theater department wants this semester's play to (. . . *pass*) ___ last semester's in attendance, it will have to run an extra night, since both nights were sold out last semester.

_____mysterious_____   10. The disappearance of twenty dollars from my wallet is (*mysteri* . . .) ___. I'm sure the wallet was in my pocket all day.

> **NOTE:** Now check your answers to these items by turning to page 179. Going over the answers carefully will help you prepare for the next two practices, for which answers are not given.

Sentence Check 2

Using the answer line provided, complete each *italicized* word in the sentences below with the correct word part from the box. Use each word part once.

_____magician_____
_____volunteer_____   1–2. The (*magic* . . .) ___ called for someone from the audience to come up on the stage and be sawed in half. My impetuous° sister was the first to (. . . *unteer*) ___.

_____homogenized_____
_____surface_____   3–4. If peanut butter is not (. . . *genized*) ___, making it the same throughout, the oil separates and rises to the (. . . *face*) ___.

_____ Francophile _____

_____ marvelous _____

5–6. Thomas is such a staunch° (*Franco . . .*) ____ that he thinks everything French is (*marvel . . .*) ____. If he ever moves to France, he should find it easy to assimilate° there.

_____ octogenarian _____

_____ decades _____

7–8. My neighbor is a(n) (. . . *genarian*) ____, but he's so robust° you'd never guess he's lived eight (. . . *ades*) ____ just by looking at him.

_____ conduct _____

_____ leaden _____

9–10. Superman has x-ray vision but still can't see through lead—so one criminal decided to (*con . . .*) ____ his illicit° business in a room with (*lead . . .*) ____ walls.

Final Check: *Grandpa and Music*

Here is a final opportunity for you to strengthen your knowledge of the ten word parts. First read the following selection carefully. Then complete each *italicized* word in the parentheses below with a word part from the box at the top of the previous page. (Context clues will help you figure out which word part goes in which blank.) Use each word part once.

As a younger man, my grandfather had a beautiful singing voice, and he loved to talk about his three (. . . *ades*) (1)_____ decades _____ (from age 20 until 50) as a loyal member of a group called the (*Gold . . .*) (2) "_____ Golden _____ Voices."

When the original seven members of the group heard him sing solos in his church, they invited him to join them, not realizing that he couldn't read music. He was determined not to let this be a liability°, and he worked hard to (*e . . . ate*) (3)_____ educate _____ himself about music and become a proficient° (*music . . .*) (4)_____ musician _____. He wanted to join the group for two reasons: he loved singing, and he had a crush on its lively young pianist.

After Grandfather became a member, the (. . . *et's*) (5)_____ octet's _____ success began to (. . . *pass*) (6)_____ surpass _____ all expectations. Their voices, he used to say, were so (. . . *geneous*) (7)_____ homogeneous _____ and so cohesive° that they sometimes sounded like a single voice singing all eight parts. Eventually, the group became so popular that the singers performed for pay, rather than just (. . . *unteering*) (8)_____ volunteering _____ their services. The zenith° of their musical careers, said Grandpa, came when the group was invited to perform with the (. . . *harmonic*) (9)_____ Philharmonic _____ Society; the opportunity to collaborate° with this famous orchestra made all eight singers euphoric°.

In retrospect°, though, Grandpa would always say that his own greatest success was marrying that (*vivaci . . .*) (10)_____ vivacious _____ young pianist. It's probably superfluous° to add that they made beautiful music together.

| Scores | Sentence Check 2 _____ % | Final Check _____ % |

Enter your scores above and in the **Vocabulary Performance Chart** on the inside back cover of the book.

The box at the right lists twenty-five words from Unit Four. Using the clues at the bottom of the page, fill in these words to complete the puzzle that follows.

Word box:
annihilate
atrophy
belligerent
chide
decorum
deprivation
diabolic
dissipate
emanate
espouse
extricate
holistic
indolent
inherent
integral
mitigate
nonchalant
noxious
panacea
placebo
rejuvenate
staunch
tenuous
utilitarian
yen

ACROSS

1. Made or intended for practical use
4. To free from a tangled situation or a difficulty
5. To support, argue for, or adopt (an idea or cause)
7. Correctness in behavior and manners
8. To thin out or scatter and gradually vanish; drive away
9. To destroy completely; to reduce to nothingness
11. A substance containing no medicine, which the receiver believes is a medicine
14. Quick or eager to argue or fight; hostile; aggressive
19. Lazy; avoiding work
20. To wear down, lose strength, or become weak
21. To scold mildly
22. Firm; loyal; strong in support
23. Calm, carefree, and casually unconcerned

DOWN

2. Necessary to the whole; belonging to the whole
3. To make (someone) feel or seem young again
6. To flow out; come forth
7. Lack or shortage of one or more basic necessities
10. Emphasizing the whole and the interdependence of its parts
11. Something supposed to cure all diseases or evils
12. Very cruel; wicked; demonic
13. A strong desire; craving
15. Harmful to life or health
16. To make less severe; relieve
17. Having little substance or basis; weak; poorly supported
18. Existing as a natural or essential quality of a person or thing; built-in

134

PART A

Choose the word that best completes each item and write it in the space provided.

_____diabolic_____ 1. Fairy tales, such as "Hansel and Gretel" and "Cinderella," have given stepmothers a reputation for being ___.

    A. holistic   B. diabolic   C. unassuming   D. unprecedented

_____exhilaration_____ 2. Hang-gliding produces a feeling of ___ that few other activities can match.

    A. exhilaration   B. decorum   C. connotation   D. atrophy

_____emanates_____ 3. Superstitious people believe that a cold, clammy wind ___ from the "haunted" house on Elm Street.

    A. synchronizes   B. vindicates   C. emanates   D. mitigates

_____synchronize_____ 4. To ___ their movements so well, the dancers must practice doing the steps together for hours.

    A. chide   B. extricate   C. mitigate   D. synchronize

_____decorum_____ 5. Rules of ___ change over the years. For instance, my grandmother says that a lady always wears a hat to church, but few young women do so nowadays.

    A. analogy   B. decorum   C. panacea   D. placebo

_____dilapidated_____ 6. When my sister's new boyfriend came chugging up in a(n) ___ van with no windows, my father offered to pay for a taxi.

    A. exorbitant   B. objective   C. dilapidated   D. unprecedented

_____subversive_____ 7. In order to find a ring of spies trying to learn military secrets, the government agent pretended to be involved in ___ activities.

    A. indolent   B. unilateral   C. holistic   D. subversive

_____denunciation_____ 8. After keeping her angry feelings about her brother bottled up for months, Lana finally exploded with a ___ of his irresponsible ways.

    A. yen   B. criterion   C. panacea   D. denunciation

_____annihilate_____ 9. It's amazing how I can ___ a thousand mosquitoes with bug spray, and an hour later another thousand appear.

    A. espouse   B. annihilate   C. facilitate   D. vindicate

_____noxious_____ 10. Neighbors of the chemical company became suspicious that ___ fumes were coming from the plant when several of them became mysteriously ill.

    A. utilitarian   B. unassuming   C. noxious   D. imperative

(Continues on next page)

PART B

On the answer line, write the letter of the choice that best completes each item.

_B_ 11. My mother considers baked custard a **panacea**. According to her, it
    A. is the worst-tasting thing in the world.   C. should be saved for special occasions.
    B. cures everything from flu to a broken heart.   D. tastes good, but is not good for us.

_D_ 12. A truly **unprecedented** event would be
    A. an eclipse of the sun.   C. the landing of humans on the moon.
    B. a musical as good as *West Side Story*.   D. a TV interview with an alien life form.

_A_ 13. Right after his heart attack, Alec's grip on life was so **tenuous** that his doctors
    A. did not expect him to live.   C. were amazed at his quick recovery.
    B. admired his fighting spirit.   D. realized the heart attack had been mild.

_A_ 14. When my boyfriend of two years dumped me, I wasn't surprised to hear my **staunch** friend say,
    A. "He wasn't good enough for you, anyway."   C. "Would you mind if I started dating him?"
    B. "I don't want to hear about it."   D. "It was probably your fault."

_B_ 15. "Under the word '**indolent**' in the dictionary, there should be an illustration of my cat," claimed Ari. "All day long, Tabby
    A. hunts and kills mice and insects."   C. eats as though she were starving."
    B. lies in the sun. Then she takes a nap."   D. purrs, licks my hand, and begs to be petted."

_C_ 16. Commenting on the **exorbitant** prices in the restaurant, Willy said,
    A. "No wonder the restaurant is popular—it's such a bargain!"
    B. "The prices don't make sense—why is the lobster less expensive than the spaghetti?"
    C. "A cup of soup here costs more than a full meal anywhere else!"
    D. "Nothing is cheap, but nothing is very expensive either—the prices are reasonable."

_B_ 17. Wanting to **assimilate** to life in Mexico, Brenda
    A. arranged to return to the United States.
    B. enrolled in intensive Spanish classes, ate Mexican food, and made Mexican friends.
    C. bought lots of souvenirs to send to her friends in the United States.
    D. rented an apartment in an American community where she could speak only English.

_B_ 18. When Brett asked Rhonda for a date, this was her **nonchalant** response:
    A. "No, Brett, I do not want to go out with you. Not today, not tomorrow, not ever."
    B. "OK, that sounds good."
    C. "I . . . well . . . I'm just not sure . . . I might have other plans . . . can I get back to you later?"
    D. "Oh, wow, that'd really be great! I'm so excited—I can't wait!"

_C_ 19. Because Ben and Susan had asked for **utilitarian** wedding gifts, a group of friends bought them
    A. whoopee cushions, rubber chickens, and fake spiders dangling from long threads.
    B. silk bedsheets, French champagne, and Russian caviar.
    C. a set of dishes and silverware.
    D. dozens of roses to decorate their apartment.

_D_ 20. After the terrorist attacks of September 11, 2001, the United States formed a **coalition** of
    A. American flags displayed on streets, in front of homes, and in the windows of businesses.
    B. photographs of the thousands of people who had been killed.
    C. promises to find and punish those who were responsible for the attacks.
    D. countries that agreed to join with the United States in its battle against terrorism.

Score   (Number correct) _____ x 5 = _____%

PART A

Complete each item with a word from the box. Use each word once.

A. **atrophy**	B. **belligerent**	C. **connotation**	D. **criterion**	E. **deplore**
F. **deprivation**	G. **extricate**	H. **inherent**	I. **objective**	J. **placebo**
K. **rejuvenate**	L. **scenario**	M. **unilateral**		

inherent   1. Danger is a(n) ___ part of police work.

objective   2. Judging people by their appearance makes it difficult to be ___ about their personalities.

criterion   3. One ___ I use in selecting clothing is that an item be made out of a comfortable fabric.

deprivation   4. After Chrissy stayed awake studying for seventy-two hours, sleep ___ caused her to start having double vision and to hear voices that weren't there.

extricate   5. The little boy's foot was so firmly caught in the folding chair that it took three adults to ___ him.

rejuvenate   6. My mother was feeling twice her age before her trip to Arizona, but the relaxing vacation really ___(e)d her.

deplore   7. Although I ___ the conditions that face children born to drug addicts, I don't know what to do to help.

atrophy   8. The day after surgery, the nurses got Alonso out of bed and walking, so that his muscles would not begin to ___.

scenario   9. To make his case to the jury, the lawyer went through a possible ___ of the events leading up to the murder.

unilateral   10. Neither Jessie nor Mel would make a(n) ___ move to end their feud, so the silence between them continued.

belligerent   11. When I bumped the car in front of me as I was parking, the other driver emerged and stormed toward me in a most ___ manner.

connotation   12. The dictionary definition of home is "a place in which one lives," but for many people the word has ___s of comfort and family.

placebo   13. When little Sarah couldn't sleep, her mother gave her a ___ and called it a "magic sleeping potion." It was a glass of milk tinted red with food coloring.

(Continues on next page)

PART B

Write **C** if the italicized word is used **correctly**. Write **I** if the word is used **incorrectly**.

___I___ 14. I have such a *yen* for meatloaf that whenever it's served, I leave the table immediately.

___C___ 15. A genuine affection for young people is an *integral* part of being a successful teacher.

___C___ 16. It is *imperative* that my mother get her cholesterol level down, as she is now at high risk of a heart attack.

___I___ 17. Nadia's ankle injury is severe, but the doctor told her a couple of days of bed rest will *exacerbate* the sprain enough so that she can walk again.

___I___ 18. It was bad enough being grounded, but my father is going to *mitigate* my punishment by stopping my allowance.

___C___ 19. The defendant, accused of murder, proclaimed his innocence and was *vindicated* when a man who looked just like him confessed.

PART C

On the answer line, write the letter of the word that is the **synonym** of the boldfaced word.

Example: ___B___ **utilitarian**   A. useless   B. practical   C. late

___C___ 20. **chide**   A. avoid   B. praise   C. scold

___A___ 21. **proficient**   A. expert   B. unskilled   C. famous

___A___ 22. **orthodox**   A. traditional   B. thoughtful   C. radical

PART D

On the answer line, write the letter of the word that is the **antonym** of the boldfaced word.

Example: ___A___ **utilitarian**   A. useless   B. practical   C. late

___C___ 23. **analogy**   A. solution   B. similarity   C. difference

___B___ 24. **unassuming**   A. humble   B. boastful   C. curious

___B___ 25. **dissipate**   A. scatter   B. gather   C. exclude

Score   (Number correct) _____ x 4 = _____%

Enter your scores above and in the **Vocabulary Performance Chart** on the inside back cover of the book.

Each item below starts with a pair of words in CAPITAL LETTERS. For each item, figure out the relationship between these two words. Then decide which of the choices (A, B, C, or D) expresses a similar relationship. Write the letter of your choice on the answer line.

D   1. CHIDE : CARELESS STUDENT ::
     A. praise : kidnapper   C. respect : thief
     B. reward : money   D. promote : hardworking employee

C   2. COMMENSURATE : APPROPRIATE ::
     A. complex : simple   C. confidential : secret
     B. compatible : unsuitable   D. conscious : asleep

B   3. NOXIOUS : APPLE ::
     A. poisonous : arsenic   C. sweet : watermelon
     B. fattening : tea   D. sour : lemon

A   4. SCENARIO : MOVIE ::
     A. outline : essay   C. cover : book
     B. closing : play   D. grade : test

D   5. DEPLORE : SIN ::
     A. praise : crime   C. forget : forgiveness
     B. foretell : predict   D. seek : wisdom

C   6. OBJECTIVE : JUDGE ::
     A. treacherous : jury   C. knowledgeable : teacher
     B. sluggish : rock group   D. obedient : parent

C   7. UTILITARIAN : FRYING PAN ::
     A. useless : doorway   C. decorative : wallpaper
     B. electrical : water pipes   D. portable : foundation

B   8. UNPRECEDENTED : FAMILIAR ::
     A. injurious : accidental   C. abundant : plentiful
     B. horrible : pleasant   D. questioning : curious

D   9. EXHILARATION : WALKING ON AIR ::
     A. anxiety : being cool as a cucumber   C. ambitious : drifting along
     B. weariness : being fresh as a daisy   D. depression : being down in the dumps

C   10. ESPOUSE : DENOUNCE ::
     A. dislike : enemies   C. complain : praise
     B. study : learn   D. distrust : doubt

(Continues on next page)

_A_ 11. INHERENT : ACQUIRED ::
   A. instinctive : learned
   B. learned : remembered
   C. reluctant : unwilling
   D. desired : lost

_A_ 12. FACILITATE : MAKE EASIER ::
   A. postpone : delay
   B. speak : speech
   C. exaggerate : understate
   D. fence : post

_C_ 13. BELLIGERENT : PEACEFUL ::
   A. hostile : angry
   B. frail : weak
   C. powerful : feeble
   D. warlike : aggressive

_A_ 14. DEMEANOR : CALM ::
   A. hair : red
   B. height : weight
   C. eyes : glasses
   D. fingers : hand

_B_ 15. INDOLENT : LAZYBONES ::
   A. good-natured : sorehead
   B. boastful : showoff
   C. soft-spoken : loudmouth
   D. shy : backslapper

_C_ 16. EXTRICATE : FREE ::
   A. read : write
   B. add : subtract
   C. pledge : promise
   D. ignore : celebrate

_B_ 17. ANALOGY : COMPARISON ::
   A. anatomy : music
   B. anthology : collection
   C. astronomy : medicine
   D. anonymity : fame

_C_ 18. HOLISTIC : WHOLE ::
   A. skeptical : positive
   B. physical : mental
   C. fragmentary : part
   D. weekly : monthly

_D_ 19. PLACEBO : SUGAR PILL ::
   A. health : vitamins
   B. prescription : subscription
   C. leaf : lettuce
   D. dwelling : igloo

_B_ 20. PROFICIENT : INCAPABLE ::
   A. talented : artistic
   B. fake : genuine
   C. immaculate : reputation
   D. perceptive : observer

Score   (Number correct) _____ x 5 = _____%

Enter your scores above and in the **Vocabulary Performance Chart** on the inside back cover of the book.

PART A

Listed in the left-hand column below are ten common word parts, followed by words in which the parts are used. In each blank, write in the letter of the correct definition on the right.

	Word Parts	Examples	Definitions
D	1. **-cian, -ian**	politician, librarian	A. Loving; lover; friend
I	2. **dec-**	decathlon, decimal	B. Eight
E	3. **duc, duct**	ducal, conduct	C. Having; full of; characterized by
J	4. **-en**	woolen, golden	D. A person with a certain ability or a certain kind of knowledge
H	5. **homo-**	homogeneous, homosexual	E. To lead; guide; draw off
B	6. **oct-, octo-**	octagon, octopus	F. Over; above; additional
C	7. **-ous**	famous, serious	G. To will; choose
A	8. **phil, -phile**	Philadelphia, Anglophile	H. Same; similar
F	9. **sur-**	surface, surplus	I. Ten
G	10. **vol**	volunteer, voluntary	J. Made of

PART B

Using the answer line provided, complete each *italicized* word in the sentences below with the correct word part from the box. Not every word part will be used.

A. **-cian**	B. **dec-**	C. **duct**	D. **-en**	E. **homo-**
F. **octo-**	G. **-ous**	H. **-phile**	I. **sur-**	J. **vol**

_____homonym_____ 11. To explain to my brother what a (. . . *nym*) ___ is, I gave him a demonstration. "Look, David. I just ate the *whole* doughnut. I didn't leave even the *hole* for you."

_____December_____ 12. In the ancient Roman calendar, (. . . *ember*) ___ was the tenth month.

_____conductor_____ 13. The (*con . . . or*) ___ led the orchestra in a lively encore.

_____morticians_____ 14. In addition to technical knowledge, (*morti . . . s*) ___ must know how to be sympathetic and comforting.

_____ridiculous_____ 15. When a new calendar system was adopted in England in 1752, many people felt it was (*ridicul . . .*) ___ that the day after September 2 was suddenly September 14.

(Continues on next page)

PART C

Use your knowledge of word parts to determine the meaning of the **boldfaced** words. On the answer line, write the letter of each meaning.

___A___ 16. That brilliant two-year-old just played a scale, a straight **octave**, on the piano.

      A. an eight-note scale   B. a three-note scale   C. a ten-note scale

___B___ 17. We all ate a **surfeit** of food at Thanksgiving dinner.

      A. what we chose   B. an excess   C. less than usual

___A___ 18. José carried the water in an old **oaken** bucket.

      A. made of oak   B. broken   C. large

___C___ 19. Ever since visiting Germany, Carl has been a real **Germanophile**.

      A. a student of Germany   B. an expert on Germany   C. an admirer of Germany

___B___ 20. Pauline cleaned the entire apartment yesterday. She did it of her own **volition**.

      A. with her own supplies   B. by choice   C. on her day off

Score	(Number correct) _____ x 5 = _____ %

Enter your scores above and in the **Vocabulary Performance Chart** on the inside back cover of the book.

Unit Five

disparity	obsequious
forestall	omnipotent
insidious	opportune
insinuate	permeate
interrogate	retribution

Ten Words in Context

In the space provided, write the letter of the meaning closest to that of each **boldfaced** word. Use the context of the sentences to help you figure out each word's meaning.

1 disparity
(dĭ-spăr′ə-tē)
-noun

- There's an enormous **disparity** between the multi-million-dollar incomes of top executives and the modest paychecks most people earn.
- Shirley and Jason don't let the **disparity** in their ages weaken their marriage, but Jason's mother isn't happy with a daughter-in-law her own age.

<u>B</u> *Disparity* means   A. a combination.   B. a contrast.   C. a closeness.

2 forestall
(fôr-stôl′)
-verb

- The owners of the failing store hoped that the huge sale would bring in enough cash to **forestall** bankruptcy.
- When the environmentalists were unable to **forestall** the destruction of the forest by legal means, they lay down in front of the developer's bulldozers.

<u>A</u> *Forestall* means   A. to keep from happening.   B. to predict.   C. to pay for.

3 insidious
(ĭn-sĭd′ē-əs)
-adjective

- Lyme disease is **insidious** because although it is very serious, it starts with a nearly invisible tick bite, and its early symptoms are mild.
- Many people fear that farm chemicals have **insidious** effects. The chemicals don't seem harmful, but cancer rates have started to increase.

<u>B</u> *Insidious* means   A. badly timed.   B. subtly harmful.   C. all-powerful.

4 insinuate
(ĭn-sĭn′yōō-āt′)
-verb

- He didn't come right out and say it, but Mr. Shriber **insinuated** that someone in the class had gotten hold of the test ahead of time.
- "You always find time to help Sandy with her homework," my sister said to me, as if to **insinuate** that I was flirting with Sandy.

<u>A</u> *Insinuate* means   A. to hint.   B. to wish.   C. to state directly.

5 interrogate
(ĭn-tĕr′ə-gāt′)
-verb

- Before the police **interrogated** the suspect, they informed him of his right not to answer their questions.
- "You never just ask me if I had a nice time with my date," Tyrell complained to his parents. "Instead, you sit me down at the kitchen table and **interrogate** me."

<u>A</u> *Interrogate* means   A. to ask questions.   B. to delay.   C. to abuse.

6 obsequious
(ŏb-sē′kwē-əs)
-adjective

- Each of the queen's advisers tried to be more **obsequious** than the others, bowing as low as possible and uttering flowery compliments.
- Marge constantly flatters the boss, calls him "sir," and agrees loudly with everything he says. However, her **obsequious** behavior only annoys him.

<u>B</u> *Obsequious* means   A. unequal in rank.   B. overly eager to please.   C. methodical.

144

7 omnipotent
(ŏm-nĭp′ə-tənt)
-*adjective*

● Small children think of their parents as **omnipotent**—able to do anything, control everything, and grant whatever a child might wish for.

● The American government is designed so that no one branch can be **omnipotent**. Congress, the President, and the Supreme Court share power and hold each other in check.

_C_ *Omnipotent* means   A. totally good.   B. willing to serve.   C. all-powerful.

8 opportune
(ŏp′ər-tōon′)
-*adjective*

● Althea thought that her parents' anniversary would be an **opportune** time to announce her own engagement. They could have a double celebration.

● The job offer came at an especially **opportune** time. I had just decided that I might like to work for a year or so before returning to school.

_A_ *Opportune* means   A. appropriate.   B. difficult.   C. early.

9 permeate
(pûr′mē-āt′)
-*verb*

● The strong scent of Kate's perfume soon **permeated** the entire room.

● The weather was so rainy and damp that moisture seemed to **permeate** everything: curtains hung limply, towels wouldn't dry, and windows were fogged over.

_B_ *Permeate* means   A. to harm.   B. to penetrate.   C. to make unclear.

10 retribution
(rĕ′trə-byōo′shən)
-*noun*

● Some "sins" in life have their own built-in **retribution**. For example, if you get drunk, you'll have a hangover; if you overeat, you'll gain weight.

● For much of human history, before science could explain diseases, many people believed that any illness was a **retribution** for immoral behavior.

_C_ *Retribution* means   A. an inequality.   B. an obstacle.   C. a penalty.

Matching Words with Definitions

Following are definitions of the ten words. Clearly write or print each word next to its definition. The sentences above and on the previous page will help you decide on the meaning of each word.

1. ___obsequious___   Overly willing to serve, obey, or flatter in order to gain favor

2. ___insinuate___   To suggest slyly

3. ___retribution___   Something given or done as repayment, reward, or (usually) punishment

4. ___disparity___   An inequality or difference, as in ages or amounts

5. ___insidious___   Working or spreading harmfully but in a manner hard to notice; more harmful than is evident at first

6. ___permeate___   To flow or spread throughout (something)

7. ___opportune___   Suitable (said of time); well-timed

8. ___forestall___   To prevent or hinder by taking action beforehand

9. ___omnipotent___   All-powerful; having unlimited power or authority

10. ___interrogate___   To question formally and systematically

CAUTION: Do not go any further until you are sure the above answers are correct. Then you can use the definitions to help you in the following practices. Your goal is eventually to know the words well enough so that you don't need to check the definitions at all.

Sentence Check 1

Using the answer line provided, complete each item below with the correct word from the box. Use each word once.

A. **disparity**	B. **forestall**	C. **insidious**	D. **insinuate**	E. **interrogate**
F. **obsequious**	G. **omnipotent**	H. **opportune**	I. **permeate**	J. **retribution**

permeate   1. When our dog was sprayed by a skunk, the smell soon ___(e)d the house.

forestall   2. To ___ complaints about unrepaired potholes, the township set up a "pothole hotline" and promised to fill in any reported hole within two days.

opportune   3. Because no one else's hand was raised, I considered it a(n) ___ moment to ask a question.

interrogate   4. In many countries, political prisoners who are being ___(e)d by the secret police are likely to be tortured in an attempt to force answers from them.

retribution   5. When the Earl of Essex plotted against his queen, Elizabeth I of England, ___ was swift and harsh: she had him beheaded for treason.

disparity   6. "There seems to be quite a ___," Shannon objected to the car dealer, "between your cost and the sticker price."

insidious   7. The effects of certain prescription drugs, such as Valium, can be ___. People who take them may slip into addiction without being aware of it.

omnipotent   8. According to legend, King Canute—an ancient ruler of England, Denmark, and Norway—thought he was ___. He actually ordered the tide to stop rising.

insinuate   9. Instead of directly saying "Buy our product," many ads use slick images to ___ that the product will give the buyer sex appeal, power, or prestige.

obsequious   10. The headwaiter's manner toward customers who looked rich was ___. Ignoring the rest of us, he gave them the restaurant's best tables and hovered over them, all smiles.

NOTE: Now check your answers to these items by turning to page 179. Going over the answers carefully will help you prepare for the next two practices, for which answers are not given.

Sentence Check 2

Using the answer lines provided, complete each item below with **two** words from the box. Use each word once.

disparity
insinuate   1–2. The wide ___ between men's and women's pay in the company led to a protest by the women. The management tried to squelch° the protest and ___(e)d that the women were subversive° and were trying to ruin company morale.

insidious
permeate   3–4. The noxious° chemical spray used to eradicate° tentworms had ___ effects: after killing the worms, it gradually seeped down, ___(e)d the soil, and poisoned Duck Lake.

retribution

opportune

5–6. The ex-convict was filled with rancor°. As ___ for his years in prison, he planned to attack, at the first ___ moment, the judge who had sentenced him.

omnipotent

forestall

7–8. The remote control of my DVD player makes me feel ___. I can ___ any imminent° disaster—a fire, a flood, an earthquake, a sordid° crime—by pressing a button and stopping the movie dead.

interrogate

obsequious

9–10. In a job interview, use discretion°. Don't react as though you're being ___(e)d by the police; but don't be ___ either, as if the interviewer were a king or queen and you were a humble servant.

Final Check: My Devilish Older Sister

Here is a final opportunity for you to strengthen your knowledge of the ten words. First read the following selection carefully. Then fill in each blank with a word from the box at the top of the previous page. (Context clues will help you figure out which word goes in which blank.) Use each word once.

Anyone who thinks older sisters protect younger ones has never heard me tell about my sister Pam. There's no great (1)_____disparity_____ in our ages—Pam is only three years older—but throughout our childhood she was always able to beat me at cards, at jacks, at all board games. This seemingly unlimited power to win made me think of her as (2)_____omnipotent_____. I obeyed all her orders ("Relinquish° that lollipop!") and accepted all her insults ("You're grotesque°!" "You're positively repugnant°!") in the most timid, (3)_____obsequious_____ manner. Privately, I longed for revenge.

When Pam made up her mind to tease or trick me, there was nothing I could do to (4)_____forestall_____ her plans. And she never missed a(n) (5)_____opportune_____ moment to terrorize me. When our old dog growled, for no reason, at the empty air, she would (6)_____insinuate_____ that evil spirits must have (7)_____permeate_____(e)d the atmosphere, saying, "Dogs, you know, can sense the supernatural." Once I made the mistake of revealing that crabs terrified me. After that, I was inundated° with photos of crabs, drawings of crabs, even labels from cans of crabmeat. In retrospect°, though, her most diabolic° trick was giving me some "chocolate candy" that I impetuously° gobbled up. It turned out to be Ex-Lax. After that, if Pam offered me anything, no matter how innocuous° it looked, I always (8)_____interrogate_____(e)d her: "What is it really? Do you still have the wrapping? Will you take a bite first?" But this episode also had a more (9)_____insidious_____ effect: for years, I was afraid of new foods.

Now that we're grown, Pam has greatly improved. She no longer likes to torment me, and she even seems contrite° about the past. However, I still sometimes think up various scenarios° of (10)_____retribution_____ in which I am the older sister, and at last I get my revenge.

Scores	Sentence Check 2 _____ %	Final Check _____ %

Enter your scores above and in the **Vocabulary Performance Chart** on the inside back cover of the book.

complement	implement
discreet	impromptu
fastidious	inference
flout	intuition
heinous	obtrusive

Ten Words in Context

In the space provided, write the letter of the meaning closest to that of each **boldfaced** word. Use the context of the sentences to help you figure out each word's meaning.

1 complement
(kŏm′plə-mənt)
-verb

● The new singer's voice **complemented** the other voices, rounding out the group's sound.

● A red tie would **complement** Pedro's gray suit and white shirt, giving the outfit a needed touch of color.

_A_ _Complement_ means   A. to go perfectly with.   B. to reach out for.   C. to overpower.

2 discreet
(dĭ-skrēt′)
-adjective

● Once the teacher realized Jared could not read well, she made discreet efforts to give him extra help. She didn't want to embarrass him in front of his classmates.

● "Be **discreet** about these drawings, Wilson," the boss said. "Don't show them to just anyone. We don't want another company stealing our designs."

_B_ _Discreet_ means   A. honest.   B. cautious.   C. obvious.

3 fastidious
(făs-tĭd′ē-əs)
-adjective

● Tilly was a **fastidious** housekeeper who vacuumed every day, dusted twice a day, and never allowed so much as a pencil or safety pin to be out of place.

● A **fastidious** dresser, Mr. Lapp never leaves his home without looking as if he has just stepped out of a fashion magazine.

_C_ _Fastidious_ means   A. working quickly.   B. having insight.   C. very particular.

4 flout
(flout)
-verb

● My neighbors were evicted from their apartment because they **flouted** the building's rules. They threw trash in the hallway, had loud all-night parties, and just laughed at anyone who complained.

● The men in the warehouse are **flouting** regulations about eating on the job. Wastebaskets are filled with sandwich wrappers and empty chip, pretzel, and nacho bags.

_A_ _Flout_ means   A. to mock and defy.   B. to put into effect.   C. to show off.

5 heinous
(hā′nəs)
-adjective

● The child murderer's final **heinous** act was taunting the victim's father as the guilty verdict was announced.

● Millions of people were shocked recently by news reports of a **heinous** act: a woman had locked her little daughter in the basement and starved her to death.

_A_ _Heinous_ means   A. wicked.   B. unplanned.   C. detailed.

6 implement
(ĭm′plə-měnt′)
-verb

● NASA expects to **implement** a plan to return astronauts to the moon by 2020.

● Brett is full of ideas about starting his own business, but he never follows through and **implements** them.

_B_ _Implement_ means   A. to recall.   B. to put into effect.   C. to criticize.

7 impromptu
(ĭm-prŏmp′tōō′)
-*adjective*

- My speech at my cousin's birthday dinner was **impromptu**; I hadn't expected to be called on to say anything.
- When Maya discovered that she and Barry had both brought guitars to the party, she suggested an **impromptu** duet.

<u>A</u> *Impromptu* means   A. not rehearsed.   B. not very good.   C. very quiet.

8 inference
(ĭn′fər-əns)
-*noun*

- Ruby said with a wink, "Did you notice how Uncle Joe's hair has miraculously grown back?" My **inference** was that he was wearing a toupee.
- "Where did you buy these pork chops?" asked Harry. "Why? What's wrong with them?" Maria asked, making the **inference** that he didn't like them.

<u>B</u> *Inference* means   A. a statement.   B. a conclusion.   C. a secret.

9 intuition
(ĭn′tōō-ĭsh′ən)
-*noun*

- "I paint by **intuition**," the artist said. "In a flash, I see how a work should look. I don't really think it out."
- "The minute I met your mother," my father said, "my **intuition** told me that we'd get married someday."

<u>C</u> *Intuition* means   A. careful study.   B. memory.   C. instinct.

10 obtrusive
(ŏb-trōō′sĭv)
-*adjective*

- The huge, sprawling new mall seemed **obtrusive** in the quiet little country town.
- My brother's stutter is often hardly noticeable, but when he is nervous or in a hurry, it can become **obtrusive**.

<u>A</u> *Obtrusive* means   A. overly obvious.   B. unplanned.   C. greatly improved.

Matching Words with Definitions

Following are definitions of the ten words. Clearly write or print each word next to its definition. The sentences above and on the previous page will help you decide on the meaning of each word.

1. _____flout_____ To treat with scorn or contempt; defy insultingly

2. _____intuition_____ Instinctive knowledge; hunch

3. _____implement_____ To carry out; put into practice

4. _____obtrusive_____ Undesirably noticeable

5. _____discreet_____ Wise in keeping silent about secrets and other information of a delicate nature; prudent; tactful

6. _____impromptu_____ Performed or spoken without practice or preparation

7. _____heinous_____ Extremely evil; outrageous

8. _____inference_____ A conclusion drawn from evidence; an assumption

9. _____complement_____ To add (to something or someone) what is lacking or needed; round out; bring to perfection

10. _____fastidious_____ Extremely attentive to details; fussy

CAUTION: Do not go any further until you are sure the above answers are correct. Then you can use the definitions to help you in the following practices. Your goal is eventually to know the words well enough so that you don't need to check the definitions at all.

Sentence Check 1

Using the answer line provided, complete each item below with the correct word from the box. Use each word once.

A. complement	B. discreet	C. fastidious	D. flout	E. heinous
F. implement	G. impromptu	H. inference	I. intuition	J. obtrusive

intuition   1. Rachel's ___ told her not to date a man who kept tropical fish in his bathtub.

flout   2. After Rudy ___(e)d his 11 p.m. curfew—breezing in at 2 a.m. with a cheerful "Hi, folks!"—his parents took away his car keys for a month.

heinous   3. In the American system of justice, anyone charged with a crime, no matter how ___ the offense, is entitled to be defended by a lawyer.

impromptu   4. The ___ press conference turned out to be a bad idea. The senator should have planned his remarks beforehand.

discreet   5. "Loose lips sink ships" was a famous World War II slogan. It warned Americans to be ___ and not say anything that might reveal military plans.

implement   6. To ___ their plan for a surprise attack on the girls' club, the boys needed squirt guns and a gallon of grape juice.

fastidious   7. The writer Ernest Hemingway had a "tough guy" image but was ___ about using words; he rewrote the ending of one novel forty-four times.

complement   8. Wendy is an excellent hair stylist, because she doesn't just cut hair. She also advises her customers about which hairstyle will ___ their features.

inference   9. Alicia signed her card to Manuel "Warm regards." Manuel's ___ was that she meant "I feel *only* warm regards, not love."

obtrusive   10. The new partition between the restaurant's smoking and nonsmoking sections looks ___. Some plants or flowers might help it blend in better.

NOTE: Now check your answers to these items by turning to page 179. Going over the answers carefully will help you prepare for the next two practices, for which answers are not given.

Sentence Check 2

Using the answer lines provided, complete each item below with **two** words from the box. Use each word once.

intuition
fastidious
1–2. Although Anne is one of my best friends, my ___ tells me we would not be good roommates. She's so ___ that she irons her bedsheets, while I'm notorious° for giving my apartment sporadic° cleanings—like once a year.

complement
impromptu
3–4. The dark, rumbling voice of the bass ___(e)d the high, sweet tones of the soprano as they sang a(n) ___ but flawless duet. Having just met, they were surprised and delighted at how good they sounded together.

discreet
inference
5–6. What Kay actually said was, "It would be ___ not to discuss the missing funds in front of Debra." But she meant us to make this ___: "I think she stole them."

_____ implement _____   7–8. Connoisseurs° of science fiction love one movie in which evil alien invaders
_____ heinous _____   decide to annihilate° all life on Earth. The aliens ___ this ___ plan by
                                       constructing a "space shield" that cuts off all sunlight.

_____ flout _____   9–10. There seems to be a conspiracy° to ___ the rule, "No sidewalk vendors on
_____ obtrusive _____   government property." The vendors have set up their stands in an ___ spot—
                                       right in front of City Hall.

Final Check: *Harriet Tubman*

Here is a final opportunity for you to strengthen your knowledge of the ten words. First read the following selection carefully. Then fill in each blank with a word from the box at the top of the previous page. (Context clues will help you figure out which word goes in which blank.) Use each word once.

In 1849 Harriet Tubman—then in her late twenties—fled from the (1)_____ heinous _____ brutality she had endured as a slave. Aware that a lone black woman would be a(n) (2)_____ obtrusive _____ figure among ordinary travelers, she traveled on foot and only at night, over hundreds of miles, to reach Pennsylvania. There, for the first time in her life, she was free, but her parents, brothers, and sisters remained behind in Maryland, still slaves. Harriet decided to go back for them—and, over the next ten years, for many more.

Harriet had several qualities that (3)_____ complement _____(e)d each other and facilitated° her mission. First, because she was knowledgeable and had good (4)_____ intuition _____, she could always sense when an opportune° time for an escape had arrived, and who could and couldn't be trusted. Second, she was (5)_____ fastidious _____ about planning; she always worked out a plan to the last detail before she (6)_____ implement _____(e)d it. Third, she was flexible, capable of taking (7)_____ impromptu _____ action if an unexpected problem arose. Time and again, when a disaster seemed imminent°, she was able to forestall° it. For instance, when she learned that slave-hunters had posted a description of a runaway man, she disguised him as a woman. When the slave-hunters turned up at a railroad station, she fooled them by having the runaways board a southbound train instead of a northbound one. Fourth, she was (8)_____ discreet _____ about her plans. She knew how important it was to be reticent°, since anyone might be a spy. Often, her instructions about where and when to meet were not actually stated, but were (9)_____ inference _____ s in the songs and Bible stories she used, familiar to those waiting to escape. Fifth, she was physically strong, able to endure extended periods of deprivation°; she could go for a long time without food, shelter, or rest.

Harriet Tubman (10)_____ flout _____(e)d the unjust laws of an evil system, but she was never captured, and she never lost a single runaway. She led more slaves to freedom than any other individual—over three hundred—and her name is venerated° to this day.

Scores	Sentence Check 2 _____%	Final Check _____%

Enter your scores above and in the **Vocabulary Performance Chart** on the inside back cover of the book.

auspicious	rebuke
expedite	redeem
extenuating	subordinate
fraudulent	transgress
innuendo	vehement

Ten Words in Context

In the space provided, write the letter of the meaning closest to that of each **boldfaced** word. Use the context of the sentences to help you figure out each word's meaning.

1 auspicious
(ô-spĭsh′əs)
-adjective

● The beginning of the semester was **auspicious** for Liza; she got an A on the first quiz and saw this as a promise of more good grades to come.

● Jen and Robert's marriage plans did not get off to an **auspicious** start. They couldn't agree on what kind of ceremony they wanted or which guests to invite.

_C_ *Auspicious* means   A. deceptive.   B. indirect.   C. favorable.

2 expedite
(ĕks′pə-dīt′)
-verb

● Express lanes in supermarkets **expedite** the checkout process for shoppers who buy only a few items.

● To **expedite** payment on an insurance claim, be sure to include all the necessary information on the form before mailing it in.

_A_ *Expedite* means   A. to hurry up.   B. to reduce the cost of.   C. to delay.

3 extenuating
(ĕk-stĕn′yoō-ā′tĭng)
-adjective

● I know I promised to come to the surprise party, but there were **extenuating** circumstances: my car broke down.

● When my father had a heart attack, I missed a final exam. Due to the **extenuating** circumstances, the professor agreed to let me take a makeup exam.

_A_ *Extenuating* means   A. providing a good excuse.   B. assigning blame.   C. encouraging.

4 fraudulent
(frô′jə-lənt)
-adjective

● Leroy was jailed for filing **fraudulent** income tax returns. He had been cheating the government for years.

● The art dealer was involved in a **fraudulent** scheme to pass off worthless forgeries as valuable old paintings.

_B_ *Fraudulent* means   A. inferior.   B. dishonest.   C. careless.

5 innuendo
(ĭn′yoō-ĕn′dō)
-noun

● People weren't willing to say directly that the mayor had taken a bribe, but there were many **innuendos** such as "Someone must have gotten to him."

● When Neil said, "Emily's home sick. Again," he was using an **innuendo**. He really meant that she was just taking another day off.

_C_ *Innuendo* means   A. a sharp scolding.   B. an obvious lie.   C. a suggestion.

6 rebuke
(rĭ-byoōk′)
-verb

● When the puppy chews the furniture, don't hit him; instead, **rebuke** him in a harsh voice.

● Although my father scolded me many times in private, I'm grateful that he never **rebuked** me in public.

_A_ *Rebuke* means   A. to criticize.   B. to make excuses for.   C. to hit.

7 redeem
(rǐ-dēm')
-verb

- Tuan's parents were angry with him for neglecting his chores, but he **redeemed** himself by washing and waxing their car.
- Cal was suspended from the basketball team because of his low grades, but he **redeemed** himself the next semester by earning a B average.

B *Redeem* means   A. to reveal.   B. to make up for past errors.   C. to punish.

8 subordinate
(sə-bôr'də-nĭt)
-adjective

- As a waiter, I take orders from the headwaiter, and he's **subordinate** to the manager of the restaurant.
- The federal District Courts are lower than the United States Court of Appeals, which in turn is **subordinate** to the Supreme Court.

A *Subordinate to* means   A. lower than.   B. a substitute for.   C. superior to.

9 transgress
(trăns-grĕs')
-verb

- Adam **transgressed** by eating an apple Eve gave him; God punished them both.
- Kianna knew she had **transgressed** against family wishes when she sold the ring her grandmother had given her.

C *Transgress* means   A. to benefit.   B. to tell a lie.   C. to commit an offense.

10 vehement
(vē'ə-mənt)
-adjective

- I knew my parents would not be happy about my plan to take a year off from school, but I didn't expect their objections to be so **vehement**.
- When Nell's boyfriend angrily grabbed her, she responded with **vehement** fury. Yelling "That's the last time you'll ever touch me!" she walked out on him.

A *Vehement* means   A. strong.   B. secret.   C. unjustified.

Matching Words with Definitions

Following are definitions of the ten words. Clearly write or print each word next to its definition. The sentences above and on the previous page will help you decide on the meaning of each word.

1. innuendo   An indirect remark or gesture, usually suggesting something belittling or improper; an insinuation; a hint

2. expedite   To speed up or ease the progress of; make easier

3. rebuke   To scold sharply; express blame or disapproval

4. vehement   Intense; forceful

5. fraudulent   Characterized by trickery, cheating, or lies

6. auspicious   Being a good sign; favorable; encouraging

7. extenuating   Serving to make (a fault, an offense, or guilt) less serious or seem less serious through some excuse

8. transgress   To sin or commit an offense; break a law or command

9. subordinate   Under the authority or power of another; inferior or below another in rank, power, or importance

10. redeem   To restore (oneself) to favor by making up for offensive conduct; make amends

CAUTION: Do not go any further until you are sure the above answers are correct. Then you can use the definitions to help you in the following practices. Your goal is eventually to know the words well enough so that you don't need to check the definitions at all.

Sentence Check 1

Using the answer line provided, complete each item below with the correct word from the box. Use each word once.

A. **auspicious**	B. **expedite**	C. **extenuating**	D. **fraudulent**	E. **innuendo**
F. **rebuke**	G. **redeem**	H. **subordinate**	I. **transgress**	J. **vehement**

subordinate   1. The company president is ___ only to the board of directors. She takes orders from the board, and only the board can fire her.

transgress   2. When young children ___, they may lie to cover up their misdeeds.

fraudulent   3. If you get a phone call announcing that you've won a free car or free trip in some contest you've never heard of, watch out. It's probably ___.

expedite   4. To ___ the registration process, fill out all the forms before you get in line.

redeem   5. After showing up late for the fund-raising dinner and then falling asleep during the speeches, the politician tried to ___ himself with a public apology.

auspicious   6. According to tradition, it's ___ if March "comes in like a lion" with stormy weather, because it will then "go out like a lamb."

vehement   7. Edna was ___ in her opposition to the proposed budget cuts. She let everyone in the department know just how strongly she felt.

rebuke   8. Later, Edna's supervisor ___(e)d her, saying, "No one asked for your opinion about the budget, so just get on with your work."

innuendo   9. The friendly weekly poker game grew less friendly when Travis said, "Isn't it amazing that, week after week, Bill always wins?" The ___, of course, was that Bill was cheating.

extenuating   10. "Yes, my client robbed the bank," the lawyer said, "but there were ___ circumstances. She didn't have time to wait in line to make a withdrawal."

NOTE: Now check your answers to these items by turning to page 179. Going over the answers carefully will help you prepare for the next two practices, for which answers are not given.

Sentence Check 2

Using the answer lines provided, complete each item below with **two** words from the box. Use each word once.

transgress
redeem   1–2. Reuben certainly ___(e)d against decorum° when he showed up at his sister's wedding in jeans. Later, he tried to ___ himself by giving the newlyweds an ostentatious° present.

rebuke
fraudulent   3–4. First the judge ___(e)d the charlatans° for "violating the public trust." Then he fined them thousands of dollars for engaging in ___ advertising.

auspicious
extenuating   5–6. The tour did not get off to a(n) ___ start—the singer missed the first concert. But there was a(n) ___ reason: he had developed bronchitis, and trying to sing would have exacerbated° the infection.

_____ vehement _____

_____ subordinate _____

7–8. The owner of that company is ___ in his insistence that managers implement° a plan to communicate better with workers in ___ positions.

_____ innuendo _____

_____ expedite _____

9–10. The restaurant critic wrote, "Those customers who are oblivious° to the headwaiter's outstretched hand will have an overly long wait to be seated." Her ___ implied that customers could ___ getting a table only by slipping the headwaiter some money.

Final Check: *Tony's Rehabilitation*

Here is a final opportunity for you to strengthen your knowledge of the ten words. First read the following selection carefully. Then fill in each blank with a word from the box at the top of the previous page. (Context clues will help you figure out which word goes in which blank.) Use each word once.

When he was 18, Tony was arrested for possessing a small amount of cocaine. Instead of panicking, he was nonchalant°. He didn't think of himself as having (1)____transgress____(e)d; the cocaine was just for fun, not some heinous° offense. On the way to the police station, he wasn't worried about being interrogated°. He figured he could claim that there were (2)____extenuating____ circumstances. He'd say he was just holding the stuff for a friend—maybe he'd even insinuate° that the "friend" was making him the victim of some (3)____fraudulent____ scheme—and then he'd be released right away.

But things didn't work out according to Tony's scenario°. When he told his story to the police captain, the captain's response was hardly (4)____auspicious____: "Tell it to the judge, kid. I've heard it all before." Then, turning to a(n) (5)____subordinate____ officer, the captain said, "Book him." Tony still wasn't distraught°. He just thought, "Well, my father will extricate° me from this mess. He'll (6)____rebuke____ me, of course, but after he's through yelling at me, he'll pay my bail, even if it's exorbitant°. And he knows plenty of influential people who can (7)____expedite____ the legal process so my case will be dismissed quickly." So Tony wasn't prepared for his father's (8)____vehement____ anger, or for his parting words: "You got yourself into this. Now you'll take the consequences."

With no bail, Tony had to remain in jail until his hearing took place. He was terrified, especially by the other inmates. Some were belligerent°, trying to start fights; others used (9)____innuendo____s, such as calling him "the millionaire." His inference° was that they were threatening retribution° for his easy life. He got through his nine-day stay without being attacked, though, and the experience woke up his dormant° good sense. He realized that fooling around with drugs is insidious°—his involvement would only get worse unless he turned his life around.

Therefore, at his court hearing, Tony asked to be sent to a drug treatment center, and as a first-time offender, he got his wish. Today, six years later, Tony is still "clean." He has not regressed° to his previous self-destructive behavior. And he still wonders what would have become of him if he hadn't managed to (10)____redeem____ himself.

| Scores | Sentence Check 2 _____% | Final Check _____% |

CHAPTER 28

deride	misconstrue
derogatory	paramount
fabricate	quandary
impending	turbulent
macabre	validate

Ten Words in Context

In the space provided, write the letter of the meaning closest to that of each **boldfaced** word. Use the context of the sentences to help you figure out each word's meaning.

1 deride
(dĭ-rīd′)
-verb

● One nightclub comedian **derides** members of the audience, poking fun at their looks, clothing, and mannerisms. He says they know it's just part of the act.

● Walter went on a diet after several classmates **derided** him by calling him "Lardo" and "Blimpy."

B *Deride* means 　　A. to misunderstand. 　　B. to mock. 　　C. to argue with.

2 derogatory
(dĭ-rŏg′ə-tôr′ē)
-adjective

● Lorenzo's **derogatory** remark about his boss—he called her an airhead—caused him to get fired.

● Charisse makes **derogatory** comments about Deion behind his back, saying that he's vain, sloppy, and lazy. But she never says such things to his face.

A *Derogatory* means 　　A. uncomplimentary. 　　B. mistaken. 　　C. provable.

3 fabricate
(făb′rĭ-kāt′)
-verb

● Supermarket tabloids often **fabricate** ridiculous stories, such as "Boy Is Born Wearing Green Sneakers."

● When she handed in her term paper late, Diane **fabricated** a story that her computer had crashed. The truth is that she doesn't even use a computer.

C *Fabricate* means 　　A. to avoid. 　　B. to prove. 　　C. to invent.

4 impending
(ĭm-pĕnd′ĭng)
-adjective

● Gary never studies until an exam is **impending**. If he'd start sooner, he wouldn't have to cram so hard, and he'd get better grades.

● "Because of the company's **impending** move," the office manager said, "I'm not ordering any supplies until next month, when we'll be in the new office."

A *Impending* means 　　A. approaching. 　　B. apparent. 　　C. important.

5 macabre
(mə-kŏb′rə)
-adjective

● Edgar Allan Poe's story "The Fall of the House of Usher" is a **macabre** tale in which someone is buried alive.

● The movie opened with a **macabre** scene: a row of bodies lying in drawers in the city morgue.

C *Macabre* means 　　A. confusing. 　　B. mocking. 　　C. gruesome.

6 misconstrue
(mĭs′kən-stroo′)
-verb

● Carla would like to date Matt, but when she told him she was busy last weekend, he **misconstrued** her meaning, thinking she wasn't interested in him.

● Many readers **misconstrue** Robert Frost's well-known line "Good fences make good neighbors." They think it's Frost's own opinion, but the line is spoken by an unneighborly character.

A *Misconstrue* means 　　A. to misunderstand. 　　B. to understand. 　　C. to ignore.

7 paramount
(păr′ə-mount′)
-adjective

- When you are driving on rain-slick, icy, or winding roads, good traction is of **paramount** importance, so always be sure your tires are in top condition.
- **Paramount** Pictures must have chosen its name to suggest that its movies were superior to all others.

_A_ _Paramount means_   A. supreme.   B. growing.   C. successful.

8 quandary
(kwŏn′də-rē)
-noun

- Bonita was in a **quandary**—she couldn't decide whether to return to school, take a job she had just been offered, or move to Alaska with her family.
- Aaron is in a **quandary** over financial matters: he is baffled by the problems of making a budget, handling credit, and paying taxes.

_A_ _Quandary means_   A. a state of confusion.   B. a state of anger.   C. a state of confidence.

9 turbulent
(tûr′byoo-lənt)
-adjective

- The **turbulent** air made the plane rock so wildly that passengers felt as if they were on a roller coaster.
- The Warreners' household tends to be **turbulent**. Whenever Mr. Warrener gets upset, he yells and throws things.

_A_ _Turbulent means_   A. violent.   B. distant.   C. unusual.

10 validate
(văl′ə-dāt′)
-verb

- Many people believe Columbus sailed west to **validate** the theory that the world is round. But in 1492, the fact that the world is round was already well known.
- There is no real doubt about the dangers of smoking; the claim that smoking is a serious health risk has been **validated** by many studies.

_B_ _Validate means_   A. to misinterpret.   B. to prove.   C. to invent.

Matching Words with Definitions

Following are definitions of the ten words. Clearly write or print each word next to its definition. The sentences above and on the previous page will help you decide on the meaning of each word.

1. ____turbulent____ Full of wild disorder or wildly irregular motion; violently disturbed

2. ____macabre____ Suggestive of death and decay; frightful; causing horror and disgust

3. ____quandary____ A state of uncertainty or confusion about what to do; predicament

4. ____derogatory____ Expressing a low opinion; belittling

5. ____validate____ To show to be true; prove; confirm

6. ____misconstrue____ To misinterpret; misunderstand the meaning or significance of

7. ____deride____ To make fun of; ridicule

8. ____fabricate____ To make up (a story, information) in order to deceive; invent (a lie)

9. ____impending____ About to happen; imminent

10. ____paramount____ Of greatest concern or importance; foremost; chief in rank or authority

CAUTION: Do not go any further until you are sure the above answers are correct. Then you can use the definitions to help you in the following practices. Your goal is eventually to know the words well enough so that you don't need to check the definitions at all.

Sentence Check 1

Using the answer line provided, complete each item below with the correct word from the box. Use each word once.

A. **deride**	B. **derogatory**	C. **fabricate**	D. **impending**	E. **macabre**
F. **misconstrue**	G. **paramount**	H. **quandary**	I. **turbulent**	J. **validate**

macabre   1. Mel has a(n) ___ hobby—he visits places where murders were committed.

paramount   2. We had skipped dinner in order to get to the play on time, so throughout the performance, food—not the drama—was ___ in our thoughts.

impending   3. Just before I was fired, I had a sense of ___ disaster; I could tell that something bad was about to happen.

misconstrue   4. Delia ___(e)d Miguel's friendliness as romantic interest. She didn't realize that he already had a girlfriend.

derogatory   5. When my friend said her teacher was "different," I wasn't sure if she meant the description to be complimentary or ___.

fabricate   6. Dwayne didn't show up for the final exam because he hadn't studied, but he ___(e)d a story about having a flat tire.

validate   7. In the psychology class, the students were given an interesting team assignment. They had to make some statement about human nature and then ___ it by finding supporting evidence.

quandary   8. Ivan is in a ___ over his car. He doesn't know whether to get his old car the major repairs it desperately needs, take out a loan and buy his dream car, or spend the money he has on another used car he doesn't like.

turbulent   9. The sun may seem to be shining calmly and steadily, but in fact, nuclear reactions inside the sun are causing a seething mass of ___ flames.

deride   10. A critic once ___(e)d a book he disliked by saying, "This is not a novel to be tossed aside lightly. It should be thrown with great force."

NOTE: Now check your answers to these items by turning to page 179. Going over the answers carefully will help you prepare for the next two practices, for which answers are not given.

Sentence Check 2

Using the answer lines provided, complete each item below with **two** words from the box. Use each word once.

turbulent
paramount   1–2. Many surfers prefer ___ water to calmer waves. Their ___ goal is excitement, and they get a feeling of exhilaration° from confronting a dangerous situation.

quandary
macabre   3–4. I was in a ___ over whether to study, practice the piano, or go to a movie with my friend Sal. To complicate things further, Sal wanted to see a(n) ___ horror film, and I dislike anything gruesome.

_____validate_____   5–6. When the evidence does not ___ their theories, scrupulous° researchers will
_____fabricate_____   report this honestly. But less conscientious researchers will flout° scientific
                              ethics and ___ fake "results" to appear to prove their theories.

_____impending_____   7–8. With the trial ___, the defense lawyer tried to forestall° negative news stories
_____derogatory_____   by asking for a "gag" order. The lawyer argued that if ___ stories about his
                              client's character were published, the trial would be a travesty° of justice.

_____misconstrue_____ 9–10. When Craig called Peggy "the perfect secretary," she was offended. He was
_____deride_____   complimenting her, but she ___(e)d his comment, thinking he had ___(e)d
                              her by saying she belonged in a subordinate° position.

Final Check: *Rumors*

Here is a final opportunity for you to strengthen your knowledge of the ten words. First read the following selection carefully. Then fill in each blank with a word from the box at the top of the previous page. (Context clues will help you figure out which word goes in which blank.) Use each word once.

Did you hear that K-Mart sold sweaters with baby snakes inside? The story, of course, was untrue, but it was not easy to squelch°.

How do such unrealistic rumors get started? Sometimes they are (1)_____fabricate_____(e)d. In the case of the K-Mart rumor, the story was actually fraudulent°; someone had deliberately made it up and disseminated° it to discredit the store. Often, though, a rumor starts with an innocent misinterpretation. For instance, when a magazine article drew an analogy° between a worm farm turning out bait and McDonald's turning out hamburgers, some readers (2)_____misconstrue_____(e)d this to mean that McDonald's was grinding up worms in its burgers—and the preposterous° story spread.

Rumors about individuals can start when someone makes a(n) (3)_____derogatory_____ statement or (4)_____deride_____s someone else, out of rancor° or jealousy: "Josie got an A because she's dating Professor X," or "Al isn't in class today— he left town because he knew his arrest for stealing a copy of the final exam was (5)_____impending_____." Even an innuendo°—something that's merely hinted at—can start a rumor that can do irrevocable° harm to someone's reputation: "Josie and Professor X are really quite discreet°, aren't they?" No story is too gruesome to make the rounds, not even the (6)_____macabre_____ tale of the girl whose beehive hairdo housed a black widow spider, which eventually burrowed into her brain and killed her.

Once a rumor gets started, people who hear it are sometimes in a (7)_____quandary_____. Even if there's nothing to corroborate° the rumor, they may be afraid to ignore it. And so there is a proliferation° of rumors, spreading fear, damaging reputations, and turning calm situations into (8)_____turbulent_____ ones. To stop or forestall° rumors, one thing is probably of (9)_____paramount_____ importance: before accepting any story, be sure the facts (10)_____validate_____ it.

Scores	Sentence Check 2 _____%	Final Check _____%

Enter your scores above and in the **Vocabulary Performance Chart** on the inside back cover of the book.

adroit	platitude
constituent	promiscuous
contention	repudiate
irreparable	spontaneous
pinnacle	stigma

Ten Words in Context

In the space provided, write the letter of the meaning closest to that of each **boldfaced** word. Use the context of the sentences to help you figure out each word's meaning.

1 adroit
(ə-droit′)
-*adjective*

● Doris is **adroit** in any kind of discussion or debate. She's very skillful at getting others to see things her way.

● **Adroit** chess players can make it seem as if the opponent is winning, when in fact he or she is about to lose in another move or two.

_B_ *Adroit* means   A. impulsive.   B. expert.   C. not selective.

2 constituent
(kən-stĭch′o͞o-ənt)
-*noun*

● Our senator genuinely wants to represent the citizens, so she makes serious efforts to find out how her **constituents** feel about important issues.

● Many of Councilman Hall's **constituents** live in poverty, so one way he helps those he represents is by working for programs to assist the poor.

_A_ *Constituent* means   A. someone represented.   B. someone who speaks well.   C. an officeholder.

3 contention
(kən-tĕn′shən)
-*noun*

● The artist's **contention** is that he was born in Paris, but actually he was born in a small town in Missouri.

● John's **contention** was that smoking hadn't hurt his health, but right after making that statement, he had a fit of coughing that lasted ten minutes.

_C_ *Contention* means   A. an attempt.   B. a realization.   C. a claim.

4 irreparable
(ĭr-rĕp′ə-rə-bəl)
-*adjective*

● The damage to the vase is **irreparable**. It broke into so many pieces that it cannot possibly be put together again.

● LaTanya apologized to Fred for her angry words, but I'm afraid the harm to their friendship is **irreparable**.

_B_ *Irreparable* means   A. untrue.   B. not able to be fixed.   C. unnatural.

5 pinnacle
(pĭn′ə-kəl)
-*noun*

● The rock singer seems to have reached the **pinnacle** of her career: she's at the height of her popularity, and her recordings are selling more than ever before.

● Robin felt that being elected class president was the **pinnacle** of her college years. Her parents, though, wish that she had thought of her "personal best" more in terms of academic achievement.

_A_ *Pinnacle* means   A. the highest point.   B. the starting point.   C. the end.

6 platitude
(plăt′ə-to͞od′)
-*noun*

● Some conversations are made up entirely of **platitudes**: "Good to see you." "We've got to get together sometime." "Well, take care."

● I made no response to the clerk's "Have a nice day." He meant well, but I'm tired of **platitudes** like that.

_B_ *Platitude* means   A. good advice.   B. an unoriginal comment.   C. a lie.

7 promiscuous
(prə-mĭs′kyoo-əs)
-*adjective*

● In this age of HIV and AIDS, it's more important than ever for people to be choosy about sexual partners. Being **promiscuous** can have deadly consequences.

● When it comes to women, Erik and Harry are opposites. Erik dates one woman at a time and is serious about commitment, but Harry is totally **promiscuous**.

B   *Promiscuous* means   A. faithful.   B. unselective.   C. rude.

8 repudiate
(rĭ-pyoo′dē-āt′)
-*verb*

● The actor **repudiated** his biography, saying it had been written without his consent or cooperation and that it was filled with lies.

● After the millionaire died, several people showed up claiming to be his children and demanding a share of his estate, but his real family **repudiated** their claims.

C   *Repudiate* means   A. to accept.   B. to discuss.   C. to reject.

9 spontaneous
(spŏn-tā′nē-əs)
-*adjective*

● The key to good acting is to be so well prepared that all words and actions seem natural and **spontaneous**, not rehearsed.

● When I asked Shawn to the movies, I tried to make the invitation sound **spontaneous**, as if I'd just thought of it. I didn't want him to know that I'd been planning it, nervously, for days.

A   *Spontaneous* means   A. unplanned.   B. clever.   C. irresistible.

10 stigma
(stĭg′mə)
-*noun*

● In the past, seeing a psychiatrist might harm a person's reputation, but now there's little or no **stigma** attached to seeking help for psychological problems.

● For a long time, there was a **stigma** associated with divorce. Today, of course, divorce is so common that it's no longer considered a disgrace.

A   *Stigma* means   A. dishonor.   B. an insight.   C. an argument.

Matching Words with Definitions

Following are definitions of the ten words. Clearly write or print each word next to its definition. The sentences above and on the previous page will help you decide on the meaning of each word.

1. _____irreparable_____ Not able to be repaired or made better

2. _____adroit_____ Skillful and clever under challenging conditions

3. _____stigma_____ A mark of shame or disgrace; blemish on character or reputation

4. _____repudiate_____ To deny the truth, validity, or authority of

5. _____spontaneous_____ Occurring or done as a result of a natural feeling or impulse; not forced or planned

6. _____promiscuous_____ Lacking standards of selection; having many sexual partners

7. _____pinnacle_____ A peak of achievement; topmost point

8. _____constituent_____ A member of a group represented by an elected official

9. _____platitude_____ A remark that is commonplace or has become uninteresting through repeated use

10. _____contention_____ A claim that something is true; a declaration

CAUTION: Do not go any further until you are sure the above answers are correct. Then you can use the definitions to help you in the following practices. Your goal is eventually to know the words well enough so that you don't need to check the definitions at all.

Sentence Check 1

Using the answer line provided, complete each item below with the correct word from the box. Use each word once.

A. **adroit**	B. **constituent**	C. **contention**	D. **irreparable**	E. **pinnacle**
F. **platitude**	G. **promiscuous**	H. **repudiate**	I. **spontaneous**	J. **stigma**

promiscuous   1. Some animals are ___ in their breeding habits, mating freely with no apparent effort at selection.

repudiate   2. The painting was being auctioned off as an early work of a well-known artist—until the artist ___(e)d it, saying that she had never painted it at all.

stigma   3. Eyeglasses have become so fashionable by now that there is no longer any ___ about wearing them.

irreparable   4. After the earthquake, some houses that were still standing nevertheless had to be completely destroyed; the damage to them was ___.

adroit   5. Tisha is a(n) ___ sales representative; she can convince anyone on the phone, and she can get her foot in any door.

pinnacle   6. Many people say that the plays of William Shakespeare—considered the greatest playwright who ever lived—represent the ___ of English drama.

spontaneous   7. Our football game was ___; we had no plans to play, but then we found an old football as we walked across the field.

contention   8. When Galileo made the ___ that the sun, not the Earth, is the center of our planetary system, the Catholic Church forced him to deny what he knew to be true.

constituent   9. Some elected representatives vote as the majority of their ___s wish, but others follow their own choice, even if it represents a minority opinion.

platitude   10. When Jimmy tells me about his problems, I don't know what to say. I just mumble ___s like "That's too bad" or "Oh well, I'm sure you'll work it out."

NOTE: Now check your answers to these items by turning to page 179. Going over the answers carefully will help you prepare for the next two practices, for which answers are not given.

Sentence Check 2

Using the answer lines provided, complete each item below with **two** words from the box. Use each word once.

stigma
irreparable   1–2. Serving time in prison leaves a ___ that can do ___ harm to someone's ability to find a job. Ex-convicts who try to redeem° themselves may find that any attempt to get honest work is impeded° by their record.

contention
platitude   3–4. "No matter how often I hear Kevin's ___ that he loves me," Tammy said, "it always sounds perfunctory° and insincere because he uses ___s."

_____adroit_____

_____pinnacle_____

5–6. Greta was so ___ at mechanical drawing in high school that I wasn't surprised to hear she'd reached the ___ of success as an architect.

_____constituent_____

_____spontaneous_____

7–8. Senator Harper's warm welcome to any of his ___s isn't just a sham°, meant to get votes; it's a(n) ___ expression of his genuine interest and inherent° good will.

_____repudiate_____

_____promiscuous_____

9–10. The teacher ___(e)d the idea that most animals are by nature ___, going from mate to mate. She explained that animals such as wolves, whales, pigeons, and swans stay with one mate for life.

Final Check: *The End of a Political Career*

Here is a final opportunity for you to strengthen your knowledge of the ten words. First read the following selection carefully. Then fill in each blank with a word from the box at the top of the previous page. (Context clues will help you figure out which word goes in which blank.) Use each word once.

Our mayor was not only a proficient° politician but also an extremely (1)_____adroit_____ speechmaker. Great warmth and charm emanated° from him. Whenever he spoke in front of an audience of his (2)_____constituent_____s, potential voters came away thinking, "He's one of us." His speeches always sounded (3)_____spontaneous_____, never rehearsed. When he made his way through a crowd, shaking hands, even (4)_____platitude_____s like "Great to see you!" and "What a beautiful baby!" sounded original and sincere. He seemed like a model of decorum° as well. When he would hear of the (5)_____promiscuous_____ behavior of other politicians, he would shake his head sadly over their loose conduct. He constantly appeared in public with his wife of thirty years, as if to show he was a devoted family man. Understandably, he was reelected several times.

But at the (6)_____pinnacle_____ of the mayor's career, disturbing rumors and innuendos° began to circulate. It was insinuated° that the mayor had won his first election by fraudulent° means. The manager of his first campaign became seriously ill. Knowing she was not likely to survive, she told several close friends that she wanted to disclose a guilty secret before dying. She made the (7)_____contention_____ that, during the campaign, the mayor had blackmailed his opponent. The opponent had a teenage daughter who had been caught shoplifting. Although the store owner had lectured the girl and let her go, the mayor learned of the story. He promised he would ruin the girl's reputation if his opponent did not deliberately lose the election.

The campaign manager's claims finally reached the evening news. When the mayor tried to (8)_____repudiate_____ the story, the former opponent and his daughter came forward to say it was true. The mayor could not escape the (9)_____stigma_____ of this sordid° scandal. His reputation as a man of impeccable° character was destroyed, and the damage was (10)_____irreparable_____. He lost the support of his party and even his staunch° friends, and he soon retired from politics.

Scores   Sentence Check 2 _____%   Final Check _____%

Enter your scores above and in the **Vocabulary Performance Chart** on the inside back cover of the book.

abrasive	emulate
admonish	hierarchy
antithesis	incapacitate
culmination	prognosis
docile	tumult

Ten Words in Context

In the space provided, write the letter of the meaning closest to that of each **boldfaced** word. Use the context of the sentences to help you figure out each word's meaning.

1 abrasive
(ə-brā'sĭv)
-*adjective*

- Pumice stone, a naturally **abrasive** substance, can be used for rubbing away rough spots on the feet.
- Roz has an **abrasive** personality—critical and negative. She always seems to rub people the wrong way.

B *Abrasive* means   A. simple.   B. harsh.   C. common.

2 admonish
(ăd-mŏn'ĭsh)
-*verb*

- When the guide found the hikers deep in the woods but unhurt, he **admonished** them for straying off the trail.
- Because the little girl had spent her entire allowance on candy, her parents **admonished** her for wasting her money.

B *Admonish* means   A. to lead.   B. to criticize.   C. to irritate.

3 antithesis
(ăn-tĭth'ĭ-sĭs)
-*noun*

- My taste in music is the **antithesis** of my brother's. I like heavy metal, played loud; he likes soft classical music.
- Pauline's free-spirited second husband is the **antithesis** of her first, who was a very timid and cautious man.

A *Antithesis* means   A. the reverse.   B. something superior.   C. an imitation.

4 culmination
(kŭl'mə-nā'shən)
-*noun*

- For an actor or actress, receiving an Academy Award is often the **culmination** of many years of effort, progressing from drama school to bit parts to major roles.
- The Super Bowl is the **culmination** of the entire professional football season. All the rivalries, victories, and defeats lead up to this final contest.

C *Culmination* means   A. a series.   B. a cause.   C. a final high point.

5 docile
(dŏs'ĭl)
-*adjective*

- After only a month of obedience training, our uncontrollable puppy calmed down, learned to pay attention to us, and became far more **docile**.
- Drugs and even surgery have been used in mental hospitals to make violent patients **docile**, so that they could be managed more easily.

A *Docile* means   A. obedient.   B. strong.   C. curable.

6 emulate
(ĕm'yoŏ-lāt')
-*verb*

- Jessie has always tried to **emulate** her older sister; she tries hard to do just as well as her sister—if not better—in school, at sports, and in popularity.
- Youngsters often want to **emulate** famous athletes. They train almost as hard as the champions do, with dreams of someday being as skilled as their heroes.

B *Emulate* means   A. to admire.   B. to imitate.   C. to submit to.

7 hierarchy
(hī′ər-är′kē)
-noun

- The armed forces are a clear example of a strict **hierarchy**. Everyone has a specific rank and must follow the orders of those whose rank is higher.
- Eva soon learned that all requests and suggestions had to be passed up through the levels of the company **hierarchy**. She could communicate directly with her own boss, but not with the boss's boss—let alone with the company president.

A *Hierarchy* means   A. a ranked system.   B. a training system.   C. a large system.

8 incapacitate
(ĭn′kə-păs′ə-tāt′)
-verb

- The lecture was canceled because the speaker was **incapacitated** by the flu.
- My mother can't tolerate alcohol. Even half a glass of wine **incapacitates** her; all she can do is giggle for a while and then go to sleep.

C *Incapacitate* means   A. to irritate.   B. to be concerned with.   C. to disable.

9 prognosis
(prŏg-nō′sĭs)
-noun

- Nathan's operation went well. The surgeon's **prognosis** is that Nathan will fully recover.
- Unless something can be done to reduce global warming, the **prognosis** for the environment will remain poor.

A *Prognosis* means   A. a forecast.   B. an illness.   C. an organization.

10 tumult
(too′mŭlt′)
-noun

- Spectators at a hockey match are often wild and noisy, and the **tumult** becomes even greater during a "sudden-death" overtime.
- On New Year's Eve, the **tumult** in Times Square reaches such proportions that the crowd noise can be heard a mile away.

B *Tumult* means   A. damage.   B. uproar.   C. friction.

Matching Words with Definitions

Following are definitions of the ten words. Clearly write or print each word next to its definition. The sentences above and on the previous page will help you decide on the meaning of each word.

1. ___tumult___   The noisy disorder of a crowd; a commotion
2. ___incapacitate___   To make unable or unfit, especially for normal activities; disable
3. ___docile___   Tending to give in to the control or power of others without resisting; easy to handle or discipline; willingly led
4. ___abrasive___   Able to cause a wearing away by rubbing or scraping; rough; irritating
5. ___prognosis___   A prediction of the course, outcome, or fate of something, especially a disease or injury
6. ___admonish___   To scold gently but seriously; caution; give a warning
7. ___antithesis___   The exact opposite
8. ___culmination___   The highest point or degree of a series of actions or events; the climax
9. ___emulate___   To try to equal or surpass, especially by imitation; imitate
10. ___hierarchy___   An organization of people in a series of levels, according to importance or authority

CAUTION: Do not go any further until you are sure the above answers are correct. Then you can use the definitions to help you in the following practices. Your goal is eventually to know the words well enough so that you don't need to check the definitions at all.

Sentence Check 1

Using the answer line provided, complete each item below with the correct word from the box. Use each word once.

A. **abrasive**	B. **admonish**	C. **antithesis**	D. **culmination**	E. **docile**
F. **emulate**	G. **hierarchy**	H. **incapacitate**	I. **prognosis**	J. **tumult**

tumult   1. At the rock concert, the audience grew more and more excited and out of control. There was such ___ that no one could hear the music.

abrasive   2. I ruined a nonstick frying pan by using a(n) ___ cleanser on it—the surface rubbed right off.

incapacitate   3. The runner was ___(e)d by a sprained ankle and had to miss the big race.

antithesis   4. Wendell's ideas about furniture are the ___ of mine. He likes colonial maple, but I like ultramodern tubular steel.

hierarchy   5. The ___ of the Roman Catholic Church goes from the parish priest up through bishops, archbishops, and cardinals, to the Pope at the head.

admonish   6. Mother ___(e)d us for spending too much money on her birthday gift, but we could see that she was pleased.

prognosis   7. The company is financially sick, and unless some changes are made in top management, the ___ is poor—it could go out of business.

docile   8. In the prison movie, the convicts acted very ___ while planning a riot. The guards—who weren't too bright—kept congratulating the inmates on being so well-behaved.

culmination   9. In colonial America, many people believed in and feared witches. Hysteria over "witch-hunting" reached its ___ in Salem, Massachusetts, where nineteen supposed witches were put to death.

emulate   10. "If you want to ___ Elvis Presley, fine," my mother said. "But try to match his energy and warmth onstage—not his self-destructiveness."

NOTE: Now check your answers to these items by turning to page 179. Going over the answers carefully will help you prepare for the next two practices, for which answers are not given.

Sentence Check 2

Using the answer lines provided, complete each item below with **two** words from the box. Use each word once.

antithesis
docile   1–2. The rebellious little girl, always demanding more and more autonomy°, was the ___ of her obedient, ___ sister. They were an incongruous° pair of siblings.

prognosis
incapacitate   3–4. The ___ for Dale's arthritis is not encouraging. Her doctor didn't equivocate° but told her frankly that in time it might ___ her completely.

_____hierarchy_____
_____culmination_____
5–6. Beth moved steadily up the company ___ until she was named president. This appointment, the ___ of twenty years of hard work and dedication, put her at the pinnacle° of her career.

_____emulate_____
_____abrasive_____
7–8. Cory has many good qualities that I would like to ___. But his ___ manner is a handicap; he estranges° people because he rejects any ideas that diverge° from his own.

_____tumult_____
_____admonish_____
9–10. Gil didn't expect the children's behavior in the car to be impeccable°, but the ___ in the back seat finally reached such a level that he had to ___ them.

Final Check: *Firing Our Boss*

Here is a final opportunity for you to strengthen your knowledge of the ten words. First read the following selection carefully. Then fill in each blank with a word from the box at the top of the previous page. (Context clues will help you figure out which word goes in which blank.) Use each word once.

My stint° in the bookkeeping department had lasted for three years when Jay Keller was brought in as department head. I don't expect supervisors to be pals with their subordinates°, and I don't object to being (1)_____admonish_____(e)d when I've done something wrong. Keller's criticism, however, was constant and harsh, and the office atmosphere seemed permeated° by his antipathy° toward us. His (2)_____abrasive_____ style made everyone in the department miserable. Keller was the complete (3)_____antithesis_____ of Chandra Borden, our previous boss, who had been so thoughtful and solicitous° about our needs that we all tried to (4)_____emulate_____ her. In contrast, Keller's mere presence could (5)_____incapacitate_____ us to a point where we could hardly add two and two.

Within a few weeks, even the most (6)_____docile_____ employees were becoming rebellious and starting to have subversive° thoughts. Our frustration and anger finally reached its (7)_____culmination_____ when Keller loudly belittled a new worker in front of everyone else, using such derogatory° terms ("Stupid! Airhead!") that he made her cry. Furious, we suddenly decided that our only recourse° was to go over Keller's head—to ignore the company (8)_____hierarchy_____ and, as a group, present our vehement° denunciation° of Keller directly to his boss.

Our meeting in her office began in (9)_____tumult_____, but then we settled down and told our story, trying to be as lucid° as possible so she could understand exactly what had been going on. We concluded with the contention° that ours was a deeply troubled department and that if Keller stayed, the (10)_____prognosis_____ for it was not good: everyone else would quit. That was Friday afternoon. On Monday morning, our spontaneous° action proved to be successful: we had a new boss.

Scores   Sentence Check 2 _____%   Final Check _____%

Enter your scores above and in the **Vocabulary Performance Chart** on the inside back cover of the book.

The box at the right lists twenty-five words from Unit Five. Using the clues at the bottom of the page, fill in these words to complete the puzzle that follows.

Word box:

- adroit
- auspicious
- contention
- deride
- discreet
- disparity
- docile
- emulate
- expedite
- flout
- forestall
- heinous
- impending
- impromptu
- inference
- macabre
- opportune
- permeate
- pinnacle
- platitude
- stigma
- transgress
- tumult
- validate
- vehement

ACROSS

2. To treat with scorn or contempt; defy insultingly
6. To flow or spread throughout
7. Suggestive of death and decay; frightful; causing horror and disgust
8. An inequality or difference, as in ages or amounts
9. Favorable; encouraging
12. Extremely evil; outrageous
14. To try to equal or surpass, especially by imitation
18. A remark that is commonplace or that has become uninteresting through repeated use
20. A conclusion drawn from evidence; an assumption
21. To sin or commit an offense; break a law or command
22. About to happen; imminent
23. Intense; forceful

DOWN

1. The noisy disorder of a crowd; a commotion
2. To prevent or hinder by taking action beforehand
3. Suitable (said of time); well-timed
4. A mark of shame or disgrace; a blemish on character or reputation
5. To show to be true; prove
8. Easy to handle or discipline; willingly led
10. A peak of achievement
11. A claim that something is true; a declaration
13. To make fun of; ridicule
15. To speed up or ease the progress of
16. Wise in keeping silent about secrets and other information of a delicate nature; tactful
17. Performed or spoken without practice or preparation
19. Skillful and clever under challenging conditions

PART A

Choose the word that best completes each item and write it in the space provided.

_____incapacitates_____ 1. When my foot falls asleep, it ___ me for several minutes.

    A. interrogates   B. incapacitates   C. misconstrues   D. insinuates

_____promiscuous_____ 2. The fear of AIDS has discouraged some people from being ___.

    A. fastidious   B. auspicious   C. impending   D. promiscuous

_____subordinate_____ 3. Since my uncle was made vice president of his company, he's ___ only to the president.

    A. subordinate   B. adroit   C. vehement   D. omnipotent

_____rebuked_____ 4. The mayor ___ citizens for their lack of cooperation in keeping the parks and streets clean.

    A. emulated   B. rebuked   C. fabricated   D. validated

_____permeated_____ 5. Harsh rules ___ life in Puritan New England, where people were forbidden even to celebrate Christmas.

    A. emulated   B. permeated   C. derided   D. repudiated

_____constituents_____ 6. When the public learned that the senator had accepted bribes, many of his ___ regretted having voted for him.

    A. constituents   B. pinnacles   C. intuitions   D. tumults

_____expedite_____ 7. Since I needed the tax forms as soon as possible, I downloaded them from the IRS website to ___ receiving them.

    A. insinuate   B. forestall   C. expedite   D. deride

_____omnipotent_____ 8. A novelist once commented on how wonderfully ___ a writer feels when creating "an entire universe."

    A. derogatory   B. omnipotent   C. extenuating   D. irreparable

_____prognosis_____ 9. Since petting an animal appears to lower a person's blood pressure, the ___ for survival after a heart attack is probably better for people with pets.

    A. prognosis   B. constituent   C. innuendo   D. quandary

_____complement_____ 10. Victor and Raquel ___ each other, making a perfect couple. He's rich but doesn't care about money; she's poor and cares about it a lot.

    A. complement   B. fabricate   C. implement   D. validate

(Continues on next page)

PART B

On the answer line, write the letter of the choice that best completes each item.

___A___ 11. You would be most likely to expect a **tumult** in the midst of a(n)
- A. riot.
- B. church service.
- C. living room where a family was reading.
- D. art museum.

___D___ 12. Although the prisoner appeared at first to be **docile**, prison officials soon learned he was actually
- A. laid-back, relaxed, and cooperative.
- B. highly intelligent.
- C. depressed to the point of suicide.
- D. rebellious and impossible to discipline.

___A___ 13. People generally use an **innuendo** when they want to say
- A. something critical, but in an indirect way.
- B. something highly complimentary.
- C. something that is not true.
- D. something in praise of themselves.

___A___ 14. Because Katya felt that her foreign accent was **obtrusive**, she decided to
- A. take a speech class to make it less obvious.
- B. keep it because she liked the way it sounded.
- C. assume that no one would notice it.
- D. emphasize it.

___C___ 15. Delia knew she must have **transgressed** somehow while driving to work because
- A. she got to work half an hour early.
- B. she found herself in a strange neighborhood.
- C. a police car was following her.
- D. she got to work half an hour late.

___B___ 16. To **forestall** seeing Diana at school today, Marc
- A. said nasty things to her in the hallway right before classes started.
- B. stayed home.
- C. asked her to eat lunch with him.
- D. ignored her in math class, even though she waved at him.

___C___ 17. One group of students **flouted** the library's "no unnecessary noise" rule by
- A. complaining about other students who were talking loudly.
- B. making occasional, brief whispered comments to one another.
- C. deliberately dropping heavy books on the floor and then laughing.
- D. studying in absolute silence.

___C___ 18. When Tara came to work late for the third time that week, her boss's **vehement** response was
- A. "Honey, are you having some sort of problem at home?"
- B. "Good morning, Tara."
- C. "Get out of here and stay out!"
- D. to shake her head and look disappointed.

___B___ 19. Brendan has forgotten his girlfriend's birthday. If he **fabricates** an excuse, he might tell her,
- A. "I forgot. I'm sorry. Can I make it up to you tomorrow?"
- B. "I put the money for your gift in my wallet, and someone stole it."
- C. "Birthdays! Who can remember them? They come along so often!"
- D. "If it will make you feel better, you can forget my birthday next June."

___A___ 20. My brother embarrassed me in front of my date by telling the story of the time I made dinner and the whole family got food poisoning. Later, he **redeemed** himself by
- A. telling another story about me that made me seem brave, funny, and intelligent.
- B. telling even more embarrassing stories about me.
- C. getting into a fight with my date.
- D. asking my date, "Why in the world do you want to go out with her?"

Score   (Number correct) _____ x 5 = _____%

PART A

Complete each item with a word from the box. Use each word once.

A. abrasive	B. adroit	C. antithesis	D. contention	E. emulate
F. extenuating	G. impromptu	H. inference	I. intuition	J. pinnacle
K. quandary	L. stigma	M. validate		

_____adroit_____ 1. The cockroach is ___ at squeezing into cracks because it can flatten its skeleton, which is on the outside of its body.

_____inference_____ 2. When Hal refused to kiss his wife goodbye, her ___ was that he was still angry with her.

_____abrasive_____ 3. Don't use a(n) ___ cleanser on your car. It will rub the paint off.

_____stigma_____ 4. As if being poor isn't bad enough, there is often a social ___ attached to poverty.

_____antithesis_____ 5. Last year, the town experienced a sizzling summer that was the ___ of its frigid winters.

_____intuition_____ 6. My ___ told me to stay away from anyone who called me "darling" after only five minutes of acquaintance.

_____emulate_____ 7. I tried to ___ my sister's ability to make money, but I ended up imitating only her readiness to spend it.

_____contention_____ 8. Mitch's ___ was that he deserved a higher grade in history, but I think the teacher was generous in giving him a C.

_____pinnacle_____ 9. From the mountain's snowy ___, the climbers looked down on a layer of clouds that hid the valley below.

_____quandary_____ 10. Suki is in a(n) ___ as to whether she should start college now part-time or wait until she can go full-time.

_____extenuating_____ 11. The police officer didn't consider my being late for a party a(n) ___ circumstance, so he went ahead and wrote the ticket for speeding.

_____impromptu_____ 12. Acting students often perform ___ scenes. Without a script, they must fully imagine how a particular character might speak and behave.

_____validate_____ 13. The study ___(e)d claims that drinking is strongly related to violence, providing evidence that alcohol is involved in about half of all murders in the United States.

(Continues on next page)

PART B

Write **C** if the italicized word is used **correctly**. Write **I** if the word is used **incorrectly**.

___I___ 14. The circus clown's beaming smile and *insidious* makeup made all the children at the party laugh.

___I___ 15. As *obsequious* as ever, Daniel refused to get in line for the fire drill.

___C___ 16. A baseball injury caused *irreparable* damage to Howard's left eye, which was left sightless.

___I___ 17. Just as humans often *admonish* each other by shaking hands, elephants often greet each other by intertwining their trunks.

___C___ 18. The scientist had the courage and honesty to *repudiate* his earlier theory when he discovered new evidence that contradicted it.

___C___ 19. It would be fitting *retribution* if my brother, who stays on the phone for hours at a time, had to live in some country with a twenty-year waiting period for phone service.

PART C

On the answer line, write the letter of the word that is the **synonym** of the boldfaced word.

Example: __A__ rebuke   A. blame   B. praise   C. answer

__B__ 20. **disparity**   A. equality   B. difference   C. sadness

__C__ 21. **implement**   A. reject   B. prevent   C. apply

__A__ 22. **impending**   A. approaching   B. remembering   C. fading

PART D

On the answer line, write the letter of the word that is the **antonym** of the boldfaced word.

Example: __B__ rebuke   A. blame   B. praise   C. answer

__B__ 23. **misconstrue**   A. misinterpret   B. understand   C. imagine

__C__ 24. **culmination**   A. achievement   B. disagreement   C. bottom

__A__ 25. **derogatory**   A. flattering   B. reassuring   C. insulting

Score   (Number correct) _____   x 4 = _____%

Enter your scores above and in the **Vocabulary Performance Chart** on the inside back cover of the book.

Each item below starts with a pair of words in CAPITAL LETTERS. For each item, figure out the relationship between these two words. Then decide which of the choices (A, B, C, or D) expresses a similar relationship. Write the letter of your choice on the answer line.

_C_ 1. INSINUATE : HINT ::
    A. hear : see
    B. exercise : jump rope
    C. express : communicate
    D. read : calculate

_B_ 2. INTERROGATE : QUESTION ::
    A. hide : see
    B. investigate : examine
    C. climb : descend
    D. know : guess

_A_ 3. OMNIPOTENT : HELPLESS ::
    A. sensible : unreasonable
    B. kind : helpful
    C. mighty : powerful
    D. recent : new

_C_ 4. OPPORTUNE : WELL-TIMED ::
    A. working : broken
    B. delayed : ahead of time
    C. punctual : on time
    D. frequent : rare

_D_ 5. DISCREET : DIPLOMAT ::
    A. hasty : tightrope walker
    B. frail : piano mover
    C. shy : master of ceremonies
    D. interesting : speaker

_A_ 6. FASTIDIOUS : NEGLECTFUL ::
    A. cautious : reckless
    B. worried : problem
    C. fatigued : exhausted
    D. friendly : neighborly

_C_ 7. HEINOUS : MURDER ::
    A. swift : turtle
    B. minor : catastrophe
    C. destructive : tornado
    D. tragic : joke

_B_ 8. AUSPICIOUS : FOUR-LEAF CLOVER ::
    A. threatening : butterfly
    B. ominous : broken mirror
    C. time-consuming : toast
    D. disastrous : first prize

_C_ 9. FRAUDULENT : HONEST ::
    A. foolhardy : senseless
    B. freakish : odd
    C. stale : fresh
    D. fruitful : productive

_A_ 10. SUBORDINATE : ASSISTANT ::
    A. superior : boss
    B. persistent : architect
    C. humorous : librarian
    D. noble : beggar

(Continues on next page)

B   11. DERIDE : PRAISE ::
     A. decide : ignore   C. appear : show up
     B. divide : unite   D. deliver : package

D   12. MACABRE : HORROR FILM ::
     A. old-fashioned : website   C. X-rated : sermon
     B. amusing : math lecture   D. useful : cookbook

C   13. PARAMOUNT : IMPORTANT ::
     A. early : late   C. deadly : unhealthy
     B. educational : recess   D. parallel : intersecting

C   14. TURBULENT : WAR ::
     A. evil : pear   C. tiny : atom
     B. few : pounds   D. desirable : illness

B   15. PLATITUDE : "HAVE A NICE DAY" ::
     A. gratitude : "Later."   C. invitation : "Yes."
     B. insult : "You stink!"   D. adoration : "We're through!"

A   16. SPONTANEOUS : PLANNED ::
     A. early : late   C. disappointing : imperfect
     B. large : elephant   D. expensive : costly

D   17. STIGMA : SHAME ::
     A. red cross : pirates   C. hug : protest
     B. yogurt : health food   D. medal : bravery

C   18. ABRASIVE : SCRATCH ::
     A. large : nail   C. sharp : cut
     B. pliers : tool   D. fork : spoon

D   19. INCAPACITATE : BROKEN LEG ::
     A. energize : flu   C. entertain : telephone book
     B. inform : sneeze   D. delay : traffic jam

B   20. HIERARCHY : LEVELS ::
     A. closet : room   C. petals : flowers
     B. school : grades   D. pain : medications

Score   (Number correct) _____ x 5 = _____%

Enter your scores above and in the **Vocabulary Performance Chart** on the inside back cover of the book.

Appendixes

A. Limited Answer Key

IMPORTANT NOTE: Be sure to use this answer key as a learning tool only. You should not turn to this key until you have considered carefully the sentence in which a given word appears.

Used properly, the key will help you to learn words and to prepare for the activities and tests for which answers are not given. For ease of reference, the title of the "Final Check" passage in each chapter appears in parentheses.

Chapter 1 (Apartment Problems)

Sentence Check 1

1. discretion	6. ostentatious
2. detriment	7. vicarious
3. dexterous	8. optimum
4. gregarious	9. sensory
5. scrupulous	10. facetious

Chapter 2 (Hardly a Loser)

Sentence Check 1

1. rudimentary	6. scoff
2. despondent	7. collaborate
3. instigate	8. squelch
4. zealot	9. retrospect
5. venerate	10. resilient

Chapter 3 (Grandfather at the Art Museum)

Sentence Check 1

1. lethargy	6. embellish
2. sporadic	7. juxtapose
3. subsidize	8. dissident
4. inadvertent	9. ambiguous
5. fritter	10. inane

Chapter 4 (My Brother's Mental Illness)

Sentence Check 1

1. regress	6. infallible
2. zenith	7. berate
3. euphoric	8. ubiquitous
4. relinquish	9. maudlin
5. estrange	10. impetuous

Chapter 5 (A Get-Rich-Quick Scam)

Sentence Check 1

1. diverge	6. illicit
2. charlatan	7. hoist
3. irrevocable	8. disseminate
4. dormant	9. corroborate
5. precipitate	10. proliferation

Chapter 6 (Holiday Blues)

Sentence Check 1

1. antipasto	6. extraordinary
2. revived	7. liberated
3. injection	8. Regicide
4. defrosting	9. vocabulary
5. dormitories	10. anachronism

Chapter 7 (A Phony Friend)

Sentence Check 1

1. solace	6. sham
2. impeccable	7. propensity
3. predisposed	8. fortuitous
4. solicitous	9. liaison
5. reprehensible	10. equivocate

Chapter 8 (Coco the Gorilla)

Sentence Check 1

1. oblivious	6. cohesive
2. vociferous	7. grievous
3. sanction	8. inundate
4. robust	9. attrition
5. circumvent	10. reticent

Chapter 9 (Our Annual Garage Sale)

Sentence Check 1

1. terse
2. indiscriminate
3. bolster
4. depreciate
5. tenet
6. replete
7. relegate
8. nebulous
9. sedentary
10. inquisitive

Chapter 10 (A Debate on School Uniforms)

Sentence Check 1

1. autonomy
2. ostracize
3. reiterate
4. tantamount
5. raucous
6. tenacious
7. utopia
8. bureaucratic
9. mandate
10. recourse

Chapter 11 (My Large Family)

Sentence Check 1

1. incongruous
2. reinstate
3. liability
4. indigenous
5. contingency
6. exonerate
7. prolific
8. clandestine
9. superfluous
10. egocentric

Chapter 12 (Alex's Search)

Sentence Check 1

1. confident
2. very
3. panorama
4. primary
5. direct
6. bibliotherapy
7. Synonyms
8. Hinduism
9. anonymous
10. renovate

Chapter 13 (Ann's Love of Animals)

Sentence Check 1

1. precarious
2. advocate
3. inclusive
4. imminent
5. impede
6. emancipate
7. jurisdiction
8. antipathy
9. preposterous
10. idiosyncrasy

Chapter 14 (A Costume Party)

Sentence Check 1

1. travesty
2. notorious
3. provocative
4. grotesque
5. facsimile
6. esoteric
7. mesmerize
8. perfunctory
9. austere
10. Metamorphosis

Chapter 15 (The Missing Painting)

Sentence Check 1

1. contrite
2. plight
3. symmetrical
4. connoisseur
5. verbose
6. conspiracy
7. germane
8. distraught
9. lucid
10. superficially

Chapter 16 (An Ohio Girl in New York)

Sentence Check 1

1. presumptuous
2. adept
3. sordid
4. stint
5. eradicate
6. homogeneous
7. encompass
8. stringent
9. entrepreneur
10. standardize

Chapter 17 (How Neat Is Neat Enough?)

Sentence Check 1

1. repugnant
2. magnanimous
3. masochist
4. foible
5. exhort
6. innocuous
7. rancor
8. recrimination
9. meticulous
10. flamboyant

Chapter 18 (A Cult Community)

Sentence Check 1

1. archangel
2. benefactor
3. temporized
4. travelogues
5. tenets
6. dismissed
7. postmortem
8. polygraph
9. animation
10. nominees

Chapter 19 (Halloween Troubles)

Sentence Check 1

1. chide
2. diabolic
3. integral
4. coalition
5. yen
6. commensurate
7. connotation
8. dilapidated
9. noxious
10. scenario

Chapter 20 (Thomas Dooley)

Sentence Check 1

1. deprivation
2. mitigate
3. exacerbate
4. unprecedented
5. deplore
6. utilitarian
7. objective
8. panacea
9. imperative
10. atrophy

Chapter 21 (Twelve Grown Men in a Bug)

Sentence Check 1
1. decorum
2. tenuous
3. rejuvenate
4. exorbitant
5. exhilaration
6. facilitate
7. extricate
8. espouse
9. synchronize
10. orthodox

Chapter 22 (Adjusting to a Group Home)

Sentence Check 1
1. inherent
2. dissipate
3. belligerent
4. denunciation
5. nonchalant
6. indolent
7. demeanor
8. unassuming
9. assimilate
10. unilateral

Chapter 23 (A Different Kind of Doctor)

Sentence Check 1
1. subversive
2. annihilate
3. staunch
4. criterion
5. proficient
6. holistic
7. emanate
8. analogy
9. vindicate
10. placebo

Chapter 24 (Grandpa and Music)

Sentence Check 1
1. volition
2. wooden
3. physician
4. decathlon
5. octuplets
6. homophone
7. aqueduct
8. philanthropist
9. surpass
10. mysterious

Chapter 25 (My Devilish Older Sister)

Sentence Check 1
1. permeate
2. forestall
3. opportune
4. interrogate
5. retribution
6. disparity
7. insidious
8. omnipotent
9. insinuate
10. obsequious

Chapter 26 (Harriet Tubman)

Sentence Check 1
1. intuition
2. flout
3. heinous
4. impromptu
5. discreet
6. implement
7. fastidious
8. complement
9. inference
10. obtrusive

Chapter 27 (Tony's Rehabilitation)

Sentence Check 1
1. subordinate
2. transgress
3. fraudulent
4. expedite
5. redeem
6. auspicious
7. vehement
8. rebuke
9. innuendo
10. extenuating

Chapter 28 (Rumors)

Sentence Check 1
1. macabre
2. paramount
3. impending
4. misconstrue
5. derogatory
6. fabricate
7. validate
8. quandary
9. turbulent
10. deride

Chapter 29 (The End of a Political Career)

Sentence Check 1
1. promiscuous
2. repudiate
3. stigma
4. irreparable
5. adroit
6. pinnacle
7. spontaneous
8. contention
9. constituent
10. platitude

Chapter 30 (Firing Our Boss)

Sentence Check 1
1. tumult
2. abrasive
3. incapacitate
4. antithesis
5. hierarchy
6. admonish
7. prognosis
8. docile
9. culmination
10. emulate

B. Dictionary Use

It isn't always possible to figure out the meaning of a word from its context, and that's where a dictionary comes in. Following is some basic information to help you use a dictionary.

How to Find a Word

A dictionary contains so many words that it can take a while to find the one you're looking for. But if you know how to use guidewords, you can find a word rather quickly. *Guidewords* are the two words at the top of each dictionary page. The first guideword tells what the first word is on the page. The second guideword tells what the last word is on that page. The other words on a page fall alphabetically between the two guidewords. So when you look up a word, find the two guidewords that alphabetically surround the word you're looking for.

● Which of the following pairs of guidewords would be on the page with the word *skirmish*?

(**skimp / skyscraper**)   **skyward / slave**   **sixty / skimming**

The answer to this question and the questions that follow are given on the next page.

How to Use a Dictionary Listing

A dictionary listing includes many pieces of information. For example, here is a typical listing. Note that it includes much more than just a definition.

> **driz•zle** (drĭz′əl) *v.* **-zled, -zling.** To rain gently and steadily in fine drops.
> — *n.* A very light rain. —**driz′zly,** *adj.*

Key parts of a dictionary entry are listed and explained below.

Syllables. Dots separate dictionary entry words into syllables. Note that *drizzle* has one dot, which breaks the word into two syllables.

● To practice seeing the syllable breakdown in a dictionary entry, write the number of syllables in each word below.

    glam•our _2_   **mi•cro•wave** _3_   **in•de•scrib•a•ble** _5_

Pronunciation guide. The information within parentheses after the entry word shows how to pronounce the entry word. This pronunciation guide includes two types of symbols: pronunciation symbols and accent marks.

Pronunciation symbols represent the consonant and vowel sounds in a word. The consonant sounds are probably very familiar to you, but you may find it helpful to review some of the sounds of the vowels—*a, e, i, o,* and *u*. Every dictionary has a key explaining the sounds of its pronunciation symbols, including the long and short sounds of vowels.

Long vowels have the sound of their own names. For example, the *a* in *pay* and the *o* in *no* both have long vowel sounds. Long vowel sounds are shown by a straight line above the vowel.

In many dictionaries, the *short vowels* are shown by a curved line above the vowel. Thus the *i* in the first syllable of *drizzle* is a short *i*. The pronunciation chart on the inside front cover of this book indicates that the short *i* has the sound of *i* in *ill*. It also indicates that the short *a* has the sound of *a* in *apple*, that the short *e* has the sound of *e* in *end*, and so on.

● Which of the words below have a short vowel sound? Which has a long vowel sound?

    drug _short_   **night** _long_   **sand** _short_

Another pronunciation symbol is the *schwa* (ə), which looks like an upside-down *e*. It stands for certain rapidly spoken, unaccented vowel sounds, such as the *a* in *above*, the *e* in *item*, the *i* in *easily*, the *o* in *gallop*, and the *u* in *circus*. More generally, it has an "uh" sound, like the "uh" a speaker makes when hesitating. Here are three words that include the schwa sound:

    in•fant (ĭn′fənt)   **bum•ble** (bŭm′bəl)   **de•liv•er** (dĭ-lĭv′ər)

● Which syllable in *drizzle* contains the schwa sound, the first or the second? _____*second*_____

Accent marks are small black marks that tell you which syllable to emphasize, or stress, as you say a word. An accent mark follows *driz* in the pronunciation guide for *drizzle,* which tells you to stress the first syllable of *drizzle*. Syllables with no accent mark are not stressed. Some syllables are in between, and they are marked with a lighter accent mark.

● Which syllable has the stronger accent in *sentimental*? _____*third*_____

    sen•ti•men•tal (sĕn′tə-mĕn′tl)

Parts of speech. After the pronunciation key and before each set of definitions, the entry word's parts of speech are given. The parts of speech are abbreviated as follows:

    noun—*n.*   pronoun—*pron.*   adjective—*adj.*   adverb—*adv.*   verb—*v.*

● The listing for *drizzle* shows that it can be two parts of speech. Write them below:

    _____*noun*_____   _____*verb*_____

Definitions. Words often have more than one meaning. When they do, each meaning is usually numbered in the dictionary. You can tell which definition of a word fits a given sentence by the meaning of the sentence. For example, the word *charge* has several definitions, including these two: **1.** To ask as a price. **2.** To accuse or blame.

● Show with a check (✓) which definition (1 or 2) applies in each sentence below:

The store charged me less for the blouse because it was missing a button.   1 _✓_   2 ___

My neighbor has been charged with shoplifting.   1 ___   2 _✓_

Other information. After the definitions in a listing in a hardbound dictionary, you may get information about the *origin* of a word. Such information about origins, also known as *etymology,* is usually given in brackets. And you may sometimes be given one or more synonyms or antonyms for the entry word. *Synonyms* are words that are similar in meaning to the entry word; *antonyms* are words that are opposite in meaning.

Which Dictionaries to Own

You will find it useful to own two recent dictionaries: a small paperback dictionary to carry to class and a hardbound dictionary, which contains more information than a small paperback version. Among the good dictionaries strongly recommended are both the paperback and the hardcover editions of the following:

    The American Heritage Dictionary
    The Random House College Dictionary
    Webster's New World Dictionary

Answers to the Dictionary Questions

Guidewords: *skimp/skyscraper*   Accent: stronger accent on third syllable *(men)*
Number of syllables: 2, 3, 5   Parts of speech: noun and verb
Vowels: *drug, sand* (short); *night* (long)   Definitions: 1; 2
Schwa: second syllable of *drizzle*

C. Topics for Discussion and Writing

NOTE: The first three items for each chapter are intended for discussion; the last three, for writing. Feel free, however, to either talk or write about any of the items.

Chapter 1 (Apartment Problems)

1. Athletes training for the Olympics must be **dexterous**. What are some of the other qualities—physical, emotional, and mental—necessary for them to achieve **optimum** results?

2. **Facetious** remarks often communicate serious ideas. An example is this comment by Mark Twain: "One of the most striking differences between a cat and a lie is that a cat has only nine lives." What is the serious meaning behind that remark? What might be the benefit of expressing that meaning in a joking manner?

3. Is it possible to be too **scrupulous** about following rules? Describe a situation in which someone, perhaps an authority figure, was more concerned with the rules than with the welfare of the people involved. Do you agree or disagree with that person's point of view? Explain your answer.

4. Write about a film that gave you an enjoyable **vicarious** experience. Name the film and describe at least one scene that illustrates your point. Begin with a main idea such as this: *The movie _____ gave me a great vicarious experience of being a martial-arts expert.*

5. Did you ever wish you had used more **discretion**? For example, you may have told someone you disapproved of a mutual friend's behavior and later regretted doing so. Write a paper about what you said and why you later regretted saying it. Conclude by telling what you learned from the experience.

6. Who is your most **gregarious** friend or relative? Who is the most shy? In writing, contrast these two people by describing the different ways they react to at least two or three common circumstances, such as being at parties and choosing jobs. Use examples where possible.

Chapter 2 (Hardly a Loser)

1. Do you prefer to work alone on a project, such as a report, or to **collaborate** with others? What are the benefits and drawbacks of each way of working?

2. What are some ways parents and teachers **squelch** children's confidence and creativity? What can they do to encourage children to feel positive about themselves and their abilities?

3. Throughout the ages, **zealots** have **instigated** both good and bad events. What public person or personal acquaintance do you consider a zealot? What do you think makes this person a zealot? Has his or her attitude had good effects—or bad ones?

4. We **venerate** people in a wide variety of fields, from athletics and entertainment to military and religious organizations. Write about a public figure you greatly respect, describing and illustrating the qualities and/or abilities that make you respect this person.

5. Think of a time you behaved in a way that you later regretted. Write about how you acted and how, in **retrospect**, you feel you should have behaved.

6. Has anyone ever scoffed at a goal or plan of yours? Write a paper explaining your goal or plan, the other person's comments, and how you reacted. Did you become despondent and not follow through? Or were you resilient and able to move forward with your idea despite the disapproval?

Chapter 3 (Grandfather at the Art Museum)

1. Some parents and teachers feel that young people fritter away their time on text messaging and video games. Do you agree? Explain what you feel are the good or bad effects of either or both on young people.

2. What school activity do you wish a community organization would subsidize? Would you like a program giving students internships in various workplaces? A girls' boxing program? Or something else? Explain and defend the program you name.

3. Tell about a historical, political or religious dissident you admire. What did that person oppose? What did he or she achieve? Did the person suffer for his or her views and activities?

4. The ways we embellish spaces influence how they make us feel. For instance, a hospital waiting room may be designed to calm and comfort. Write a paper describing the decor of a room with which you're familiar and the effects you think it has.

5. Write about a time you lost out on something (for example, a job) because of lethargy—you simply didn't get up enough energy to follow through. Juxtapose that story with an account of a time you pursued and achieved something you really wanted. Use this main idea: *Two very different experiences showed me that if I want something, I must take action.*

6. Have you ever made an inadvertent comment that was so inane you felt embarrassed afterward? Write a paper describing the incident and how you reacted when you realized what you had said.

Chapter 4 (My Brother's Mental Illness)

1. Have you ever relinquished a social activity in order to do homework? Or have you ever ignored homework in favor of a social activity? Were you later glad you made the choice you did?

2. Young people may feel infallible and behave in impetuous and sometimes dangerous ways. What are some examples of such behavior? How might friends help these people avoid harmful, even tragic results?

3. Do you know anyone who has regressed to an earlier behavior? For example, you may know someone who began smoking again after having quit. Why do you think this person returned to the old behavior?

4. You have probably seen—or may have been—someone publicly berated at school, on the job, or in a chat room. Write a paper about such an incident and your reaction to it.

5. Has an argument or a misunderstanding ever estranged you from a relative or an old friend? In a paper, explain the situation and what you think can be done, or has been done, to repair the relationship.

6. For many actors, winning an Academy Award is the zenith of their career. Euphoric, they give emotional, sometimes even maudlin, speeches thanking others and describing their feelings. Think of an important goal you have achieved. Then write a speech—perhaps one humorously imitating an Academy Award speech—that you could have given upon reaching your goal.

Chapter 5 (A Get-Rich-Quick Scam)

1. Gossips often disseminate a story without bothering to corroborate it with solid evidence. Has such a rumor ever been spread about you or someone you know or have heard of? Describe the rumor, and tell how it affected the person it concerned.

2. In what ways might advertising and peer pressure contribute to the illicit use of drugs (including alcohol and cigarettes) by children and teenagers? Do you think there's been a proliferation of such use lately—or a decline? What makes you think so?

3. Sometimes just one cruel word or action can cause irrevocable damage to a person. Has this ever happened to you or someone you know? Describe the incident and its effect.

4. When you were a child, did you dream about what you wanted to be when you grew up? Are these dreams dormant, or are they active? Or have you totally changed your mind about them? Write a paper describing your old dreams and how you feel about them now.

5. Have you and an old friend taken paths that diverged? In a paper, introduce your friend, and explain how your lives have gone in different directions. Here's a sample main idea for this assignment: *Because of different interests and goals, my best friend in elementary school and I have grown apart.*

6. Write a description—serious or humorous—of a way to hoist a piano, a person, a motorcycle or bike, a bag of groceries, or anything else from street level to a second-floor window.

Chapter 7 (A Phony Friend)

1. Some guests on television real-life talk shows become very emotional, even violent. Do you find such behavior reprehensible—or acceptable? In your opinion, are these demonstrations genuine, or are they mostly a sham and thus not to be taken seriously?

2. Politicians may equivocate when answering questions about controversial issues. Why do you think they do this? Can you think of any examples of such deliberate vagueness?

3. When there's a conflict between nations or between a union and a company, a liaison is generally called upon to help. Why do you think a go-between is used so often? Why don't the conflicting parties face each other without a mediator?

4. Sometimes when we're sad, a pet can give us solace when no one else can. Write a paper on the qualities that enable pets to offer such comfort, using examples you know of.

5. Do you know someone whose appearance or manners seem faultless? Do you consider a certain car or garden to be perfect? Write a paper in which you try to persuade your reader that someone or something is impeccable. Include colorful, convincing details in your description.

6. Write about someone who has a propensity to get into trouble. Include one or more detailed examples of his or her actions and the trouble that resulted. Also, explain why you think this person is predisposed to such situations. Use a main idea such as this: *My brother's habit of acting without thinking often gets him in trouble.*

Chapter 8 (Coco the Gorilla)

1. High-school and college coaches always lose players through attrition. What are some ways this happens? How, then, can a coach create a cohesive group of players and mold them into a winning team?

2. Have you ever felt inundated with school assignments? Describe study methods you have worked out to help you survive such difficult times. For instance, do you become super-organized? Do you read when you're on a bus?

3. Some students protest in a vociferous manner when required to dissect an animal. Do you think these students should be excused from the activity without being punished? Why or why not?

4. When parents divorce, the results can be grievous for their children. Some parents explain to their children why they've divorced, while others are reticent, feeling they are protecting the children by not giving the details of the breakup. Write a paper explaining which method you think is more helpful to a child and why.

5. We all want to be robust, yet we are sometimes oblivious to our own health practices. Think about your own diet and exercise patterns. Then write about two or three ways in which you can improve your chances for remaining healthy and strong.

6. Sometimes, even though we try to circumvent an unpleasant situation, we find we have no choice except to become involved. Has this ever happened to you or someone you know? In a paper, describe such a circumstance and what eventually happened.

Chapter 9 (Our Annual Garage Sale)

1. Television news is replete with images of violence and disaster. If you were in charge of news programming, would you balance negative news with reports meant to bolster viewers' spirits? If so, explain your reasoning and how you might achieve that balance. If not, explain why.

2. Some T-shirts or bumper stickers display terse statements that are serious or humorous. Which ones are your favorites? Is there one that particularly expresses a tenet by which you live?

3. Do you sometimes go through long periods of being quite sedentary? How can people include exercise in their study or work routines?

4. Some people collect items they hope won't depreciate, such as stamps. Others collect objects with little financial value, such as matchbooks. Do (or did) you or someone you know collect anything? Write a paper about the collection. How did it start? Which are its most prized items? Is it displayed, or has it been relegated to the basement?

5. Write a letter to a friend who has given only nebulous thought to a career and could end up making an indiscriminate career choice. Explain a way to go about choosing a satisfying occupation. Use some real or imagined examples to make your points clearer and more persuasive.

6. Imagine you are preparing a guide for camp counselors. One section of the guide must tell what to do in rainy weather, when children are stuck inside a room for hours. Write about three or more activities the counselor can lead to occupy the children's inquisitive minds and keep them from becoming bored and cranky.

Chapter 10 (A Debate on School Uniforms)

1. Suppose you were studying on a weeknight and your concentration was challenged by a raucous party next door. How would you cope? Under what circumstances might you feel your best recourse was to call the police?

2. While large organizations need rules, some become overly bureaucratic. Do you feel some regulations at your school interfere with the school's effectiveness? For instance, do you think registration is more complicated than necessary or that requirements are too inflexible?

3. Sometimes an organization or social group ostracizes certain people or even prevents them from becoming members in the first place. Do you think this kind of behavior is ever justified? Why or why not?

4. Some people have a tenacious desire to work things out on their own. How about you? Do you like close supervision and feedback when working on a project, or do you prefer autonomy? Write about your preference, and illustrate your points with detailed examples.

5. Imagine that in a future election, the people's mandate is to raise the voting age from 18 to 21. Write a paper opposing or supporting this decision. Give at least two reasons for your point of view.

6. What elements should a perfect society have? Write either a serious or humorous paper describing your idea of utopia. Tell what it would include and exclude, and explain your reasoning.

Chapter 11 (My Large Family)

1. On holidays, does your family prepare superfluous amounts of food in case uninvited guests show up? Describe how you or relatives overprepare (or underprepare) for such a contingency.

2. What are some characteristics and behaviors of egocentric people? In what ways might self-centeredness be a liability—or an advantage?

3. When a defendant in a criminal trial has been exonerated of all charges, he or she is set free. What difficulties do you think this person might face in attempting to be reinstated into normal life?

4. While Native Americans are indigenous to North America, most Americans have roots in other countries. Write a paper on your family's roots and movements from place to place. Trace your family as far back as you can.

5. A friendship between people who appear completely different from each other may seem incongruous. Do you know of such a friendship? Write a paper explaining the relationship and the qualities that seem contradictory. Tell what you think draws the friends to each other.

6. Have you ever had to behave in a clandestine manner to keep a surprise secret? Write about the surprise and what you had to do to hide it. Here's a sample main idea for this assignment: *Because of a surprise party, I had to become a creative liar.*

Chapter 13 (Ann's Love of Animals)

1. Some people advocate laws restricting smoking or drinking in public. Others have an antipathy toward rules restricting personal habits. Which group are you in, and why?

2. Have you ever felt emancipated when you finally finished doing something you utterly disliked? Explain what the circumstances were and how you handled them. Did you do something to celebrate your freedom?

3. Some governments have all-inclusive jurisdiction over the rights and behavior of their citizens. Tell what you think life must be like living under a highly restrictive government. How might you react to such a life?

4. Have you ever gotten lost in a forest or witnessed a violent crime? Write about the most precarious situation you've ever been in. Explain the circumstances, how you felt and reacted, and what eventually happened. Use vivid details to bring the experience to life for readers.

5. Some students become anxious when a new school term is imminent. Has this happened to you? After the term started, did you find that most of your fears were preposterous? Write a paper about your fears before and after school started.

6. Household members must learn to live with each other's idiosyncrasies. Write a paper on the peculiarities of the people you live with and how you all deal with them. You might use a main idea much like this one: *My parents, my sister, and I have several idiosyncrasies we've learned to live with and even enjoy.*

Chapter 14 (A Costume Party)

1. At the Academy Awards, some actresses always dress in a provocative manner. Why do you think they are so showy in their dress?

2. Mary Shelley's novel *Frankenstein,* the story of a scientist and his grotesque creation, has been made into a film several times. Why do you think this story continues to mesmerize people?

3. One company makes perfect facsimiles of famous paintings, down to the brushstrokes. The copies are sold for much less than the originals. Similarly, laboratory-produced gems are much cheaper than those found in nature. Why do you think people value the originals more than the less expensive copies?

4. Do you study best in a quiet, austere environment or a noisy, cluttered space—or something in between? Write a paper on the study setting you prefer. Describe the setting in detail, and tell why you feel it works for you.

5. Some students give only perfunctory attention to what happens in class. Write a letter to a teacher telling two or three ways class can be made more interesting for such students.

6. Write the first page or two of a short story, realistic or otherwise, about a notorious criminal who tries to undergo a metamorphosis in order to escape being recognized and caught by crimefighters.

Chapter 15 (The Missing Painting)

1. Group study can be helpful, but conversations may spring up that aren't germane to the study material. Do you prefer to study with friends or by yourself? Or does it depend on the circumstances? Discuss the pros and cons of both study methods, and give reasons for your preferences.

2. Even when people feel contrite about something they did, their apology may sound more like an excuse than regret. Think of examples. Why do you think it is difficult for some people to apologize?

3. To avoid being a verbose writer, watch for and eliminate unnecessary words. For practice, edit the following statements so that each is only four words: "Hattie was elected to the position of secretary." "At this point in time, I have need of a nap." "I really prefer the dark kind of chocolate." Why might connoisseurs of writing recommend this technique?

4. Were you ever so concerned about personal matters that you paid attention only superficially to your studies? Were you distraught when your limited studying led to low grades? Write about what prevented you from doing well in school and how things turned out.

5. Suppose you have a friend who refuses to recognize a problem with drugs or alcohol. Write a lucid letter that might get your friend to admit his or her plight and do something to overcome it.

6. Sometimes when nothing seems to go right, we may feel as though there's a conspiracy against us. Has this ever happened to you? Write about your experience and how it turned out.

Chapter 16 (An Ohio Girl in New York)

1. Tabloid writers and gossip shows are adept at appealing to people's interest in sordid events. Why do you think people are so attracted to the information these newspapers and shows offer?

2. Has a stint at a part-time or full-time job ever turned into a horrible experience for you? What were the circumstances? Did you quit the job or stick with it?

3. Some schools have a code that standardizes student dress. What reasons might they have for this requirement? How do you feel about dress codes, and why?

4. Some teachers have stringent standards, while others are easier to satisfy. Write a paper contrasting strict and lenient teachers. Explain, for instance, the differences in their assignments and grading methods. Also tell which type of teacher you prefer and why. You might use the following main idea: *In my experience, a _____ teacher is generally preferable to a _____ one.*

5. Write a paper explaining which habit you would choose to eradicate if you could, and why. Go on to name two or three realistic methods you could use to get rid of, or at least weaken, that habit.

6. Imagine you are an entrepreneur opening a restaurant chain. Write a description of your business. Include the restaurant's name, theme, decor, and a general description of what the menu would encompass.

Chapter 17 (How Neat Is Neat Enough?)

1. When you were a child, did your parents exhort you to eat foods you found repugnant? What were these foods, and what did you do, if anything, to avoid eating them? How do you feel about these foods today?

2. People's foibles, though innocuous, can sometimes annoy others. What foibles do your roommates or family members have that sometimes irritate you? Which of your foibles annoy others?

3. Are you meticulous about keeping your room and belongings neat, or are you more casual with your environment? Describe what your classmates would see if they were to enter your room right now.

4. Do you know, or know of, someone who is truly magnanimous? In a paper, describe that person and tell what he or she has done to deserve your opinion.

5. Sometimes people have an argument that escalates into ongoing recriminations and rancor that can last for years. Write a paper describing such a conflict and explaining what you think might be done to ease it.

6. Imagine a fictitious person who is very flamboyant. Write a paper describing this person's showy appearance and behavior. Also tell what this flamboyance might indicate about his or her nature.

Chapter 19 (Halloween Troubles)

1. What do you get a yen for that you know isn't good for you? A cigarette? Junk food? Under what circumstances do you feel this craving? Describe any methods you use for overcoming the desire.

2. Advertisers often attempt to make noxious products like cigarettes and alcohol attractive to young people. What scenarios have you seen in ads that would particularly appeal to young viewers? Do you think these ads are successful? Why or why not?

3. What abilities or traits do you think are integral to success in any field? Name these qualities and tell why you think they are so important. Who in private or public life do you think possesses these qualities?

4. Experience influences the connotations words have for us: For a pet lover, the word *dog* will have a positive meaning; for someone bitten by a dog, it may have negative overtones. Write a paper explaining the connotations one of the following words has for you: *cat, automobile, boss, chocolate, rain, spider*. Here's a sample main idea for this assignment: *The word "rain" has pleasant connotations for me.* Support your main idea with at least two personal experiences.

5. What do you feel is a big problem at your school? In a letter to a school administrator, write a proposal to create a coalition to deal with the problem. Explain who would make up the coalition, and how it might go about solving the problem.

6. Imagine a horror movie in which one or more diabolic creatures live in a dilapidated house into which someone has just moved. Write a review of that film, including colorful descriptions. Or, if you prefer, write a one- or two-page summary of the story.

Chapter 20 (Thomas Dooley)

1. When you were a child, did a special treat work as a panacea to cure emotional upsets? Is there a certain activity today—listening to music or talking to someone special—that you can count on to lift your blue moods?

2. Being objective is imperative for a judge and a jury, but it is also important in other areas of life. What are some situations when it's important for people to be objective? For instance, is objectivity important in hiring an employee? In choosing friends?

3. We are surrounded by utilitarian things: telephone wires, pencils, television sets, and so on. Name some objects that are *not* utilitarian and are kept solely for aesthetic reasons. Name some utilitarian things we may appreciate for their looks as well as for their usefulness.

4. No matter how much we like television, many of us deplore something about it. We may feel that it promotes poor values or that local news shows care more about ratings than news. Write a paper on what you most disapprove of about TV. Include detailed examples.

5. Did someone who tried to help you with a problem actually exacerbate the situation? Write about what happened and how you eventually handled your problem.

6. Have you ever worn a cast? How badly did your muscles atrophy while in the cast? Was physical therapy used to mitigate the muscle weakness? Write a paper about your experience. Tell why you needed to wear the cast and what problems or inconveniences you experienced while wearing it and after removing it.

Chapter 21 (Twelve Grown Men in a Bug)

1. When stressful situations leave you exhausted, do you wish you could get away for a while? If you could take an all-expenses-paid two-week vacation, where would you go, and what would you do to rejuvenate yourself?

2. Some people feel exhilaration when running five miles, whereas others feel it from beating a difficult computer game. What activity fills you with excitement? Explain its appeal to you.

3. What is the worst mess you've ever gotten yourself into? Have you ever made two appointments or dates for the same time and day, or agreed to do something and later wished you hadn't? Describe the situation, and explain how you managed to extricate yourself.

4. Have you ever been criticized by someone who espoused what you consider an old-fashioned sense of decorum? For instance, has a relative insisted that nose piercing is rude or that it's wrong for females to call males for a date? Write a paper about your experience. Describe the situation, the other person's opinion, and your own point of view and reaction.

5. Did you ever want something so much that you paid what seemed like an exorbitant price for it? After the purchase, did you still feel it was worth what you paid? Do you or does someone you gave the item to still own it? Write about your experience. Be sure to describe what you bought in a way that shows your reader why you were willing to pay so much for it.

6. Imagine you write an advice column. A tenth grader who has moved to a new school district asks for your ideas on how to facilitate his or her adjustment to the new school. For your column, write a letter to that person.

Chapter 22 (Adjusting to a Group Home)

1. What are your favorite ways of dissipating tensions? Going for a walk? Jogging? Meditating? Why do your methods work so well for you?

2. Have you ever had a day when you felt completely indolent? Describe how you would ideally spend such a day.

3. Many people claim that prejudice is not inherent to our nature, but is taught. Do you agree? If so, who or what do you think are the primary teachers of racism? Where have you found denunciations of racism?

4. Write a paper explaining how easy or difficult it has been for you to assimilate into new situations, such as a new school or a new neighborhood. Tell if some situations are easier for you than others and if such adjustments have gotten easier over time.

5. Write a paper about a belligerent person you've known. Tell about one or more situations in which the person's aggressiveness was a key element. You might begin with a main idea like this: *My neighbor Mr. X seems to be constantly harassing my family and other neighbors.*

6. Was a unilateral decision that involved you but excluded your input ever made by family or friends? Write about the situation, describing what happened and how you felt about not having a say in the decision.

Chapter 23 (A Different Kind of Doctor)

1. Some patients who receive placebos (instead of real medications) report good results, even cures. What do you think could account for these results?

2. Throughout history, the power of persuasion emanated from some people so strongly that they were able to influence masses of people. Name some of those people. Did any of them use their abilities for subversive purposes? Explain.

3. In focusing on the whole person, what might holistic physicians do that other doctors often do not do? For instance, what life changes might they suggest?

4. Are you a staunch fan of a particular sports team? Write a paper explaining what you like about that team. Give examples for all your claims.

5. Were you ever wrongly accused of doing something? If so, were you able to vindicate yourself? Write a paper explaining the accusation and its effects upon you. Describe in detail the way you were—or were not—cleared of blame. Feel free to use this main idea: *I learned the hard way how important it is to be careful in making accusations.*

6. Are you good at tennis? An expert baker? Write a paper on an activity in which you feel especially proficient. Describe the skill, and tell how you came to acquire it and what place it occupies in your life now. Conclude by explaining whether you intend to use the skill in a career or as a hobby.

Chapter 25 (My Devilish Older Sister)

1. Do you dislike certain activities, such as exercise or doing laundry, so much that you find ways to **forestall** doing them? Tell which activities you dislike, why you dislike them so much, and what delaying actions you take.

2. Did your parents ever ask you questions like "Where are you going?" and "Who else will be there?" How do young people react to being **interrogated** in this fashion? Are those reactions justified? Why or why not?

3. Do wonderful odors **permeate** your home at certain times of the year, such as particular holidays or seasons? Identify the aromas and the special times with which you associate them.

4. Has anything happened to you at a particularly **opportune** time? For instance, did you get a job offer just when you needed more money? Did you meet someone special right after breaking up with someone else? Write a paper describing one such time in your life, making clear just why the timing of the event was so good. Alternatively, write about an inopportune, or ill-timed, event in your life.

5. Are you good friends with someone despite **disparities** in your opinions, ages, and/or backgrounds? Write about your relationship, explaining the differences between you and how you both handle them so that your friendship is maintained. Has anyone **insinuated** that your friendship is inappropriate? If so, also tell how you dealt with the objection.

6. Have you ever wished to be **omnipotent**? Write a paper describing what you would do and why if you were all-powerful for a day. Include any **retributions** you would like to give out.

Chapter 26 (Harriet Tubman)

1. Imagine you are asked right now to give an **impromptu** speech defending this point: Sports help society. Give one example, fact, or personal experience you could use to support that point.

2. When you get dressed in the morning, are you **fastidious** about choosing accessories to **complement** your outfit? Or are you more casual about your day's attire? Picture this outfit: black shirt, black pants, and black shoes. Name one piece of clothing or jewelry for a male or a female that you feel would complement that outfit.

3. Do you trust your instincts? Tell about a time when you did *not* follow your **intuition** and wished that you had, or a time you *did* follow your instincts and you were, or were not, glad you did.

4. On New Year's Day, many people decide to begin a self-improvement program. The **inference** is that if they make a New Year's resolution, they will stick with the plan, yet it is often soon forgotten. Have you ever made a resolution (at any time of the year) and actually followed through? Write a paper explaining the resolution and how you **implemented** it. Or write about a resolution you might make in the future and the ways you could carry it out.

5. Have you ever asked a friend or family member to be **discreet** about some information and then discovered it was told to others? Write a paper about your experience and how you handled it.

6. Write the first page or two of a novel about an evil character who **flouts** society's rules. Describe the character and a **heinous** plan he or she is working on.

Chapter 27 (Tony's Rehabilitation)

1. Judges sometimes require people who have **transgressed** but are not violent to **redeem** themselves by doing community work. Do you think community work is a fair punishment? What are the advantages and disadvantages of such a penalty?

2. Some people believe that their astrological signs are **auspicious** at certain times and plan their days accordingly. Do you believe in astrology? Give your opinion and the reasons you feel as you do.

3. What do you do to **expedite** unpleasant chores such as housecleaning or yard work? Explain your methods and why they are helpful to you.

4. Have **extenuating** circumstances ever caused you to miss an important test or appointment? Write a paper about the experience. Describe the circumstances, the reaction to your missing the test or appointment, and what happened in the end.

5. Did you ever harshly **rebuke** someone and later regret it and try to remedy the situation? Write a paper about the experience. Or write about a time you were at the receiving end of **vehement** criticism and what responses, if any, you made to the **derogatory** remarks.

6. What kind of boss would you want to be? Imagine that you are a boss and have asked the workers **subordinate** to you to evaluate your performance anonymously. Write an evaluation you would like to see.

Chapter 28 (Rumors)

1. What do you think are the reasons **macabre** movies are so popular? Give some examples. What do *you* think of such movies, and how do you respond to them?

2. Children sometimes **fabricate** stories, especially when they think they've done something that might get them into trouble. How do you think parents should handle this behavior?

3. Some people are frightened by **turbulent** storms, while others enjoy a lot of lightning and thunder. What is your reaction to violent weather? If you have a pet, how does it react to thunderstorms?

4. Have you ever been in a **quandary** because you wanted to do something your family disapproved of? For example, you might have wanted to buy a car, but your parents wanted you to use the money for college. Write a paper explaining the predicament and the decision you made.

5. Has anyone ever **derided** or criticized something that was of **paramount** importance to you, such as your choice of friends, jobs, or extracurricular activities? Write about the experience, including how you reacted to the ridicule or criticism.

6. Write a paper in which you **validate** one of the following italicized statements with at least two persuasive pieces of evidence—facts, examples, or reasons from your personal experience and common sense. *About everything bad there is something good. School uniforms are a good* (or *a bad*) *idea. Music classes benefit students.*

Chapter 29 (The End of a Political Career)

1. We all hear trite remarks throughout a day. See if your class can come up with a list of five or ten especially common **platitudes**. Are there any you feel are useful even though they're not original? Can you think of new ways to express what any of them communicate?

2. Suppose an elected official **repudiates** the wishes of his or her **constituents** and votes instead according to what he or she believes is best for them. Imagine, for instance, that most citizens of a district are opposed to a certain tax, but their congressperson votes in favor of one. Do you think the official should be applauded—or criticized? Why?

3. People with low self-esteem may repeatedly make the **contention** that they cannot do anything right. What might an **adroit** counselor or friend say or do to help such people become more positive about their abilities?

4. What is the **pinnacle** of your academic career or work experience so far? Write a paper describing your best school or work achievement and its background, telling why you did it, and what you had to do to excel.

5. A scheduled event can be disappointing, and a **spontaneous** one can be extremely satisfying. Write a paper contrasting a planned event that was a letdown with an unplanned one that was wonderful. Use colorful details to show what each event was like.

6. School cliques, social circles, and other groups attach a **stigma** to certain people, such as serious students, computer nerds, or people from other countries. This kind of negative thinking can, of course, do **irreparable** harm to the people on the receiving end. Think about a stigma you strongly dislike, and write a paper telling what it is, a group that promotes it, and its effects.

Chapter 30 (Firing Our Boss)

1. Is there someone you would like to **emulate**? The person might be someone you know, a famous individual, or a character in a novel or film. Tell how you'd like to be similar to that person and why.

2. Some people like to work for a large company with a structured **hierarchy**. Others prefer to work for a small business with a more casual structure. Which of these work settings best suits your temperament and career plans? Why?

3. Do you know a couple who are the **antithesis** of one another? For instance, is your uncle very sociable and your aunt shy? Is one person in the couple **abrasive** and the other **docile**? Despite their differences, do the two people seem well suited to each other? Why or why not?

4. Has a politician, athlete, or other public person done something you strongly disapprove of? Write a letter to that person in which you **admonish** him or her and suggest a better behavior.

5. Imagine you are a counselor. Write a professional report about someone who is **incapacitated** by extreme shyness. Describe the person and tell what you think should be done to help him or her. Conclude with what the **prognosis** would be if your program is followed.

6. Graduation day is the **culmination** of years of academic, social, and athletic experiences. Imagine that you are giving a speech at your graduation ceremony. What are some memories you would share with your classmates? What are some words of advice you would give them? Write the speech you would give.

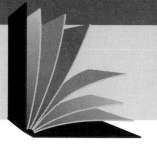

D. List of Words and Word Parts

NOTE: Word parts are in *italics*.

abrasive, 164
adept, 88
admonish, 164
adroit, 160
advocate, 76
ambiguous, 16
a-, an-, 62
analogy, 126
anima, 96
annihilate, 126
ante-, anti-, 28
antipathy, 76
antithesis, 164
arch, -archy, 96
assimilate, 122
attrition, 46
atrophy, 114
auspicious, 152
austere, 80
autonomy, 54
belligerent, 122
ben-, bene-, 96
berate, 20
bibl-, biblio-, 62
bolster, 50
bureaucratic, 54
charlatan, 24
chide, 110
chron, chrono-, 28
-cian, -ian, 130
-cide, 28
circumvent, 46
clandestine, 58
coalition, 110
cohesive, 46
collaborate, 12
commensurate, 110
complement, 148
connoisseur, 84
connotation, 110
conspiracy, 84
constituent, 160
contention, 160
contingency, 58

contrite, 84
corroborate, 24
criterion, 126
culmination, 164
de-, 28
dec-, 130
decorum, 118
demeanor, 122
denunciation, 122
deplore, 114
depreciate, 50
deprivation, 114
deride, 156
derogatory, 156
despondent, 12
detriment, 8
dexterous, 8
diabolic, 110
dilapidated, 110
discreet, 148
discretion, 8
disparity, 144
disseminate, 24
dissident, 16
dissipate, 122
distraught, 84
diverge, 24
docile, 164
dorm, 28
dormant, 24
duc, duct, 130
-ee, 96
egocentric, 58
emanate, 126
emancipate, 76
embellish, 16
emulate, 164
-en, 130
encompass, 88
entrepreneur, 88
equivocate, 42
eradicate, 88
esoteric, 80
espouse, 118

estrange, 20
euphoric, 20
exacerbate, 114
exhilaration, 118
exhort, 92
exonerate, 58
exorbitant, 118
expedite, 152
extenuating, 152
extra-, 28
extricate, 118
fabricate, 156
facetious, 8
facilitate, 118
facsimile, 80
fastidious, 148
fid, 62
flamboyant, 92
flout, 148
foible, 92
forestall, 144
fortuitous, 42
fraudulent, 152
fritter, 16
germane, 84
gregarious, 8
grievous, 46
grotesque, 80
heinous, 148
hierarchy, 165
hoist, 24
holistic, 126
homo-, 130
homogeneous, 88
idiosyncrasy, 76
illicit, 25
imminent, 76
impeccable, 42
impede, 76
impending, 156
imperative, 114
impetuous, 20
implement, 148
impromptu, 149